Also by Jerome M. Segal

Agency and Alienation: A Theory of Human Presence

Creating the Palestinian State: A Strategy for Peace

GRACEFUL
SIMPLICITY

Graceful SIMPLICITY

THE PHILOSOPHY AND POLITICS

OF THE ALTERNATIVE AMERICAN DREAM

Jerome M. Segal

UNIVERSITY OF CALIFORNIA PRESS

Berkeley · Los Angeles · London

University of California Press
Berkeley and Los Angeles, California

University of California Press, Ltd.
London, England

First Paperback Printing 2003

Library of Congress Cataloging-in-Publication Data
Segal, Jerome M., 1943–
Graceful simplicity : the philosophy and politics of the
alternative American dream / Jerome M. Segal.
p.   cm.
Originally published: New York : H. Holt & Co., 1999.
Includes bibliographical references and index.
ISBN 0-520-23600-9
1. Simplicity.   2. Simplicity—Political aspects—
United States.   I. Title.
BJ1496.S44   2003
178—dc21   2002067883

Printed in the United States of America

10   09   08   07   06   05   04   03
10   9   8   7   6   5   4   3   2   1

The paper used in this publication meets the minimum
requirements of ANSI/NISO Z39.48-1992 (R 1997)
(*Permanence of Paper*). ⊚

For Anshel and Augie,

my father and my uncle

CONTENTS

Part II
Toward a Philosophy of Simple Living

PREFACE TO THE PAPERBACK EDITION

Since the publication of the original edition, two important developments have occurred which bear special relevance to the text. The first has to do with "the politics of simplicity." When it initially appeared, *Graceful Simplicity* was intended as a challenge to a simple living movement that was highly individualistic, and largely apolitical. The simple living literature, in the main, was of the "how to" type. One after another, authors espoused the desirability of a more simple life and then set out to inform readers on the techniques of cutting back, downshifting, simplifying, reducing work, and reorienting life towards those activities and experiences of inherent value.

This "how to" literature is certainly important, and in general, reflects an often overlooked concomitant to social change. Even with ideal social and economic policies, without the individual determination that changes one life at a time, policy rarely achieves anything. This will certainly be true of any social efforts to promote a simpler, less draining, and more rewarding form of life.

At the same time advice books have their limitations. Typically the simple living "how to's" take as their starting point a dubious thesis: that we Americans have more money than we need, and that we are the victims of "artificial desires" inculcated by advertising and the general press of our consumerist culture.

One of the central theses of *Graceful Simplicity* is that this characterization of American life, while perhaps accurate for the top ten or fifteen percent of the population, largely misreads the life situation of most American families.

Yes we have more money than ever, but to say that it is, in any large part, unneeded, ignores a fundamental fact. Provided we understand efficiency as a measure of the amount of income that is required to satisfy core needs, the United States is the most inefficient society in human history. What other societies may do with less income, the United States sometimes fails to do with more. My argument, which is laid out in chapter 3, is that most American families, far from frittering away their income on trivia, are working hard, sometimes unsuccessfully, to satisfy quite legitimate needs in the areas of food, clothing, day care, college education, housing, transportation, health care, and retirement protection. The case is even more evident if we aspire to gracefulness and add the need for beauty and a bit of tranquility to the list.

Historically, the United States has seen a sharp rise in "need required income"—the amount of income required to satisfy core needs. Largely this has been ignored by economists and most social critics. Despite occasional efforts over the last hundred years to ascertain how much money one needs to live decently in America, there are no meaningful statistics on the matter. Some doubt that the issue is subject to rigorous inquiry. Even with respect to a question as basic and commonsensical as "How has the cost of living in a safe neighborhood changed during the twentieth century?" there is no place to turn for an answer. No one has ever successfully pursued the question, and few try.

We can, as a society, continue to ignore our social inefficiency of need satisfaction. We can maintain our central model that simply encourages each family to earn still more so that their needs can be more adequately satisfied. Alternatively, we can decide to focus on the growth of need required income (NRI) itself. If we choose this latter path, we will be looking towards social and economic policies that make it feasible for people to satisfy core needs with modest incomes. This, in turn, will make it possible for people to choose expanding leisure over expanding income, and to choose modest but meaningful work over more remunerative but less fulfilling activity.

To take this second path is to begin the development of a politics of simplicity. It is to set a new goal for American life: that simple living shall become a feasible option for families of average means. In short, in *Graceful Simplicity,* I argue that the simple living movement needs to take this social turn, needs to develop into a politics that goes beyond the bounds of a self-help movement.

In the three years since the appearance of the hardcover edition, exactly this change has begun to occur. In the summer of 2001, many of the leading authors and figures in the simple living movement, some that I criticize in chapter 2, joined together to form a new organization, The Simplicity Forum, to promote a transition to a simplicity-friendly society. This is all in its early stages, and whether this particular organization, of which I am a part, will endure and have a lasting impact is not the central question. What is significant is that there is a growing social awareness among some of the most prominent advocates of simple living. We are now cautiously embarked on the project of establishing a politics of simplicity. And I suspect that it will not be long before there are referenda to shorten the work week, legislative proposals to provide free public day care, and a popular demand to free ourselves from the insufferable complexity of household finances as we try to cope with the realities of medical co-payments, college education, taxation, and retirement security. Whether these threads cohere into a comprehensive re-orientation of American life is another question—but there are stirrings that were not present just a few years back.

Of a totally different magnitude, between the hardback and the paperback, something else happened. Essentially our world changed, at least here in America. On 9/11/01 terrorists flew two commercial airliners into the Trade Towers and brought them to the ground. They crashed another into the Pentagon. And only through the heroism of the doomed passengers on a fourth did we avoid the destruction of either the White House or the U.S. Capitol.

In response, the U.S. went to war in Afghanistan and destroyed the Taliban regime, though much of its leadership and that of the al-Qaida organization escaped. At home we underwent a brush with anthrax terrorism, and we still do not know whether this was truly designed to kill tens of thousands or was the work of a demented Paul Revere seeking to awaken us to the extraordinary vulnerability of our society. At this very moment, we are in the midst of a countdown towards a new war in the Middle East, possibly an American attack on Iraq. Most alarmingly, there is a growing danger that terrorists may have the capability of detonating a nuclear device within an American city.

When life itself is threatened, the focus on graceful existence may seem of secondary importance. Alternatively, when life itself is threatened, one may become particularly sensitive to whether our lives have lost touch with what is most essential. Both processes are now in play.

The traumatic events of 9/11 have, in their way, a particular bearing on the themes of this book. For many Americans, the events of that September day brought to the fore some very basic questions:

- What kind of a world are we living in?
- How could this have happened?
- Why is there this hatred of America?
- How can we prevent this from recurring, not just in the short run, but also in the long run?

As might be expected, Americans have given radically different answers to these questions. The dominant line of response has been:

- We are living in a world in which there is genuine evil.
- These events occurred because we were naive, because we had our guard down, because we did not retaliate more forcefully when terrorists started showing their disdain for American power.
- They hate us because our society has succeeded and because theirs have failed. They hate us for our freedoms, and for our economic achievements.
- To prevent this from happening again, we must make a clear example of what happens to regimes that host terrorists. To prevent this from happening again, we must wage unrelenting war against the terrorist, where necessary fighting in the shadows, without restriction.

A distinctly different line of thought is also heard, though it is far from national policy:

- The world we live in is one of great injustice and great resentment. Yes, there are horrible deeds, and cold-hearted killers, but 9/11 was not rooted in some metaphysics of evil. It developed in response to social contexts. Of particular importance is the failure of all dominant socio-economic models, including our own, to adequately respond to the deepest human needs.
- The specific events that happened are reflective of the vulnerability that exists even in the most militarily powerful nations, even

those with the most abundant economies. Indeed, because of our economic structures we may have a particular fragility. We were successfully attacked with very low-tech weapons—a small determined group with box cutters who commandeered commercial airliners.

- Why do they hate us? They hate us because of the economic and military dominance that the West has exercised over much of the rest of the world for the last several centuries. They hate us because we are in collusion with their corrupt rulers. They hate us because they see their deepest values as under attack by a form of civilization that we appear to epitomize. They hate us because they view the world in metaphysical absolutes, and see us as representing the great evil that exists.

- Can we prevent this from recurring? Perhaps not. This may just be the beginning. The terrorists of 9/11 may in the future be followed by those who will indeed have nuclear, chemical, or biological weapons of mass destruction—and they will be perfectly willing to use them to try to kill all of us. There are of course steps of self-defense to take in the short run, but real security will only emerge over a very long period of time, and only if we succeed in addressing the most basic failures of the social and global systems within which we live.

The two views represented above are not, in many ways, strictly incompatible. Indeed, many people have found themselves simultaneously holding elements of both perspectives. It is not my intent, in a new preface, to try to sort through these distinctly different responses to recent events. Nor, most definitely, do I intend to argue that the events of 9/11 have given greater credibility to any of the arguments in the book.

However, I do want to call attention to aspects of the book that connect with these most basic issues. Let me mention three:

What is America? In the opening chapter I argue that there is not, and there never has been, a single American dream. There are, and have always been, diametrically opposed conceptions of the place of money and economic largesse within the American ideal. From the beginning and up to the present day, a powerful stream in American thought has rejected the view that the purpose of economic activity is to serve as an engine that provides the cornucopia that is the good life. The alternative has been to view the economic sphere as having only a tangential relation to the good life. On this view a successful economy is not one that 'grows,' but one that at ever more modest levels of human effort successfully addresses fundamental economic needs. The good life occurs primarily outside the realms of getting and spending. The richness of this alternative tradition in American life is largely unknown to many Americans, and surely is invisible to those who only know America through the stereotypes of our own media exports. Yet it is a powerful tradition, one that, in the minds of the founding fathers, had an explicit connection to similar traditions among the ancient Greeks, as well as the early Christians.

What is the relation between the pursuit of economic abundance and social evil? After 9/11 we may listen differently to the 18th century Quaker theorist John Woolman, who argued that the worst of our social evils emerge from the desire to have more than one can produce from one's own labor. Woolman argued that slavery, exploitation, and war are all rooted in the individual's relation to money. He urged us to look to our dress, to our very clothes to see if we have not attired ourselves in a fashion that contains the seeds of the next war. Were he alive today, he would shift his gaze from clothing, which accounts for a mere 5% of household consumption, to transportation, which at 20% now exceeds what we spend on shelter. In particular Woolman would focus on the automobile, on gasoline and imported oil. He would argue that it is our pursuit of oil which has drawn us into foreign lands, just as pursuit of slaves did centuries ago. Why war with Iraq? Why are we now in danger of nuclear terrorists? Why are there vast American military encampments in the land of Mecca and Medina? Though, of course, an oversimplification, Woolman would say that we should look first at our cars. With a different transportation system, we could be out of the Middle East and perhaps in a different kind of world.

At the same time, post 9/11 one cannot read Woolman's near contemporary, Bernard Mandeville, as we once did. Mandeville, discussed at length in the interlude between Part I (on the politics of simplicity) and Part II (on graceful existence), was the author of *The Fable of the Bees.* And in his fable he articulated a very contemporary view of the world. The bees, a greedy, corrupt, and vain populace, all undergo a conversion to simple living. They become virtuous, and honest, and limited in their desires. They seek a better world, but good intentions hardly ensure good results. The effect is quite catastrophic; the once-booming economy contracts and then collapses. The denouement is not long in coming. The 'hive' is attacked and destroyed from the outside, by now more powerful invading forces. Thus, Mandeville too places the economic sphere within the larger questions of war and peace —but he reaches a very different conclusion than did Woolman. Essentially his is a world with external evils, and the bustling economy must be seen in relation to national security capabilities. If the world according to Woolman is one in which the United States would not have been attacked, the world of Mandeville is one in which only the American economy could have routed the Taliban with hardly an American combat casualty.

What is the good life? This, of course, is a central concern of the book. For most of us it is a question rarely asked. Yet post 9/11 most Americans reported that they had made some important changes in their lives. Change was largely in one direction—Americans pulled inward, toward family and friends, towards close relations, toward religion, towards the home. What came strikingly clear, at least for a blazing moment, is the fragility of our existence and the lives of those we most cherish.

Historians will tell us that war always has this effect. Such has certainly been the American experience. A determination to live a more rooted existence was evident during the Revolutionary War, the Civil War, and the First and Second World Wars. Yet the historians will also tell us that when the wars came to an end, Americans embarked on vast spending sprees, and whatever deeper insights were raised by the conflicts were soon overcome by the consumption booms that came with the peace.

To some this may seem a permanent cycle, a predictable swinging pendulum—but that is not the perspective of a genuine politics. The perspective of a politics is one of human agency; it is a commitment to the belief that first and foremost we are potential agents of change and creatures that can transform. Whether recent events have any lasting impact is something that we ourselves will determine, and for which we ourselves will be responsible. It's in our hands.

Jerome Segal
March 2002

P. S. The Simplicity Forum as its first political action has launched "Take Back Your Time Day" to focus America's attention on overwork, the time-crunch, and the new for a balanced life. It is scheduled for October 24, 2003—the date we would be finished working for the year if we had as much leisure as Europeans.

PREFACE

This book is about time, work, and money. Even as a child, I was aware that these were troubling and confusing matters. They troubled my father and mother, and they confused me.

Between 1943 and 1964, I lived at home with my parents and sisters. During that time, typically six days a week, my father would wake early in the morning. He would put on a white shirt starched rigid at the Chinese laundry. With that shirt he would wear a tie, a suit, and polished shoes. He would then leave our apartment in the Bronx and travel by subway to Brooklyn (in 1956 he learned to drive and bought his first car). I now know that when he arrived at work, he would take off the shirt, tie, suit, and shoes and change into work clothes. He was a blue-collar worker, employed in a small factory that made women's blouses.

In that factory he worked first as a cutter, then as a marker (the person who figures out how to lay the pattern on the reams of fabric so as to minimize waste), and then as the shop foreman. He always worked overtime, and often on Saturdays. He brought his pay home in a small brown envelope stuffed with tens and twenties. Coming home late, he often ate after the rest of the family had finished, and when he finished eating, he would tell stories.

Often they were the stories about what had happened that day, and inevitably he was a modern knight battling against the utter stupidity of the people around him: his boss, his fellow workers, or officials from the union (of which he was a proud member). Sometimes, however, the stories were of another world, the world that he had grown up in.

Born in a small village in Poland, he was the great-grandson of a famous Hassidic rabbi. (Years later, he and I would visit the Library of Congress and work through the several inches of card catalogue devoted to his famous ancestor). In his little corner of the world, he was something of a prince—always known in his town as the great-grandson of Rabbi K. As a youth, he rebelled against his religious background and became an ardent socialist. He was a natural leader and public speaker. By the time he was twenty-one, he had already been elected to public office and had served time as a political prisoner.

As a young man, he came to the United States as a tourist on the *Isle de France*. He came to visit his father and mother and sister, all of whom had emigrated. He came wearing hand-tailored suits, and planning to return to his life in Poland. He never went back.

At first, I suppose, his transition to life here was not very difficult. There was a vibrant Jewish socialist movement in New York. Everyone spoke Yiddish. There was a Yiddish theater (he sometimes performed), there were Yiddish papers (he sometimes wrote). He met my mother. She taught him English. She, too, was a socialist. She was also beautiful and a dancer. He had friends; he had relatives; he had ideals; he had a political movement. He lived in Manhattan.

Gradually, it all changed. My father had never pursued a career, had never even gone to college. He was devoted to the "movement" and took jobs just to earn some money. When I was growing up everything was different. The Depression was over. World War II was over. He was married, had two children, and was living in the Bronx. My mother stopped dancing. She took care of the house and, ultimately, four children. My father, for the most part, stopped his political activity. There were fewer friends. Mostly, it seemed, life was about making a living and supporting a family. He worked hard. He earned good money. But, he resented the work and resented what had happened to him. I remember he paid careful attention to how I was doing in school; he used to say, "Work now and you won't have to work later."

I did apply myself at school, but one of the great things about my childhood was time away from school. I was able to spend my summers with another branch of my mother's family. My mother's oldest sister never married. Having no children of her own, she became the extra parent of the children of her younger sisters. She owned a small cottage that was part of a summer cooperative some forty miles north of New York City. For years, my family would spend July at the cottage, and my mother's younger sister and family would spend August. My father chafed at the ambiguous arrangement, feeling neither guest nor owner. Ultimately my family spent the summers in the Bronx, passing many hours in the park nearby.

Fortunately, it was arranged that I would continue to spend my summers at the cottage, living with the family of my mother's younger sister. If our income bracket was lower middle class, theirs was what used to be called "working class." But my uncle wasn't a factory worker like my father, he was an artist. My cousins' family lived in Greenwich Village and paid $60 a month rent.

My uncle was a bit of a buffoon, but he was also a true magician. He saw the magic in the most ordinary things, and he could awaken you to that magic. He built a tiny frog pond in the woods—a place to sit on large stones and watch the tadpoles as they grew their legs. The cottage was on a hillside, and he spent a decade, perhaps it was two decades, transporting dirt from the front of the house to the back of the house, so that eventually there was level ground for a driveway and for a turn-around area. What fun it was to work with him in the August sun, sweating and straining to fill a homemade cart with front-of-the-house dirt. The other kids in the area used to come over just to join in the project.

Around the cottage we had some of the best raspberries that ever grew. In the July morning sun, we would walk a step or two out the door and gather jewels for our cereal. The cottage had neither phone, TV, nor even radio. It had just one bedroom, and at night we rigged up all sorts of sleeping places and shared what beds and couches we had. Most of the time, we had no car. My aunt was a great cook, and though no one said grace at any meal, there was a kind of pagan reverence at mealtime—a kind of food worship we all took part in. It wasn't about overeating, nor was it about being thankful for having food. It was about the food itself—about how good the bread was, even about how good the old family knife was that my uncle used to cut the bread. Great pleasure was found in the ordinary activities and things that surrounded and filled our lives.

But, it certainly wasn't all sweetness and light. Both families had their internal problems and considerable craziness. My mother did not work outside the home and, for many years, neither did my aunt. Both of them suffered from the isolation. For both of them, money was always an issue. For years, my parents fought about it. I was aware that my aunt watched every penny. Indeed, during the summers, she took note of everything I ate and made sure that I was not costing more than my parents were contributing for my keep. Indeed, some of the worse moments in the family, some that ended up estranging people for years, turned on the issues of money and property.

For years I passed between these two families who had gone different routes with respect to work and time and money, both of whom had failed to square the circle. The issues they struggled with never go away. When I was in college, I completed a double major, philosophy and economics. My economics honors thesis was about John Kenneth Galbraith's *The Affluent Society*. That was thirty-five years ago, and nowadays, struggling over whether to send my eight-year-old to private or public school, I'm still wrestling with the question of money and time. During those thirty-five years, I have worked in various venues, first as an academic philosopher, then as a congressional aide and administrator of the House Budget Committee's Task Force on the Distributive Impacts of Economic Policy, then as a policy analyst in the U.S. Agency for International Development, now as a peace activist concerned with the Israeli-Palestinian conflict, and as a research scholar at the University of Maryland's Institute for Philosophy and Public Policy. Through all of these positions, the topic of money and the role it plays in our lives as a society and as individuals follows me. This book is my attempt to answer questions I've had through the years about what we are looking for in life and how to capture it.

I've shared all the autobiographical material that I am going to in this book in the preface. Yet in its way, all of its content remains intensely personal. It is about something that many of us continue to feel and continue to struggle with daily, and the choices we make regarding what we expect from our jobs and our lives.

In the world today there is considerable confusion and uneasiness about how to live, in particular about those dimensions of life that are sharply impacted by the economic realm. Whether it be questions of overload, of hectic lifestyles and harried existence, or issues of materialism and consumption, or concerns over interpersonal competition, careerism, overwork, loss of leisure, or loss of security—there is a widespread skepticism that our fast-paced, mass-consumption society represents the highest form of human social development. On the most visceral level, for many of us, something just doesn't feel right. We have lost any semblance of graceful existence, and we sense it, even if we can't articulate it.

As an American, it is the United States and the Western tradition that I know best. Thus, while these issues are of global concern, middle-class life in the United States provides the contemporary context for much of my discussion. But, in spite of the examples I use that pertain mainly to life in the United States, this inquiry into simple living should be of particular interest to those in wealthy countries, such as France and Japan, where much that they cherish is under pressure, whether it be two-hour lunches, the small shops that give life to city streets, or family traditions and bonds that provide shape and meaning to the cycle of life. Equally, what is discussed should have special relevance to those in low-income countries. We in the United States and in other rich lands have, somewhere along the line, made a wrong turn. We are not quite sure where it was, in part because we are not sure where we are. Yet, even without fully diagnosing our own situation, there are clear mistakes that we have made that others can learn from.

The subtitle of this book is "Toward a Philosophy and Politics of Simple Living." Given that, the plan of this book is the reverse of what might be expected. I start with politics and end with philosophy. I take it as given that there is a widespread desire for a simpler way of life. Books on simple living abound; magazines regularly feature stories on people trying to "cut back"; there are simple-living web sites and simplicity support groups. Part I concerns itself with how we can move toward the simpler lives we crave. Its central thesis is that this is not merely something to be pursued on the personal level. The missing half of the equation is a politics of simplicity. Contrary to those who offer advertising, consumer culture, or even human nature as an explanation of why we never feel we have enough, I argue that we have created a very inefficient society—one in which our very real and legitimate economic needs can be met only with high levels of income. As a result, it is very hard to work less when this means a lower income for your family. This is a problem that we must address as a society, through new ways of thinking about economic and social policy.

In Part II, I explore elements of a philosophy of simple living. My main concern there is whether, at bottom, we are simple creatures with simple needs. I consider the nature of genuine wealth. I call for a form of simple living that I term "graceful simplicity," and from which the title of this book emerges. Gracefulness is one of those elusive concepts of great power; like "love," it is not easy to say exactly what it is, but we can feel its absence like a pain in the heart. The absence of gracefulness captures much of what is wrong with the way we live and our sense that things have gotten "hard," whether it be hard to make ends meet, hard times within the family, or the hard edges of our daily interactions. This is not a problem easily righted. Achieving gracefulness is always a challenge. To live gracefully, in both its inner and outer dimensions, is to have mastered an art.

The central theme of the book is that we cannot think coherently about economic life unless we situate all that is economic within a broader conception of human existence. Since this is not how we typically think of the economy and economics, we need to go back to basics and ask, "What is an economy for?" This question, I suggest, cannot be properly answered unless we can also answer some of the questions that once animated philosophers, such as "What is the nature of human happiness?" and "What is true wealth?"

The reader is advised that I allow the discussion to go where it needs to, without paying much respect to familiar boundaries that restrict any given book's subject matter to certain topics. Thus, in the course of the inquiry, I consider diverse matters that are generally not found between the same covers: for instance, Aristotle's views about money, strategies for giving up paid employment, the virtues of Sabbath observance, and the extra financial costs associated with shifting from one to two wage earners. While initially this may be a bit disconcerting, I believe the variety of topics I touch upon gives strength to the argument, making it something of a web, tacked down at many points.

Two crosscutting themes recur throughout the text: the importance of the aesthetic dimension of life, and the central role of the services that people provide for each other. Let me address these in turn.

The choice of the term "graceful simplicity" is intended to give emphasis to the aesthetic dimension—by this I mean far more than surrounding oneself with beautiful objects. Gracefulness is a way of being in the world, and there is an aesthetics of time that is violated when we live in constant rush, when our lives are a succession of agenda items, when we live like someone racing through the supermarket with a shopping list. To live well means giving things the time they deserve, be it time for the children, one's spouse and lover, one's friends, or the garden.

Taking the time to do things right strengthens our ability to live more simply. Slowing down and achieving a human pace brings out the value in the things we have and the things we do. Living in a beautiful environment, whether it be a beautiful city or the unspoiled countryside, has a similar power to liberate us from the imperative to consume. Rather than retreating to the isolated self-created environment of home and possessions, we are drawn toward a shared public space.

Our need for beauty also forms part of the discussion of household budgets, and of our need to escape to places of beauty. In a broader sense, aesthetics is also at the heart of the notion of Sabbath observance—a cultural/religious construct that seeks to enable all, rich and poor alike, a one-day-a-week opportunity to experience gracefulness within time.

The second theme that laces its way through the book is the issue of services—the centrality to the good life of the things that people do for one another—paid or unpaid. The contexts in which this arises are quite distinct. In the final chapter, when taking up the question "What is real wealth?" I respond that real wealth primarily resides in access to the services of others and to modes of activity in which you can be of genuine service as well.

In the Greece of Aristotle, for those who were privileged, it was indeed easier to live gracefully on a modest income, because graceful living rested on three forms of inequality: the subjugation of women, slavery, and vast economic inequality. At that time substantial numbers of people were channeled into lives devoted only to serving the needs and pleasures of others. Even today, in Third World countries we often find that people in the middle class live more gracefully than they do in the United States, because they can afford to hire servants. Ultimately, this is much of what people seek when they seek riches. Yet in this sense it is logically impossible to have a rich society, because no matter what the economic abundance, it is impossible for everyone to have servants and yet not themselves be servants.

The most significant progress that mankind has made over the last two thousand years is on the level of moral ideas. In thought, and, to a considerable extent, in practice, we have made progress in overcoming the presumption that only a limited set of people possess transcendent potentials. Today everyone affirms their right to seek genuine fulfillment. On one level this is at the heart of many of the contemporary struggles within the household and over the role of women. But it also bears on the issue of living simply, of living in a way that does not give rise to an excessive need for the services of others, and, thus, it motivates the search for a form of graceful existence that can be widely attained. This is the primary goal of the politics of simplicity.

Taken more deeply, however, what people need is not merely to be the recipients of services, and to be freed from roles of subservient service providers. In addition, we have a need for the meaning and creative expression that comes through the services we provide to others. Viewed through this lens, a politics of simplicity offers a distinctly different understanding of what the output of an economy is. Rather than thinking of economic output as a gigantic heap of material goods and work as a labor input, instead, the economy is better conceived as the creator (and destroyer) of life roles. The material outputs are the means of our subsistence. What is really important are the forms of service interaction, the forms of work that a society provides, paid and unpaid.

This, in turn, circles back to the issue of time. When we give to things and to each other the time that is deserved, the meaning of service provision is transformed. When we act in haste, whether it be at work or with friends, our activity and ultimately our very being becomes a mere means to some intended outcome. When this is our general way of being in the world, we have failed in what Thoreau identified as the great enterprise—to make living poetic.

ACKNOWLEDGMENTS

I owe a debt of gratitude to quite a few people; foremost is to my wife, Naomi Nim. Special thanks also go to my brother-in-law Arthur Pincus, without whose enthusiasm for the project, early assistance, and good advice, I probably would not have written this book. And thank you Rick Wolff for your good advice.

Norbert Hornstein and Robert Sprinkle were good enough to read the manuscript in its early stages and provided very helpful suggestions. To David Crocker I owe not only thanks for reading the manuscript, but appreciation for our long intellectual comradeship.

Numerous friends and colleagues provided help directly or indirectly. To Arthur Evenchik, Sue Dwyer, David Ludden, Chuck Schneiderhan, Kate Cook, Dennis Gartner, Frithjof Bergmann, John Farmer, Michael Neuschatz, Jan Goldberg, and Lara Sao Pedro: thank you, one and all. And thank you to Joel Fishman at Bedford Book Works for your good sense and to Amelia Sheldon at Henry Holt for your good humor and good edits.

I also want to express my appreciation to the Pew Charitable Trusts for their support for the Institute for Philosophy and Public Policy at the University of Maryland for an Institute-wide project on consumption and, more generally, to my colleagues at the Institute for many years of discussion and fellowship.

Finally, I am uniquely indebted to my son, Max, my primary connection to the simple joys of life, who never lets me forget that there is nothing simple about being a parent.

PART I

TOWARD A POLITICS OF SIMPLICITY

Chapter One

_____

TWO WAYS OF THINKING ABOUT MONEY

In popular imagery, especially when seen from afar, America is often portrayed as singing a single song, as if there were only one meaning to the American Dream. This is not so. The ambivalent response that many in the world have toward American life is mirrored in an ambivalence that many Americans have toward their own life, and this is an essential part of the American tradition, even when people are "making it" in America. There is always that nagging question, "Is this really the way to live?"

Long before there was an America, there were two American Dreams, and they reflect two ways of thinking about money. In Western thought, from the very beginning to the present day, people had doubts about the real value of riches and the things money can buy. There has always been a conflict between the view that "more is better" and the view that "just enough is plenty."

This divide is reflected in two very different visions of the good life. It is the underlying thesis of this book that the Alternative Dream, the dream that rests upon the attainment of a simple life, is the sounder vision.

ARISTOTLE'S CHALLENGE TO OUR WAY OF LIFE

This book is about contemporary life, but I want to start with Aristotle for two reasons. First, because his challenge to a money-oriented form of life remains as powerful today as it was 2,300 years ago. Second, because, for all his wisdom, Aristotle never had to wrestle with the problems we face. So many of the contemporary problems that prevent people in the middle class from enjoying the good life emerge from three forms of genuine moral and social progress that Aristotle never envisioned: the elimination of slavery, the liberation of women, and the affirmation of the right of ordinary working people to self-fulfillment. Seeing both the strengths and weaknesses in Aristotle gives us a clearer perspective on our own situation.

Aristotle's *Politics* is surprising in that it opens with a discussion of the household. But this is exactly the right touchstone for both politics and economics. The household is a central ground of the good life, and all economic arrangements must be judged by whether they enable the household to perform its function as locus and support for the human good. This is one of the central messages of this book: we must put the proper functioning of the household at the center of the way we think about economic life.

The core issue, as Aristotle puts it, is property and "the art of acquisition"—that is, how people make a living. He starts with the observation that there are a variety of different modes of subsistence, and that this gives rise to a variety of different ways of life. This is as true among animals as it is of humans. Some animals live in herds, and others live in isolation. Some eat plants and others meat. Among human beings, Aristotle identifies five "natural" ways of life: pastoral, farming, fishing, hunting, and, interestingly, piracy. What he calls "true wealth" is acquired through these activities and consists of the amount of household property that suffices for the good life. This he regards as a limited amount. We can call this the perspective that "just enough is plenty."

In distinction to these modes of acquisition that supply the household with its needs, there is a second form of the art of acquisition, which Aristotle believes to be "unnatural":

> The other form is a matter only of retail trade, and it is concerned only with getting a fund of money, and that only by the method of conducting the exchange of commodities.
>
> The acquisition of wealth by the art of household management [as contrasted with the art of acquisition in its retail form] has a limit; and the object of that art is not an unlimited amount of wealth.[1]

The difference is between an approach to acquisition that views it as functional to the life of the household and one in which it takes on a life of its own, such that it reproduces unchecked without regard to the larger life of the organism, and ultimately undermines that life—the very description of what we now understand as cancer.

What Aristotle presents in these lines isn't just an academic distinction, but a clash between two different ways of life, each captured by a way of thinking about money. In the first, money and the things one can buy with it play an important but limited role. Life is not about money. It is not about getting rich. It is about something higher, whether it is philosophy, or art, or the pursuit of knowledge, or participation with one's fellow citizens in the ever-absorbing process of governing the democratic polis. Every person lives within a household, and the household has its economic needs—but the point is to attain only what is sufficient to enable one to turn away from money-getting and undertake the real activities of life.

In this first vision of life, only some ways of making a living are viewed by Aristotle as acceptable. His list of farmer, hunter, fisherman, herdsman, or pirate has an arbitrary quality to it. What is important is what these choices are intended to rule out. The one thing you cannot do is spend your life grubbing for money. You do not become a businessman, a retail trader, a man of commerce. These all represent a kind of slavishness to money. Nor (one would hope) do you find yourself so destitute that you must work for someone else, for that, too, is a form of slavery. The good life requires some degree of good fortune. Ideally for Aristotle, you are born financially independent.

But how do people manage to go so wrong about money? How does it gain such control over their lives? Aristotle suggests that this emerges from a deep misconception about the nature of human happiness; it is this that leads to the focus on the pursuit of higher and higher levels of consumption and of the higher income necessary to sustain them.

Aristotle identifies what he terms "external goods"; these externals include wealth, property, power, and reputation. These are the elements that make up the standard vision of success both then and now. To these, Aristotle contrasts elements of character, what he terms the "goods of the soul," fortitude, temperance, justice, and wisdom.[2] This is a familiar distinction, between inner and outer, between matters of worldliness and matters of virtue. We continue to make these distinctions when we are reflective, not so much about our own lives, but when we think about what we want for our children—are we more concerned that our children be rich and success-ful or that they develop into good human beings? We tell them that these "externals" are not what is really important in life, and we hope that they will listen.

Aristotle tells us that happiness "belongs more to those who have cultivated their character and mind to the uttermost, and kept acquisition of external goods within moderate limits."[3] Those who lose in life are those "who have managed to acquire more external goods than they can possibly use, and are lacking in the goods of the soul."[4] (For "soul" we might substitute "character" or "mental health.")

Of course, one might say, "Why the either/or? Why not have both?" But Aristotle, and many others, have thought that we really do have to choose. In explaining the relationship between externals and the good life, Aristotle tells us: "External goods, like all other instruments, have a necessary limit of size . . . any excessive amount of such things must either cause its possessor some injury, or at any rate, bring him no benefit."[5]

This passage, which has been overlooked by many historians of economics, implicitly is the first statement of the principle of diminishing marginal utility. We might remember from introductory economics that marginal utility is the extra utility (or happiness, satisfaction, pleasure, fulfillment) that someone gets from each successive unit of something. Marginal utility generally declines; the pleasure from the first ice-cream cone is greater than from the second, and most of us can hardly eat a third.

Aristotle is saying that with all external goods, we find that the more we have, the less utility we receive from each additional amount, and that at some point "any excessive amount" does us no good and may even harm us.

Actually, Aristotle's view of what nineteenth-century economists would identify as the "utility curve" is quite radical. As we acquire more and more things, not only does the total utility (i.e., happiness, satisfaction) level fail to rise beyond an upper bound (as in classical presentations of the diminishing character of marginal utility), but the total utility level may actually diminish, implying that the marginal benefit attached to excessive amounts of external goods diminishes beyond the zero level and actually becomes harmful. Translated into a thesis about money, Aristotle's formulation tells us that beyond a given level, additional increments of money are not only useless, but negative in their effect. Translated into a thesis about the society at large, it suggests that economic growth beyond a given point is actually harmful to human happiness. It is a straightforward rejection of the idea that "more is better."

Aristotle goes further in his account. The problem is not merely of the sort that John Kenneth Galbraith described (twenty-three centuries later) in *The Affluent Society*, where economic life is compared to life on a squirrel wheel, each of us fruitlessly expending time and resources but not getting anywhere as the wheel just spins faster and faster. For Galbraith the indictment is that we are wasting our time and energy, and thus wasting our lives.

For Aristotle the issue is even more serious than a life of wasted pursuit. The pursuit of higher and higher levels of income results in a distortion of the personality, such that we never come to be the persons that we most truly are; we are divorced from our truest selves. Instead people are "led to occupy themselves wholly in the making of money . . . using each and every capacity in a way not consonant with its nature."[6]

When Aristotle says "the lower form of the art of acquisition has come into vogue," he is quietly telling us that he sees his own civilization threatened by a new and troubling vision of the place of money in the good life. He is giving voice to concerns that, centuries later, in religious form and in America, will be repeated in the form of fiery jeremiads issued from the pulpit.

Though he might have, Aristotle doesn't use phrases such as "we have lost our souls"—instead he speaks of a distortion of human capacities. He offers an example:

> The proper function of courage, for example, is not to produce money but to give confidence. The same is true of military and medical ability: neither has the function of producing money: the one has the function of producing victory, and the other that of producing health. But those of whom we are speaking turn all such capacities into forms of the art of acquisition, as though to make money were the one aim and everything else must contribute to that aim.[7]

Consider this comment about "medical ability"—Aristotle is talking about what it is to be a doctor. What we once expected to encounter when we went to the doctor was someone whose motivation centered around the inherent value of medicine—the health of the patient. What we did not expect, and once would have been repelled by, was to have encountered a businessman in a white coat or an entrepreneur with aides who are specialists in billing practices. When this happens across the board, when everything is about money, a civilization is cracking apart.

It should be clear that Aristotle's critique is not merely about certain specific economic activities (e.g., retail sales as opposed to production). It is an indictment of a general outlook and form of life. When these become dominant in society, the object of criticism is then the entire form of social life or civilization.

Such a civilization, and I believe Aristotle would include much of the modern world in this category, is to be condemned as representing a distortion of human nature and a general thwarting of the possibility of human fulfillment.

When every human capacity gets placed at the service of obtaining money, *we ourselves are transformed and distorted*.[8] That's why you can't have it all—why there is conflict between the two American Dreams—who "you" are changes through the choices you (and your household) make toward matters of acquisition, careers, "success." Within the Aristotelian framework, to say that our capacities, that is, our selves, are separated from their proper function, is to say that we are thus denied self-actualization or human fulfillment. It is also to say that we are thus denied the possibility of living well; for to live well for Aristotle is to express one's richest potentials at high levels of excellence.

It is easy to miss the full significance of this, as the Aristotelian vocabulary is not our own. But we can shift the language a bit. Perhaps we would speak of a life so absorbed in moment-to-moment gain and careerism that one loses or never deeply develops a sense of oneself and never lives the life he or she intended to. In the end, one is left with a sense of emptiness and waste. It's captured in the bumper sticker that reads: "No one ever died wishing they had spent more time at the office."

These matters largely fall by the wayside in contemporary thinking about the economic realm. Instead we hear a very different story, one in which we come to the economic realm as well-formed consumers. We have multiple wants and desires. There are limited resources. Producers compete for our spending money by creating the products that best satisfy our desires. In an efficient system, the companies that serve people's desires most adequately and efficiently make profits; the others disappear. The result is more and more consumer satisfaction. As consumers we are said to be sovereign. But to participate in the process, we must sell our labor services to those who can make best use of them. Thus, we take jobs that pay more, and we are enabled to buy more. When the system is working well, some of what is earned is reinvested, and the economy grows, gaining greater capacity to produce. Incomes rise and the level of consumption rises within, making us even better off than we were before.

In contrast we can identify an approach that might be termed Aristotelian:

+ There is no distinct economic realm.
+ Economic institutions and policy must be judged in terms of how they affect the good life and the healthy personality.
+ The central institution to be supported by economic life is the household (which in turn supports worthwhile activity in the larger world).
+ The good life is not one of consumption, but of the flourishing of our deepest selves.
+ Absorption in a life of acquisitiveness distorts the personality out of all recognition.
+ What we need for our well-being is only a moderate supply of material goods. As we acquire more, material possessions are of diminishing value.

Ultimately the additional contribution to the good life of having more money reaches zero, and even becomes negative.

Aristotle, in his analysis of the limited place of money in the good life, and in his emphasis on how absorption in acquisition undermines both the healthy personality and the good life, can be seen as the intellectual father of a philosophy of simple living.

But before leaving Aristotle, we must recognize the other side of the picture. Aristotle was not a believer in the general equality of all men and women. Though he did not hold a racial theory, he believed that there were some people who were "natural slaves" in that they lacked the capability of governing themselves. Of course, at some point in life—when we are children—we all lack this capability. But Aristotle believed that a significant class of adult males, and women generally, lacked the capability to govern themselves.

These views about the naturalness of slavery and the subservience of women turn out to have an intimate relationship to the question of simple living, and to graceful living in particular. Later in the book I will consider the question "What is real wealth?" Ultimately I want to argue that most wealth resides in the ability to draw on the services of other people, and this is especially true of that wealth which contributes to graceful living. We normally think of such wealth as residing in financial assets (e.g., money, stocks, bonds, real estate), but it can equally reside in relationships (e.g., friendship, parent-child relationships, marriage). It can also reside in institutionalized relations of unequal power such as slavery, rigid class distinctions, and the domination of women. When one has access to the services of others through such institutional structures, it is indeed easier to live well, even gracefully, with less money; one has found nonmonetized ways of accessing valued services. The great challenge is to find a way to live simply, gracefully, and well, not only without excessive dependence upon money, but without reliance on unjust social institutions.

For Aristotle, this never really clicked into place. While he recognized that not all who were in fact slaves were of a "slavish nature," he did not challenge slavery itself. It is similar when he considers the situation of artisans; that is, skilled craftsmen employed in making the artifacts of everyday life. He speaks of the mechanical type of artisan as being subject to a "limited servitude," by which he means that the artisan is in parts of his life subject to the will of his master. But then, in contrast to the situation with slaves, Aristotle tells us that while "the slave belongs to the class of those who are naturally what they are; . . . no shoemaker or any other artisan, belongs to that class."[9]

Here Aristotle makes two points of great importance. First, artisans—and, we can say, most working people—are subject to a limited servitude; their lives bear some significant resemblance to slavery. (Twenty-three centuries later people would speak of "wage slavery.") Second, Aristotle says that no artisan is "naturally" what he is. That is, such limited slavery is unnatural.

Aristotle should have concluded from this that there is something unnatural, or at least inadequate, about the polis, understood as the sum of the socio-economic processes and structures within which Greek life occurred. He fails to do so. In his discussion of the limited slavery of workers, there is no proposal for an alternative social arrangement, despite the fact that he sees the way the institution is incompatible with the fulfillment of the deeper potentials of those who labor within it. This, I believe, emerged from an unexamined assumption that such must necessarily be the case if we are to have a social order in which there are at least some people who are fully developed and living a free and flourishing existence.

There is a passage in Aristotle in which he considers the possibility of a world in which it would not be necessary for people to work in partial or full enslavement. But he offers this speculation not as a future that might some-day be, but as a fantasy that cannot be. Thus, it shows why things must be as they are:

> There is only one condition in which we can imagine managers not needing subordinates, and masters not needing slaves. This condition would be that each (inanimate) instrument could do its own work, at the word of command or by intelligent anticipa-tion . . . as a shuttle should weave of itself and a plectrum should do its own harp playing.[10]

It is revealing that he speaks here of the "needs" of managers and masters, rather than of the needs of slaves and people who work for a living. In part this merely shows the partial blindness of even the greatest minds, but it also reflects his inability to foresee the actual occurrence of major sustained tech-nological progress. It is too much to expect that he could have truly foreseen full automation—where the machines operate on their own. But he might have had a vision of the continued increase in the productivity of labor.

Given that Aristotle was clear about the limited value of acquiring more and more, he would have been led to the alternative use of productivity increases: not to have more and more, but to allow the ordinary person to work less and less in order to produce that limited output that is required for the good and free life. In short, through productivity growth there is a poten-tial that can be put in the service of self-actualization for the ordinary person. It is such productivity growth that allowed us to go from the twelve-hour day to the eight-hour day, and opens the possibility of the six-hour day, or the three-day weekend. For a hundred years this was part of how we used pro-ductivity growth; we stopped doing this sixty years ago. Had he seen the deeper potentials of all people, Aristotle would have seen the polis of his day not as a model for humankind, but as modeling only in the life of its free male citizens, a life that someday might be available to all, provided that we used that productivity growth, not for ever-increasing amounts of unneces-sary goods, but for the elimination of slavish forms of activity.

Put in other terms, for Aristotle the existence of mass poverty does not emerge as a problem. With his acceptance of the naturalness of slavery and the subservience of women, and his acquiescence to the limited servitude of workers, the socioeconomic framework of the polis fits neatly into a theory of human development. The polis is the environment with which human fulfillment occurs. The situation of the vast majority of persons simply falls by the wayside, as not raising any pressing problems. Having limited potential, they reach their full development within subservient roles. Indeed, it is really not until the eighteenth century that the equality of ordinary people in their entitlement and potential for achieving the highest levels of human development are embedded within the structures of political ideology and action. And it is not until the twentieth century that equality begins to be substantially extended to women.

What Aristotle did do, however, remains of enormous importance. He challenged the idea that acquiring more and more things was good for the individual. He set his critique of commercial and acquisitive forms of life within a theory of human development that stressed the exercise and perfection of distinctly human capacities, capacities that are distorted and stunted if we allow economic pursuits to dominate our lives.

Appreciating the virtues of Aristotle along with his limitations is particularly important for a balanced appreciation of the problem inherent in our own way of life. We live in a society that, as a result of both economic growth and social struggle, is substantially along the way to overcoming historic legacies of slavery, mass poverty, and the subjugation of women. Yet many of the problems that we face, problems that make it more difficult to achieve simple living, emerge because of these legacies and transitions. But they also endure because we have lost sight of much that Aristotle has to teach us with respect to the place of the economic within the good life: *The point of an economy, even a dynamic economy, is not to have more and more; it is to liberate us from the economic—to provide a material platform from which we may go forth to build the good life. That's the Alternative American Dream.*

SIMPLE LIVING AND AMERICAN DREAMS

We entirely mistake our own history if we think of simple living as some recent fad. The idea of simple living has always been part of the American psyche—sometimes central, sometimes only a minor theme, but always present. From the earliest days of the American experience, advocates of simple living have challenged consumerism and materialism.

Simple living, especially in America, has meant many things.[11] For Christians the central inspiration for a life of simplicity has been the life of Jesus. In the hands of the Puritans, this emerged as a life of religious devotion, a lack of ostentation, and plenty of hard work. It was certainly not a leisure expansion movement as it is today. Nor was simple living a matter of individual choice; sumptuary laws invoked the power of the state to restrict consumption display, and economic life was regulated to limit the role of greed in human affairs.

In the hands of the Quakers, the concept of the simple life underwent an evolution. For the Puritans, at least part of the motivation for sumptuary laws was to prevent those in the lower classes from putting on the manners of those above them; among Quakers, the restrictions on display and consumption became more widely applicable. Most important, the pursuit of luxurious consumption was linked to a broad range of injustices and social problems, including alcoholism, poverty, slavery, and ill treatment of the Indians. Here, perhaps, are the origins of a radical politics of plain living— the belief that if people adopted the simple life, all of society would be transformed.

The key Quaker theorist of the simple life was John Woolman. Central to Woolman's thought was the recognition that people could be "necessitated to labour too hard." He focused on the plight of those who did not own their own land but rented it from large estates. If the rent was too high, the amount of labor required of the poor would oppress them and draw them away from the proper affairs of life. But rent was an intermediate concern; what was really at issue was the extent to which one person would be required to labor so that another might have superfluous luxuries. Woolman wrote, "Were all superfluities, and the desires of outward greatness laid aside," then "moderate labour with the blessing of Heaven would answer all good purposes . . . and a sufficient number have time to attend on the proper affairs of civil society."[12] Thus, he maintained that "every degree of luxury of what kind soever and every demand for money inconsistent with divine order hath some connexion with unnecessary labour." Woolman called on his listeners to follow the example of Jesus in simple food and dress. He saw their desire for luxurious consumption as the core motive that resulted in the practice "of fetching men to help to labour from distant parts of the world, to spend the remainder of their lives in the uncomfortable conditions of slaves." He also identified selfishness as the cause of past wars, telling us to "look upon our treasures, and the furniture of our houses, and the garment in which we array ourselves, and try whether the seeds of war have nourishment in these our possessions, or not." Were Woolman alive today, it is likely that he would extend his critique, arguing that excessive consumption, and the desire for it, is at the root of both the drug and environmental problems we face. Indeed, Woolman would probably have been receptive to the idea that the harsh poverty of many Third World countries emerges from the excessive consumption of the rich nations.

In the mid-1700s, in the years prior to the Revolution, the ideas of simple living and democratic government were intertwined. For many of the leaders of the Revolution, however, the ideal was not the simple life of Jesus, but the simple life of the self-governing citizens of ancient Greece and Rome. Key figures in the revolutionary period, in particular Samuel Adams, were deeply concerned about the relationship between our political health and the individual pursuit of luxury. The rebirth of democracy in the world brought with it an interest in the ancient Greek and Roman experiments, and why they disappeared. There was a concern (as there is today) with the virtue of officeholders. Genuine democracy seemed incompatible with too great an absorption in getting rich. There was great fear of the corrupting influences of unbridled commercialism. When the colonists boycotted British goods, it was not just a tactic of the independence movement; Britain was viewed as the Great Satan, exporting the corruptions of capitalism.

In their correspondence, John Adams and Thomas Jefferson assessed the prospects for building a nonmaterialist society. Jefferson emphasized civic virtue, and looked to public policy, in particular state-supported schools and values education, as the foundation of such a society. Adams viewed this as unrealistically "undertaking to build a new universe." He himself feared economic growth, however, and argued for preventing both extreme poverty and extravagant riches. Both men feared rather than celebrated boundless economic opportunity.

Benjamin Franklin's views on these questions are also worth noting; they, too, have a contemporary echo. In Franklin we have an unusual mixture: the espousal of frugality, hard work, and restrained consumption as the vehicles for getting ahead, the central patterns of behavior that will lead to wealth. Thus, in the preface to *Poor Richard's Almanac*, which was reprinted in fourteen languages under the title *The Way to Wealth*,[13] Franklin writes, "But dost thou love Life, then do not squander Time; for that's the stuff Life is made of." And "If Time be of all Things the most precious, wasting Time must be, as Poor Richard says, the greatest Prodigality." Franklin was concerned with how the average person might remain free in his own life, his own master. "Employ thy Time well, if thou meanest to gain Leisure." He warns of the perils of spending and in particular of borrowing. The great thing is to save. "We must add Frugality, if we would make our Industry more certainly successful. A Man may, if he knows not how to save as he gets, keep his Nose all his Life, to the Grindstone, and die not worth a Groat at last. . . . If you would be wealthy . . . think of Saving as well as Getting." Note that here Franklin is advocating simple living as a means to future wealth, quite a different reason than those that animated Woolman.

Franklin warned that the dangers of excessive consumption are easily missed. And he was quite demanding in what he viewed as "excessive." He wrote, "You may think perhaps, that a little Tea, or a little Punch now and then, Diet a little more costly, Clothes a little finer, and a little Entertainment now and then, may be no great Matter; but remember what Poor Richard says, Many a Little makes a Mickle. . . . A small Leak will sink a great Ship."

He continued, "The artificial Wants of Mankind thus become more numerous than the Natural. . . . When you have bought one fine Thing, you must buy ten more, that your Appearance may be all of a Piece. . . . 'Tis easier to suppress the first Desire, than to satisfy all that follows it. . . . What Use is this Pride of Appearance, for which so much is risked, so much is suffered? It cannot promote Health, or ease Pain; it makes no Increase of Merit in the Person, it creates Envy, it hastens Misfortune."

Franklin rails against going into debt. Credit cards would have seemed to him the instruments of our undoing. "What Madness must it be to run in Debt for these Superfluities! . . . think what you do when you turn in Debt; you give to another Power over your Liberty. . . . Preserve your Freedom; and maintain your Independency: Be Industrious and free; be frugal and free."

While Franklin spoke to the individual, in American history, the mode of response to the dominant commercial culture has often been communal. Americans have been utopian, not in the sense of speculation on utopia, but in the actual establishment of a community wherein this dominance by the economic is overcome. Utopian thought has a long and rich history, much of it European. But it was in America, both before and after the founding of the United States, that the impulse to go ahead and just create that better world was the strongest.

Though the formation of these communities was not unique to the

American experience, the abundance and constancy of utopian communities does appear to be distinctly American. Indeed there has not been a single year in the history of the United States without communes. One recent study of American communes concluded:

> The extent and continuity of the communal phenomenon had no equal outside the United States. . . . In modern times the United States is the only place where voluntary communes have existed continuously for 250 years.[14]

Two features of these utopian communities are particularly noteworthy. First, with few exceptions, they were communes. Property was typically held in common, and sometimes income was pooled. And second, they were typically not merely residential sites, but work sites as well. The community collectively owned land and capital, and the community both provided for itself and collectively produced for the outside world. Thus, virtually all of these communities challenge the boundaries between household and workplace that had begun to emerge in the seventeenth century. In doing so as a community, through the holding of the common property of the unified home/work site, they were reestablishing the extended establishment-family. In a sense, these communities could be seen as large establishment-households.

The uninterrupted history of utopian communes throughout American history speaks of an ongoing practical discourse that seeks through actual life experiments to break the boundaries between home and economy, and to replace the harsh marketplace relations of worker/master, of owner/employer, with a simpler life within a "circle of affection." In the mid-1800s such communes flourished. In some ways this period prefigured the communes, vegetarianism, nudism, and animal rights efforts of the 1960s.

Filled with a sense of adventure and experiment, but of a more individualist bent, was Henry David Thoreau. In *Walden* he looked about him and saw mostly foolishness—people not knowing how to grab hold of the gift of life. He reveled in the energy of youth and in its ability to find out what older generations had never seen.

> Practically, the old have no very important advice to give the young, their own experience has been so partial, and their lives have been such miserable failures. . . . Here is life, an experiment to a great extent untried by me. . . . If I have any experience which

I think valuable, I am sure to reflect
nothing about.[15]

With words that had echoes of Aris
necessities are few, yet we subject oursel
world that had taken the wrong turn. "
trifling in comparison with those whic
they were only twelve and had an en
enslaves us. "I see young men, my townsmen, wh
inherited farms, houses, barns, cattle and farming tools; for the
easily acquired than got rid of." Of most men Thoreau says, "they begin digging their graves as soon as they are born. . . . Men labor under a mistake. The better part of the man is soon ploughed into the soil for compost." We must take better care of ourselves, of our potentials. "The finest qualities of our nature, like the bloom on fruits, can be preserved only by the most delicate handling. Yet we do not treat ourselves nor one another thus tenderly." We miss that which is best in life. "Most men, even in this comparatively free country, through mere ignorance and mistake, are so occupied with the factitious cares and superfluously coarse labors of life that its finer fruits cannot be plucked by them."[17]

Yes, the necessities must be met, "for not till we have secured these are we prepared to entertain the true problems of life with freedom and a prospect of success."[18] But "most of the luxuries, and many of the so called comforts of life are not only not indispensable, but positive hindrances to the elevation of mankind. With respect to luxuries and comforts, the wisest have ever lived a more simple and meager life than the poor."[19] He tells us that "none can be an impartial or wise observer of human life but from the vantage ground of what we should call voluntary poverty."[20] The dictates of wisdom call for "a life of simplicity, independence, magnanimity and trust."

For Thoreau it is not necessity that enslaves us. Rather we have become the "slave-drivers" of ourselves, "the slave and prisoner of [our] own opinion of [ourselves]." Once we have satisfied our necessities, rather than laboring for superfluities, it is time to "adventure on life." But few undertake this adventure. Instead, "the mass of men lead lives of quiet desperation." It is from a disease of the spirit that Thoreau recoils, one that people may not even be aware of. "A stereotyped but unconscious despair is concealed even under what are called the games and amusements of mankind. There is no play in them. . . ."[21]

u called Americans away from their overabsorption with
, from their self-subjugation to a life of toil. Unlike earlier
simple living, he was not calling people to religion or to civic
ent; rather he was calling us as individuals to find our own nature,
ne ourselves at a higher level of experience. He called for simple living
rder to enable the life of the mind, of art, literature, poetry, philosophy,
nd an almost reverential engagement with Nature.

Interest in simple living was harder to find in the post–Civil War period, but it reemerged powerfully toward the turn of the century. There was a reaction against materialism and the hectic pace of urban life. In those days it was *The Ladies' Home Journal* (of all things) that led the charge against the dominant materialist ethos. Under a crusading editor, Edward Bok, it served as a guide for those in the middle class seeking simplicity. By 1910, the *Journal* had a circulation of close to 2 million, making it the largest-selling magazine in the world. This period also witnessed a movement of aesthetic simplicity. It was influenced by the English thinkers John Ruskin and William Morris, and recognized that only in a world which appreciated fine crafts would there be jobs for fine craftsmen. It is from this mileau that we have the "mission" furniture, much sought by antique dealers today.

One dimension of the renewed interest in simple living was a "country life" movement that sought to use modern technology to improve country life for the small farmer and to keep young people on the farm. Later, in 1933, the Department of the Interior created a Division of Subsistence Homesteads to resettle the urban and rural poor in planned communities based on "handicrafts, community activities, closer relationships, and coop-erative enterprises." About one hundred such communities were established, most of them failing in their grand design to replace individualism with "mutualism."

After World War II, as after World War I, the Civil War, and the Ameri-can Revolution, there was a surge in consumption, and simple living receded into the background. But again in the 1960s there was a critique of the afflu-ent lifestyle and a renewed interest in plain living. In the 1970s, with the energy crisis, this merged with a broad environmentalism. Many saw the energy crisis not as an economic or political problem to be overcome, but as an occasion for a spiritual renewal that would turn us away from the ram-pant materialism of modern life. One of these was President Jimmy Carter.

"We worship self-indulgence and consumption," Carter declared, taking his place in a great American tradition of social criticism. "Human identity is no longer defined by what one does but by what one owns." And, like earlier critics, Carter lamented the emptiness of such an existence. "We've discovered that owning things and consuming things does not satisfy our longing for meaning."

Carter saw the problem as residing in what he termed "a mistaken idea of freedom"—one in which we advocate "the right to grasp for ourselves some advantage over others." He called on Americans to unite together in a crusade of energy conservation:

> We often think of conservation only in terms of sacrifice . . . solutions to our energy crisis can also help us to conquer the crisis of spirit in our country. It can rekindle a sense of unity, our confidence in the future, and give our nation and all of us individually a new sense of purpose.[22]

This was his so-called "malaise" speech, and while it failed as an effort to transform the national spirit, and certainly failed Carter politically, it did capture well the link between environmental concerns and simple living that many Americans continue to feel today. Carter was followed by the Reagan and Bush administrations, during which no similar critique was heard. But now, at the turn of the millennium, there is renewed interest in simple living, if not in the White House, then at least in the heartland.

This quick historical survey reveals that "simple living" has meant many things. There is an anticonsumptionist core in much American thinking on this subject, but great diversity with respect to the human good and the place of work, religion, civic engagement, nature, literature, and the arts. Concern with simple living has been largely apolitical at some times, and at others the heart of a general political and social vision.

Today, when there is once again a great interest in simple living in America, it is mainly an apolitical enthusiasm. Most, though not all, of the literature is of a "how to" variety, offering advice on how to live more rewardingly with less money. The attainment of a simpler, more meaningful life is seen as an individual project, not as a matter of collective politics. In the chapters that follow I will explore the limitations of this individualistic approach and argue for a "politics of simplicity."

SIMPLE LIVING AND POVERTY

The question sometimes arises, "What is the difference between simple living and poverty?" Several responses are possible. One calls attention to the
difference between voluntarily choosing to live in a certain way and having
to. This is certainly of great importance. Often enough, people who adopt
simple living have the ability to earn more income if they choose. Thus, there
is an actual and psychological freedom that attends their life. This freedom is
not part of the life experience of those trapped in poverty. It is true that not
all of the poor are "trapped"; some people do manage to escape from poverty.
On the other hand, a person is not truly poor if the exit is readily available.

Yet this emphasis on freedom can go only so far. First, there are situations
in which the choice to live a simple life is not reversible, situations in which
an exit to higher levels of consumption may not be readily at hand. Second,
the core of the distinction cannot rest on whether the condition is chosen. We
can imagine situations in which for one reason or another (e.g., as a penance)
someone chooses to live in irreversible poverty. Alternatively, there are people who have been born into a community or culture based on a tradition of
simple living. Simple living is consistent with there being no choice, no
awareness of alternatives, and, under some conditions, with no opportunity
for opulent living.

The essential matter is not how people come to simple living as opposed to
poverty, but a difference that resides in the life itself. Even with no knowledge of how someone got there, it should be possible to distinguish poverty
from simple living, just by examining the life people do live.

One approach might be to say that it is a matter of degree, that simple living occupies a place between poverty and middle-class life. Thus, as government agencies sometimes do, we can define poverty arbitrarily in terms of a
certain level of income (e.g., the poverty line for a family can be set at 60 percent of median family income). And proceeding in this way, we can also
define simple living in terms of income, as a tier that exists between poverty
and middle-class status.

While this has the virtue of clarity and precision, it offers little insight.
Moreover, there are many variants of simple living, and while some operate
above the income levels used to define poverty, others may be below.

Let me offer a different answer. The touchstone here is to ask, "What is it
for a life itself to be impoverished?" As soon as the issue is put in this way,
one must ask, "Impoverished in what dimensions?" The human good is too

diverse to try to capture either its richness or its poverty in a single dimension. For instance, we can identify five forms of impoverishment:

- *Material impoverishment*, meaning inadequacies of goods and services such that the individual experiences (or is exposed to) disease, hunger, starvation. This could be caused by inadequacies of monetary income, inadequacies of public investment, inadequacies of human support systems, or even simply by bad luck.
- *Intellectual impoverishment*, meaning an inadequacy of education and/or absence of interactions with others so that the individual does not partake in a life of the mind. This can be brought about through lack of schooling leading to illiteracy, or more commonly a culture of intellectual isolation.
- *Spiritual impoverishment*, meaning the absence of any transcendent meaning in the experiences or activities of the individual. This might include, but certainly should not be limited to or defined in terms of, religious experience.
- *Aesthetic impoverishment*, meaning the absence of beauty within the person's life, whether it be the beauty of material possessions, the natural environment, the urban world, or the absence of ceremony.
- *Social impoverishment*, meaning an absence of central relationships, of friends and loved ones.

Who are "the poor"? There is no single answer. The term covers a wide diversity of people and circumstances. In material terms, it may refer to the average person in a poor African country. There the central facts may be a persistent inadequacy of food and clean water, yet at the same time there may be a vibrant communal, family, and religious life. Alternatively, we may be speaking about the poor in the United States; yet this, too, may refer to highly varied circumstances. There is a great difference between hardworking sharecropper families in Mississippi, with limited income and education, on the one hand, and young inner-city street hustlers, without fathers, in a drug culture, amid gangs and prostitution. Both may face low levels of life expectancy, the sharecropping family from malnutrition, the inner-city drug users from a high probability of either getting shot or acquiring AIDS from shared needles.

When simple living is advocated, it is generally implicit that material needs are met. Today's popular simple living literature focuses strongly on how we can meet our material needs with limited financial means. This, however, must be thought of as a precondition for simple living—by achieving relative independence from material need, one is freed to create a life that is rich in some nonmaterial sense. The central distinction is not between simple living and material poverty (indeed, these can overlap) but between simple living and a life that is impoverished in one or more of its multiple nonmaterial dimensions.

Thus understood, the richness of simple living rests upon the material and nonmaterial wealth we both possess and successfully actualize, wealth that may be public or private, cultural or natural, aesthetic, religious, intellectual, interpersonal, or psychological. It may reside in the capabilities of our families and communities, in our relationships with others, or more narrowly within ourselves, as our human capital, psychological and physical.

From this it follows that simple living is not merely a matter of downsizing, of living on less, or of working less. It's possible to do that, and have the result be nothing more than a general impoverishment. Simple living is not the residue that emerges when one consumes less; it is an achievement. It is what can emerge when as a result of subjecting the material dimension to a larger vision, one succeeds in creating a life that is rich and exciting in its aesthetic, intellectual, spiritual, and social dimensions.

Chapter Two

INDIVIDUALISTIC STRATEGIES FOR SIMPLE LIVING

While I shall strongly argue for social and economic policies for enabling lives of simplicity, in the end, achieving the simple life is not something that can be done *for* people. It is something that people have to want, have to value, and have to bring about in their own lives. Social and economic policies may powerfully affect the extent to which people will be successful in fashioning simpler lives, but unless the achievement of simple living is a personal project, it is unlikely to be achieved regardless of what policies are adopted.

As a personal project, attaining simplicity has two distinct but interpenetrating dimensions. First, there are the choices we make in leading our lives and in constructing our personal environment, choices and behavior with respect to consumption, work, income, leisure, family, friends, and so on. Second, distinct from what we do, there is the question of who we are—matters that bear on our values, our emotions, our motivational structures.

In Part II of this book I consider certain basic questions that anyone wrestling with these matters ultimately has to contend with, questions such as "What is true wealth?" and "How should we think about money?" In the present and next chapter, I am assuming a desire for a simpler life; my central concern is to try to find the appropriate balance point in looking toward both personal and political strategies for simple living. In the end, we will need both.

RECONSTRUCTING OUR PERSONAL ENVIRONMENT

Much of the current literature on simple living is concerned with the first issue—how, through wise choices, can we create a personal environment in which we can live well with limited material means? This literature is extensive and contains useful advice. Here I will limit myself to a few issues of general importance.

TIME

Simple living and the harried life are incompatible. Yet for most of us in the contemporary economy, there never seems to be enough time. We rush from one thing to the next, constantly burdened by a thousand tasks on our personal agendas. If we make some progress against those agendas, it is only momentary. Our plight is like that of someone with a vast lawn and a push mower, unable to relax on his estate for more than a second. The grass starts coming up again the very instant it is mowed in an absurd contemporary version of the punishment of Sisyphus.

We live lives that are out of balance, lacking in proportion and moderation. Given the limited time and energy available to us, we have too many things to do. If we think of this predicament as one that people can solve, or at least ameliorate, through personal choices rather than social change or personal transformation, then the use we make of time will be a central issue.

The good life requires true leisure: not just time that we are not on the job, but time that is free from pressing demands. We seek freedom from an excessive amount of both paid and personal work. Simple living doesn't necessarily mean a quiet life. It can be filled with challenge and excitement. But it does give recognition to the importance of having sufficient time to go slowly, and to do things right—whether we are eating a meal, talking with a friend, telling a story to a child, or walking the dog.

What, then, can the average person do both to find more time and to reduce the demands upon his time?

WORKING LESS

Working less is an obvious response, yet for many it seems a nonanswer. If we focus on paid employment, and if we focus on the household, rather than individuals, then it is clear that the trend is markedly in the other direction—households are working *more* not less. The major factor driving this trend has been the entry of women into the formal workplace.

For most working couples, it is not possible to go back to having one wage earner. The loss of income would be too great. In any case, such a change would be unacceptable, if it meant that women were once again relegated to the home. But suppose it were possible for a working couple to go from two full-time jobs to two half-time jobs (or even two three-quarter-time jobs). For those who chose to do so, this would open significant possibilities for a more graceful existence.

There are major workplace constraints that prevent people from making these kinds of arrangements. To begin with, most jobs don't come with this kind of divisibility. They typically come as total packages of full-time or not at all. The choice workers face is most often between a full-time job or some very different kind of job at half-time. But even if people had such choices open to them, and could fine-tune the amount of work they would do, most would not choose to do less if it meant less income. The decision to free up additional time by working less is, for most of us, not fundamentally a decision about how much to work, but a decision about how much to consume.

CONSUMING LESS

Except for people who are very poor, there really is no mystery about how to consume less than we do. For instance, in 2000, 60 percent of American families had an income of less than $62,000. So for people whose family income is $100,000 a year or $200,000 a year, and who can't see how they can consume less, the answer is simple: live like the rest of us!

For those families who earn $60,000 a year, the answer to how to live on less is also simple: Live like the 50 percent of American families who in 2000 earned less than $51,000 a year. And so it goes. There are always plenty of people who do live on less—indeed, a lot less—than we do.

The problem, however, is also simple: we don't want to. We don't want to give up what we have. Indeed, most of us want even more.

Throughout history there has always been a "simple-living literature" that seeks to convince people that the toll of their present way of life is too great, and that there is a better kind of life they could be leading if they were to consume less. Such a life would allow them to work less or at least do different work, and to have significantly more leisure time.

What is interesting (and, I will argue, mistaken) about much of the contemporary simple-living literature is that it also seeks to show people how vast changes can be done relatively painlessly. For instance, the authors of the bestselling *Your Money or Your Life* argue that, contrary to people's initial perception, there is a great deal of room for change. In this we find the echoes of Ben Franklin: a strong focus on what the individual can do for himself, a detailed concern with money and budgets, a recognition that Time is life itself. Yet while Ben Franklin's voice emerges here, we can also hear Thoreau. The larger objective of earning more, consuming less, saving and investing, is not to be wealthy, but to be able to escape from paid employment altogether, and thus to do in life those things that are most meaningful to you as an individual.

Your Money or Your Life offers more than one hundred specific suggestions for spending less money. Some of these recommendations, whatever else one might say about them, seem unlikely to make a significant difference in the overall household budget for middle-income families:

- ✦ share magazine subscriptions with a friend
- ✦ bring your own shopping bags to the store (5-cent discount)
- ✦ go to matinees rather than evening shows

This is "small potatoes stuff"—even if we get a 5-cent shopping bag discount every day of the year, we save only $18.25, and each matinee saves only $3.50—if we see ten movies a year, that's $35.

Other suggestions do have potential for moderate financial impact. And while such ideas might not work for many people, for some they represent sound practical wisdom:

- ✦ start a neighborhood tool swap
- ✦ buy everything for cash, thus avoiding high interest rates on credit cards
- ✦ buy airline tickets well in advance

+ buy in bulk
+ trade clothes with friends who wear the same size

Finally, there are some pieces of advice that could have a major impact on how much people spend. For instance:

+ move to a part of the country where housing is inexpensive
+ live close to work and give up that second car
+ hold on to your car for a significantly longer time
+ don't send your children to college
+ live in a mobile home

Some suggestions—such as living within walking or biking distance from work (and thus dramatically cutting transportation costs)—are indeed very sound, but not everyone will be able to follow them. Similarly, it is easy to say "move to parts of the country where the cost of living is lower," but where are the mid-career jobs when you are forty or fifty? Moreover, if large numbers of people followed the advice, these areas would suddenly become much more expensive.

The big-ticket items offer big savings because they either forgo certain major purchases or put them off for long periods of time. Sometimes this makes sense (e.g., holding on to the old car a little bit longer), but often enough such choices can involve major costs in quality of life. It is one thing to give up the second car when it is truly unneeded, but to do so when two parents work, and when you live far from public transportation, imposes a major disruption.

The most startling suggestion—not sending your children to college—undoubtedly could change the economics of everyday life. Consider, for instance, a family of four with an income of $50,000. Suppose that over the years they have built up a nest egg of $200,000 to send their two kids to college. If, instead, they sent the two kids out to work, or just off on their own, this would indeed transform their lives. On the economic front, they could invest the $200,000 and perhaps earn a 10 percent return of $20,000 a year. This might make it possible for them to change to more fulfilling but lower-paying jobs, or to reduce work time by 40 percent (assuming they had that option).

It might also trigger some other changes—for instance, permanent estrangement from their children, astonishment and criticism on the part of friends and relatives, guilt and recriminations between the two, and so forth. What this example makes clear is that some of the biggest expenditures families face are not merely "consumer choices." Rather, they are expressive of a moral order that engages fundamental values, including what it is to be a parent and the nature of mutual obligations within the family.

This is not to say that our current perspectives and understandings are 100 percent correct and need not be challenged, but rather that household budgets are indeed very serious matters. Yes, it is easy to find small changes on the margins, but often enough the big structural elements concern the most fundamental issues of life.

Whether we are talking about small savings or large, it is clear that some cost-cutting measures will move us further away from, rather than closer to, the gracefulness that is lacking in our lives. I would put living in a mobile home in this category. Similarly, some of the suggestions make sense only as part of a thoroughgoing shift to an alternative way of life. While they save some money, they do so by increasing the amount of personal work time. In this category I would put bargain hunting, cutting discount coupons, learning auto maintenance, acquiring needed auto parts and paying a mechanic to install them, and doing your own home repairs. Unless you start out with extensive leisure time, or you earn very little, it is hard to see how the money saved would allow one to work so much less that there would be a net increase in leisure time. Thus, these suggested activities only make sense if they themselves are regarded as inherently fulfilling. Their validity depends upon an ability to enter into a substantially different life culture—one in which "saving money" becomes imbued with significant meaning.

While most people can find some relatively easy places to cut back, this generally does not result in truly substantial savings, savings of the sort that would allow them to work significantly less. Thus, these small economies offer little relief from the time pressure that many of us experience. To get beyond this point typically requires a willingness to radically transform one's social world, perhaps to leave one's present subculture and find a new community of meanings. Throughout history, this is exactly what was intended by many who raised the call for simple living—certainly Thoreau was seeking to leave much of mainstream American life behind.

There is no doubt that this can be done. Moreover, given the underlying affluence of our society, the costs and risks associated with "dropping out" are less problematic than at any other point in history. You can go this route.

You will not starve, and there will be public schooling for your children. Quite possibly, you will be able to create a more vibrant life than otherwise. This has always been the promise of simple living, and it remains in place today.

I seek in no way to disparage this option, nor to suggest that it is not possible. My point, rather, is to make clear that this approach, which relies upon personal economizing, involves important trade-offs—trade-offs that most people are not going to make. If we are seriously looking for approaches that will actually change the lived experience of mainstream life in this country, we have to go well beyond personal economies. As will be argued in subsequent chapters, we have to change social policies.

WORKING LESS THROUGH FINANCIAL INDEPENDENCE

The goal of the nine-step process detailed in *Your Money or Your Life* is to achieve financial independence. This is attained by delayed gratification, by deferring any reduction in work time made possible by cutting back on expenditures. Instead of working less, the idea is to save and invest the unexpended income. In time, one will achieve financial independence, defined in terms of the "cross-over point" where the interest you are earning from your investments equals your expenditures. This allows you to quit your paid employment. The anticipation of reaching this stage plays an important role in the process. "Think about what would happen if you knew that you would have to work for money for a limited, foreseeable length of time (say, five years) instead of that vague limbo of working until traditional retirement."[23]

This is an extraordinarily ambitious goal—to reach a point, very early in life, at which you are truly financially independent, at which you no longer need to work for a living. To do this does not require that your investment income fully equal your present expenditures, because some expenditures are required only when you have paid employment (e.g., work clothes, transportation, eating lunch out). Added to these savings are those that come from the list of one hundred ways to cut back. All we need, it seems, is the fortitude of Ben Franklin.

In this pursuit of financial independence, there are distant echoes of Aristotle's judgment that most of the ways of making a living are unhealthy to the human spirit, and that subjecting oneself to the will of others at the workplace is a form of limited servitude. Unfortunately, vastly more than in previous periods in history, we live within a system of employment where we earn our money by selling our labor time to others. They define the activity. They define the hours. They establish the product and the production process. It is to further their objectives that they pay us, and it is to their will that we subject ourselves. To not see this as enslavement, perhaps because work conditions are pleasant, is only to fit well into the system. It is to be what Aristotle referred to as "a natural slave."

From this perspective, the pursuit of financial independence through simple living reflects Aristotle's judgments about the ignoble nature of a lifetime of paid employment and about the limited funds that the household really needs. This rejection of paid employment is coupled with a Thoreau-like desire for independent leisure, and implemented through a Franklin-like determination to work hard and attend carefully to budgets and savings.

Your Money or Your Life (which has sold approximately 700,000 copies) holds out the prospect that financial independence can be attained after approximately five years. If this is so, then with discipline, through simple living and a short period of savings and investing, we can all live simply without paid employment thereafter.

In the next few pages I will explain why this represents a vast overstatement of what is possible. But lest the reader get too discouraged, it should be borne in mind that freedom from any need to work for a living is much more than we need to reorder our lives.

The key promise in all this is that the process can be completed relatively quickly. If it takes twenty or thirty years, then the life it offers gets to look too much like normal retirement, and the entire project becomes distinctly less attractive. There are three factors that determine how quickly you can reach this point of financial independence:

- ✦ the rate of return on the portfolio of investments
- ✦ the amount that you are saving and investing each year (which can be expressed as a percentage of current income)
- ✦ your level of expenditures once you quit working altogether (which can also be expressed as a percentage of current income)

Clearly a great deal will depend upon the rate of return on investments. This, in turn, will depend upon the kind of investments one makes. Typically, the safer the investments, the lower the rate of return. U.S. Treasury bonds pay a lower rate of interest than do AAA-rated corporate bonds, and these pay lower rates than do BBB-rated corporate bonds. On the other hand, when you invest $1,000 in a Treasury bond, you know you will get back the $1,000 plus interest. If there is significant inflation, however, the $1,000 that is returned when the bond matures will be worth much less, and similarly, the fixed interest payment will also have less and less purchasing power. To avoid this, people often invest in real estate and common stocks, which provide them with real assets that appreciate in value. Typically for someone intending to retire at a specific date, investment counselors suggest a mixed portfolio of stocks and bonds.

The authors of *Your Money or Your Life* favor the safety of Treasury bonds—but this is quite problematic. Over the last forty years, the interest on Treasury bonds has generally been only about 2 percent higher than the rate of inflation. Let us assume a mixed portfolio weighted in the direction of common stocks, and assume that the portfolio assets keep pace with inflation, and that the portfolio pays a real rate of return of 5 percent. Historically, this is quite a good return. To this, as part of the program for financial independence, let us assume that each year you add to the portfolio a fixed percentage of your income, which is also keeping pace with inflation.[24]

Let us assume that if you didn't work at all, through a combination of lower taxes, elimination of costs associated with work, and generally reduced expenditures, you could live on half your current income. How long will it take before the portfolio earns each year one-half of your current income, allowing one to quit working for a living?

Unfortunately, much longer than you would wish. The following table shows how many years it would take to build up a nest egg that would give you an investment income (at 5 percent) that would equal half of your present income:

AT 5% REAL RATE OF RETURN ON INVESTMENTS			
Percentage of current income saved and invested: 10%	20%	33%	50%
Number of years until investment income reaches ½ current level of income: 37	26	19	14

Fourteen years of saving 50 percent of their income is, for most people, an impossible task. There are, however, a few people in situations where this is possible—for instance, couples without children who are earning $100,000 or even $150,000. With a decision to live simply, they can find enormous amounts of money to save and invest. But clearly, this applies to only a small group.

The situation changes importantly, however, if you assume riskier investments and great success. For instance, given a real rate of return of 10 percent, the table looks like this:

AT 10% REAL RATE OF RETURN ON INVESTMENTS				
Percentage of current income saved and invested:	10%	20%	33%	50%
Number of years until investment income reaches ½ current level of income:	19	13	10	7½

This is quite different. Attaining financial independence in seven and a half years is a remarkable feat. However, only a draconian reduction of consumption would allow you actually to save 50 percent of your income. What the table shows, however, is that there are other, more doable possibilities. For instance, if you can manage to save 20 percent of your income, then after thirteen years one can attain financial independence. This is certainly relevant to a larger group of people. But still, it is of limited value to most of us, for several reasons. First, the savings level (20 percent) is very demanding unless you are really making very high levels of income. Currently Americans save less than 4 percent of their income. Secondly, maintaining this level of discipline for thirteen years represents a good deal of discipline and planning. Some people can do this, but certainly not everyone. Third, for those with average or more modest incomes, even though costs are lower if you are not working, it would be extremely difficult to live at only 50 percent of current income. And finally, to assume a permanent real rate of return of 10 percent is far too optimistic. At this rate, if you set aside $10,000 for your child when he is one year old, when he is fifty, that $10,000 would have doubled seven times, growing to $1,280,000 after adjusting for inflation. Unfortunately, we can't count on it.

In recent years, the extraordinary rise in common stock prices have given people a false image of what is generally possible over the long run. The newspapers are filled with ads for mutual funds, boasting that over the last five or ten years these funds have risen at 20 percent or 30 percent annually. But the significance of this must be put in perspective.

When you buy stock, you are buying a small percentage of a profit-making enterprise. Its underlying financial value lies in its future profits stream. Over the decades corporate profits have risen largely in pace with the growth of the general economy—approximately 3 percent to 4 percent a year, after accounting for inflation. In recent years, corporations have gotten a somewhat larger percentage of the overall income pie, but over the long haul, corporate profits will rise in sync with the general expansion of income. The great run-up in stock prices has put stocks increasingly out of touch with the underlying profitability of the enterprises. Ultimately, such bubbles burst.

It should be realized that the great rise in common stock prices has occurred primarily because the baby boomers have achieved middle age, and thus more money is being put into investments and savings than is being taken out. In time, this process will reverse; the retirement of baby boomers will bring about a great decline in stock prices.

From the point of view of someone seeking to attain financial independence through stock purchases, the critical issue is not the market value of the portfolio, but rather the dividend income it provides. On the average, corporations reinvest approximately half of their profits and pay out half to shareholders as dividends. As the ratio of stock price to earnings rises, the ability of the corporation to pay substantial dividends decreases. Thus, a corporation with a ratio of stock price to per share earnings of 25 to 1 could pay out a maximum of 4 percent in dividends. If the ratio rises to 50 to 1, it can pay out a maximum of 2 percent. For people seeking to live on dividends from a stock portfolio, the great run-up of the stock market has not changed the fact that in general corporate earnings and thus dividends advance at a relatively mundane pace.

Of course, you could always plan to hold a stock portfolio until it increases tenfold in value and then sell it to buy high-yielding bonds on which to retire. And no doubt some people can accomplish this. But it is clear that, in principle, no general strategy can be found here. If large numbers of people were to try to sell their stock portfolios, they would drive the prices down.

Thus, in a variety of ways, the promised "pot at the end of the rainbow"—

total financial independence—except for very committed people, or people in very unusual circumstances, remains just that—at the end of the rainbow.

But from this we should not dismiss the importance of attention to budgets and savings. The promise of attaining short-term financial independence works only for a few, but short-term financial independence is far more than what most people need in order to achieve a major transformation in their lives. For many the objective is not to be totally free from paid employment; for many their jobs are the best parts of their lives. The problem is that the workplace asks too much of us; the objective is not the elimination of employment, but its reduction.

Thus, even moderate savings, those that collectively shave 10 percent or 15 percent from our annual expenditures, can have a dramatic impact for some people. If translated into extra leisure time, a 10 percent reduction in consumption means working 10 percent less—for instance, not working Friday afternoons. If employers were accommodating, you wouldn't have to wait years; this could occur as soon as you reduced consumption.

Or, alternatively, if you are willing to delay the reduction in work time and you cut expenditures by 10 percent, work full-time, and invest it—even at a moderate 5 percent return—after fourteen years, another 10 percent is coming in through interest and dividend earnings. At that point you would be able to have an income equal to 90 percent of full-time earnings, but need only work 80 percent of full-time. There are many ways to enjoy this benefit, assuming again that employers were accommodating. One option for a married couple with children might be to take Fridays for themselves—to have a day to be together, to do some of the things they love, and to rediscover their love for each other. Alternatively, they might take extra vacation time equal to the 20 percent of full-time work they were liberated from—20 percent of fifty-two weeks comes to over ten weeks more vacation—enough to make a very big difference. Or they might just shift to a six-and-a-half-hour workday.

Even if not translated into less work, a small decline in consumption expenditures may be quite significant in promoting psychological ease.

In Dickens's *David Copperfield*, Mr. Micawber (in English currency) graphically declares:

Income of $100 + Expense of $101 = misery
Income of $100 + Expense of $99 = happiness

There is an important point here. For many people who feel under constant financial pressure, the relationship between income and expenses is not wildly out of whack—after all, over the long haul it is very hard to spend much more than one earns. Rather, it is simply a little out of balance. But that small matter is itself the source of constant tension about purchases and constant hassle and conflict about overspending and overdrawn accounts.

Thus, while there may be for most of us no painless way to bring about a vast reduction in our personal need for money, modest changes that simply bring expenses and income into a stable balance can be enormously liberating.

More generally, a strategy of spending a little less and investing the savings can then make a very important contribution to graceful existence, even if major (e.g., 50 percent, 100 percent) reductions in work time are out of reach for most people.

MOVING MORE DIRECTLY TOWARD A LESS HECTIC LIFE

The various money-saving proposals just considered were motivated by a simple logic: if you spend less, then either now or in the future you will be able to work less. The goal was to reduce work time, and thus expand time available for friends and family and for those life activities you always wanted to do. For those fortunate enough to have found work that continues to be inherently rewarding right up to the last hour on the job, this motivation for cutting back does not apply. But there is a second set of concerns that often does, indeed, which may sometimes be most applicable to those who are deeply involved with their work.

In contemporary usage, "simple living" does not always mean living on a modest income. In some instances, it means leading a life that is less hectic and stressful. Thus, one bestselling book, *Simplify Your Life*, is subtitled *100 Ways to Slow Down and Enjoy the Things That Really Matter*. Here emphasis falls not on saving money but on eliminating the time crunch and escaping from a hectic, overburdened existence. It is a "how to" book primarily about how to reduce the amount of time we spend on things that are not really important—or that may be important individually, but that, taken together, require more time than we can give. The idea is to fashion a life in which we will have less on our minds, adopting a more limited agenda, making choices among the vast multiplicity of concerns that constantly pull us this way and that.

As promised the book suggests one hundred ways to save time, save money, reduce complexity, and get in touch with aspects of the good life. Here is a sample.

To free up time for the good things in life:

+ work where you live; live where you work
+ get rid of the lawn
+ move to a smaller house
+ adopt a carefree hair style
+ turn off the TV
+ shop for groceries once a week (use computer-organized grocery shopping)
+ buy in bulk
+ begin one-stop shopping (rather than going to multiple stores)
+ structure the house for quick cleaning
+ leave your shoes at the door (less cleaning)
+ use patterned carpets (less cleaning)
+ use a food tray (less cleaning)
+ get rid of houseplants
+ don't have people over for dinner unless it's potluck; go out to eat together
+ change your clothes less frequently between washing
+ don't make your bed
+ stop sending Christmas cards
+ stop shopping for presents (recycle presents you get)
+ get up early in the morning
+ resign from organizations whose meetings you can't stand

Clearly this is a mixed list. Some ideas, such as living close to work, are no doubt attractive (if not always feasible). But many of them, as with some of the money-saving ideas examined above, hardly seem to be great ideas. Not having friends over for dinner unless it's potluck offers a cramped vision of friendship and hospitality. Using food trays and patterned carpets so the dirt doesn't show hardly represents an attractive mode of life.

From a historical point of view, it is quite true that our culture has high standards of cleanliness; in particular, we eschew body odors. Perhaps this is something we can be liberated from. But for many people, choosing to walk around in what they and others perceive as smelly clothes is actually asking quite a bit.

Rather than doing less for one's friends, we might turn it around and seek to release time precisely in order to be able to do more for friends. For instance, rather than viewing birthdays and holidays as nuisances that suck time away from what we really want to do, perhaps we should be seeking a life that provides the time to do such things comfortably and more meaningfully. Rather than not shopping for gifts, perhaps we might seek more time so that we truly find the right gift for someone we care about.

It is only in some instances that reducing personal work time yields clear benefits. Where, if anywhere, can an individual household find such time savings? One major category has to do with traveling to work. Here, for those who can live close to their jobs, the time savings are potentially enormous. Someone who moves or changes jobs so as to have a fifteen-minute trip to work rather than a forty-five minute trip saves an hour a day, or five hours a week. Over fifty weeks this comes to 250 hours—an amount equivalent to over six weeks of vacation.

In some lives this is possible, and the implications are quite significant. But for most people, there are reasons why they live where they do. For families with two wage earners, moving closer to one job may mean moving farther from another. It may mean needing more income for a more costly neighborhood, or else living in a less desirable neighborhood. These are trade-offs that people may decide to make, and in some cases, in pursuit of a more graceful existence, they are trade-offs that should be made. But, for most people, there are no easy choices.

Another set of suggestions among the one hundred aren't primarily about saving time, but have to do with weeding out, with getting things down to a limited number of essentials. This category has an obvious intuitive appeal. There are some people who self-generate vast amounts of work for themselves. They take work home unnecessarily, and they make numerous commitments, virtually overloading the circuits. Under those circumstances, there is some point to a personal injunction or resolution to slow down. Perhaps there is something of this dimension in all of our lives—a discretionary area in which, if we were careful about the extent of our commitments, we would find ourselves less pressed.

The specific suggestions in *Simplifying Your Life* include the following:

✦ reduce the clutter, box it, date it, and after three years toss it
✦ sell the damn boat
✦ build a simple wardrobe
✦ drop call waiting
✦ stop the junk mail
✦ get rid of the car phone
✦ travel light
✦ get rid of all but one credit card
✦ stop newspaper delivery

Again, this is something of a mixed list. Why, for instance, should someone stop newspaper delivery? The reason, it seems, is that there is too much bad news in the paper. The author refers to "the negative information that complicates life without enhancing it" and maintains that "cutting back on the negative you're subjected to every day is a positive step towards simplifying your life."

It's not fully clear how "negative" information complicates your life; presumably the idea is that one's peace of mind is disturbed by knowledge of problems. In this there are echoes of an old theme—that eating of the fruit of the tree of knowledge leads to banishment from the Garden of Eden. True, Adam and Eve lived the simple life, but there are many varieties of simple living, and not all of them are tied to blissful ignorance.

Indeed, the real challenge may lie in the other direction—how can we become not merely aware of the world, but engaged in a project of its transformation, without abandoning our own ability to live gracefully? Here, too, the secret may lie in pacing—in not rushing into the fray, intent on quickly making the world right, but recognizing instead that the labor we do for a better world is a lifelong project. Like those who plant trees that will bear fruit only when they are gone, or those who worked on building cathedrals that took one hundred years to complete, we engage in projects of social transformation that connect the generations. The problems of the world are our opportunity to take up the load gracefully and to carry on—as part of life, not in opposition to it.

HASSLE AND CONFLICT AT HOME

The simple life is not something that emerges as a matter of course when work is reduced and leisure time expanded. Such changes only open a space of possibility. By themselves, they are insufficient. One impediment to simplicity of life, one that illustrates how difficult it is to attain, is domestic tension. Here I do not mean the extreme case of conflict where a household is rocked by verbal and often physical battles. Rather, consider the low-intensity conflict that can pervade a relationship between two adults struggling to retain distinct identities and yet seeking to make the common project work.

Whatever else the household is, it is a complex economic unit, an entity that holds property in common, that pools income, that empowers several members to consume, that requires collective decision making in certain areas, that allocates labor tasks, and that requires that the adults, implicitly or explicitly, define its income, expenditure, and investment objectives and engage in self-discipline to meet those standards.

It is thus nonsense to imagine that the home is a refuge outside the hurly-burly of economic life. Rather, in going from home to work, we make our daily passage from one economic unit to another. Indeed, the complexity of the first unit, the household, is for the individual vastly greater than that of the formal workplace where lines of authority and tasks and rewards are relatively clear. One recent study suggests that many people find the workplace to be a refuge from the demands of the household, which makes the time we spend at home more burdensome than before.[25]

Viewed as a complex economic enterprise, the household is an obvious source of conflict and tension. Living within such units, we nonetheless seek to make them the central locus of a graceful existence. This seems a project almost destined to fail.

Of special bearing on the issue of conflict is the question of roles and expectations. In a society in which there are long-established and widely internalized social roles, especially roles within the family, it is clear to all what is expected of each. This does not mean that people always fulfill these expectations, or that there is no conflict. And certainly it is substantially a myth that there ever was a genuine shared acceptance of roles, rather than domination by the advantaged.

Nonetheless, there is no doubt that in contemporary American life, we find an unparalleled absence of clear social definition with respect to work roles within the home. There are today few established norms regarding most of the household duties. Who works inside and who outside? How is work inside divided up? Who cooks, cleans, shops? Whose responsibility is it to think about what needs to be done? Who thinks about the long-range financial health of the household? Are there separate bank accounts? And investments?

In short, the work and financial aspects of household management are up for grabs, with each couple having to grope in their unique way toward a solution that works for them. Given that the issues here are intensely symbolic, having to do with women's emergence from domination, they are not purely private matters. Rather, for better or worse, one of the great causes of human history, the liberation of women, continues to be played out within each household. Thus, the stage is set for perpetual conflict, be it low-level tension or explosions leading to divorce. Sometimes the issues are of inherent importance, but, often enough, they are over power and selfhood itself.

In all this—and often unmentioned in simple-living books—is the issue of children. Even the list of one hundred suggestions for simplification from *Simplify Your Life* does not advise people not to have children. And while *Your Money or Your Life* suggests possibly forgoing a child's college education, the authors stop far short of suggesting forgoing children altogether. Yet it is very clear that if you want a simpler life, nothing interferes as thoroughly, at least in some respects, as the decision to have children.

The relationship of parenting to simple living is more complex than it might seem at first. For many people, having children provides the strongest motivation, as well as unique opportunities, to achieve a simple life, rooted in an appreciation of what they have been given. Having children can put one in touch with miraculous aspects of human development and emergence—it offers something indeed to be appreciative about, as well as being an opportunity to gain perspective on what really matters. It can put one back in touch with the simple, central realities of existence. Exposure to a child's laughter and pleasure reminds one that the good life is not dependent upon acquisition.

Further, having children creates a sphere in which people give of themselves—perhaps for the first time—without any sense of what they expect to get in return. They give gracefully, experiencing what it is to be genuinely committed to the well-being of something beyond themselves. In short, child rearing is not inimical to simple living. The challenge is to turn the equation around, to draw on the potential of the relationship with the child to build for oneself a richer life.

MONEY AND A PHILOSOPHY OF LIFE

Achieving any form of simple living is not easy. Whether the issues are saving money or saving time, or the problems of political engagement or the problems of parenting, there are no easy answers. There are some good ideas out there, such as the importance of budgeting carefully and making long-term investments, but many of the ideas found in the self-help literature do not offer much for the ordinary people who may not be seeking to enter a new subculture, but who desperately want to find a way to make their existing lives work better for themselves and their families.

In all this, the central issue is money. If we are willing to have a lot less, we can radically transform our relationship to work and family; we can radically change the way we spend our time. Aristotle was right—the open-ended pursuit of more is a disease; beyond a certain point, seeking more and having more is destructive of life. But where is that point? How much is enough?

There is no general answer to this question. It is not just that each individual answers the question differently. The amount of money we need is dependent on the answers we, as individuals, give to the deepest questions of human existence. Depending on how we answer these questions, it is possible to dispense with virtually all money and yet retain a peaceful self-possession.

There have always been religious and philosophic traditions that have emphasized human transformations that liberate us from a concern with externals. Consider, for instance, how it would affect your attitude toward money if you came to view life through the eyes of the Greek and Roman Stoics, who wrote:

> For this is your duty, to act well the part that is given to you; but to select the part, belongs to another.[26]

and,

> Seek not that the things which happen should happen as you wish; but wish the things which happen to be as they are, and you will have a tranquil flow of life.

and,

> In everything which pleases the soul or supplies a want or is loved remember to add this to the (description, notion); what is the nature of each thing, beginning from the smallest? . . . If you are kissing your child or wife, say that it is a human being whom you are kissing, for when the wife or child dies, you will not be disturbed.

This is wide, sweeping advice to stop caring about anything. We are told to accept all as it comes, not even wanting things to be different from the way they turn out, and to anticipate in every encounter, and in every relationship, that each treasured object or loved person will, ultimately, be lost to you.

Clearly, if people adopted this outlook, they would think about money in a very different way. Indeed, not just money, but virtually everything that people seek in life will appear in a different light, and we would be indifferent to having or not having.

This is a form of simple living, but not one that is particularly attractive. Tranquillity of mind is not the only good. What is espoused here is not life—life requires engagement. " 'Tis better to have loved and lost/Than never to have loved at all" is to me the sounder sentiment.

What is wrong here is not the idea that our problems may emerge from the fact that we care about the wrong things, or that we give too much importance to some things. What is wrong here is that there is no balance, no discrimination. As such, although there may have been people who have lived this way, the lifestyle offers little of general value.

Indeed, even in its heyday, its general usefulness was questioned. Ancient critics of Stoicism maintained that what the Stoics called for was beyond human capabilities. And, indeed, it seems that sometimes the Stoics themselves so regarded their project. Thus, Seneca at one point says that the Stoic wise man may be ranked above even the Gods in that he achieves his godlike calm through his own efforts at transformation. Seneca thought that such people emerged rarely, just one in many years. From our point of view, this is the basic point. The issue is not whether the Stoic attitude is possible at all, but rather whether it has any general applicability. And here Seneca's characterization of it as "greatness which transcends the limit of the ordinary and common type" is right on target. Stoicism in its most extreme variants is a program of human transformation that, even if we did not reject it because of its substance, is irrelevant because it commends transformations that are beyond the capacities of the ordinary person.

Today the advocacy of simple living is not linked to philosophies or religious ideals that make such great transformative demands upon the average person. History has seen many such philosophies, but we must conclude that few can meet their demands, and that, in any event, such movements are rarely sustained beyond the initial fervent generation. What we need is a much more realistic approach to simple living, one that can work, in a sustained manner, for much of the population.

With its individualist approach, the contemporary simple-living movement, even if asking of us far less than the Stoics, often asks more than is realistic. Its general thrust is merely that we don't need all that "stuff" we accumulate. The working assumption—and here, I believe, is where it goes wrong—is that in the rich countries of the world, except for pockets of poverty, the most fundamental economic needs of the population have long since been met. Insofar as people in rich countries continue to feel hard-pressed economically, the causes are said to lie in the dynamics of affluence and overconsumption.

Galbraith argued along these lines in *The Affluent Society* when he identified the forces of advertising and emulation as central to the psychological dynamic that keeps the affluent consumer always wanting more, even when legitimate needs have been met. That, for Galbraith, is how the squirrel wheel works.

It is this general picture that produces the notion that simple living is readily attainable. If our legitimate economic needs have already been met, then once we have been freed from the hold of artificial desires, it should be easy for us to contentedly scale back our consumption, work less, expand our leisure, and build meaningful lives.

Certainly there is some truth to this picture. Human beings have an enormous capacity to want more, and nothing so whets the appetite as seeing what the other fellow has. Housing is a good example of this. If you live in a $150,000 house and visit a friend who lives in a $250,000 house, it is very easy to imagine how nice it would be to live that way, to have what your friend has. The same is true of the person living in the $250,000 house, should he visit a friend in a $400,000 house. Indeed, there seems to be no upper limit to what might be desired. On the rare occasion when I have been inside a million-dollar home, it wasn't hard to develop a mental picture of how nice it would be to live there. So I don't mean to dismiss altogether the claim that we suffer from an escalation of appetites.

Recent statistics add further support. For instance, the National Association of Home Builders estimates that in the year 2000, the average American house will have 2,500 square feet, up significantly from 1,900 in 1977. One part of this process, it seems, is that couples are expanding the size of their homes, *after their children move out*—quite the opposite of what might be expected based on their reduced need.[27]

More problematic is that there seems to be a ratchet effect. We can readily imagine having more, but once we have experienced it, it is very hard to see how we can live with less. Thus, the family living in the $150,000 house would find it terribly difficult to move in the other direction and live in a $100,000 house—even though there are millions of Americans who do so.

Further, it seems hard to deny American affluence when we compare ourselves to the condition of most of mankind. We have a per capita gross national product (GNP) of $30,600 per year, while in India the level is $2,149.[28] We might be concerned with relative poverty and inequality within our own society, but what is that in comparison to the absolute poverty found throughout the world.

Nonetheless, neither the existence of mechanisms of escalating desire nor the undeniable difference between the levels of consumption in the United States and the absolute poverty that exists in much of the Third World shows that in countries such as the United States economic need has long been overcome. Contrary to the long tradition among simple-living advocates, I want to argue that most Americans feel hard-pressed economically *because they are.*

Thus, while on the one hand I believe that from a material point of view we are rather simple creatures, with only a limited set of needs, I do not believe that the primary reason we are unsatisfied is that we are the victims of either marketeers or our own psychology. To the contrary, I will argue that, even in America, fundamental economic needs are either unmet or can be met only at high levels of income and consumption. And if this is so, then suggesting to people that they deal with their problems individually, by working less, earning less, and consuming less is quite tricky. Taken modestly this may be sound advice, but beyond that, for many it may be asking people to make a bad situation even worse.

Chapter Three

THE MONEY WE NEED

Of course, Aristotle was right. We don't have an open-ended need for money, and if we act as if we do, we undermine the possibility of the good life. But the key question remains open: "How much do we need?" Getting clear on this is essential. If, in fact, we Americans have considerably more than we need, then attaining simple living is primarily an individual project. It is a matter of coming to a correct understanding of what matters in life, of gaining control over our desires, of knowing how to cut back, and of doing so. If, in fact, our need for money, our sense that perhaps we need even more of it, is not ersatz, is not the result of some deep misconception about what matters in life, and is not merely a matter of our victimization at the hands of Madison Avenue, then attaining lives of greater simplicity is also a social or political project. In this case, it is a matter of creating a society that enables or facilitates the lives we seek to lead.

Obviously, there is no single answer that is true for all people. Clearly, there are those who live in conditions of genuine material poverty. Equally clearly, if someone earns a million dollars a year and feels that he "needs" every penny of it, and that he spends only for "essentials," then we have an individual in need of liberation from his own desires. The issue is whether this latter picture is a generally accurate image of the lives of 75 percent, 50 percent, 10 percent, or 1 percent of the population of this country.

WHAT DO WE SPEND OUR MONEY ON?

Total consumer expenditures in the United States divide up as follows:[29, 30]

✦ Housing	⅓
✦ Transportation	⅕
✦ Food	⅐
✦ Personal insurance/pensions (includes Social Security)	⅒
✦ Health care	1/20
✦ Clothing	1/20
✦ Entertainment	1/20
✦ Other	⅒

These are averages, and some variation emerges when we examine different income groups and household types. Nonetheless, this broad spending pattern is remarkably uniform across the population. Consider the following chart that shows the percentage of expenditures devoted to various categories for households at different income levels:

CONSUMER EXPENDITURES BY INCOME GROUP[31]

	Pretax Income of Consumer Units		
	$15–20,000	$40–50,000	over $70,000
Housing	32.9%	30.4%	30.2%
Transport	19.2%	20.6%	17.6%
Food	15.4%	14.7%	11.4%
Insurance	4.4%	10.2%	15.6%
Clothing	4.8%	4.7%	5.3%
Health	8.1%	5.1%	3.8%
Entertainment	3.7%	4.7%	5.2%

With only minor exceptions, the rank ordering of spending categories is the same across the income spectrum. Regardless of income level, the areas of housing, clothing, and entertainment show almost no percentage variation. Transportation is also relatively stable, dropping off only with the highest income group. The really big difference is in the area of insurance, which includes personal insurance, pension contributions, and Social Security. For upper-income groups these "security" expenditures rise to a very significant percentage of expenditures. This rise is made possible by decreases in other areas, most notably, the areas of food and health.

It is very interesting that American households, across the income stream, maintain largely similar patterns of spending. If one believed in the frivolity of most consumption expenditures above modest levels, one might have expected to see an area such as entertainment rising steadily as a percentage of income, perhaps for people in the upper-income brackets becoming a very large part of overall consumption. That this does not occur, of course, does not prove that much of American consumption is not frivolous—it might be frivolous across the board. Still, the constancy of the spending pattern should make one cautious about such assumptions.

It is of central importance to remember that most Americans do not have the high incomes that are sometimes projected in media images. In 2000, median household income was $42,148 and only one in five households had an income of over $81,960. Roughly 50 percent of total income went to this top 20 percent of households. Some 57 percent of all households had incomes below $50,000. While the top fifth of households had an average pretax income of $141,621, for the second highest quintile, the average was $65,727. While such numbers must look astonishingly high to people in poor countries, from the inside, for someone who lives here, they are more sobering.

The term "households" includes single individuals, couples without children, and large family units. The average levels meld together those on opposite ends of the income spectrum. It is more informative to consider that social unit which remains at the societal core, even if less so than in previous generations: married couples with children. This group encompasses over 100 million people, about 41 percent of the total population.[32] *If we look at median income, we find that in 2000 median income for married couples with children was $63,110; at this level of income, consumption expenditures are roughly $48,700.*[33, 34] It is useful to keep this figure in mind. If the median American two-parent family with children is spending $48,7000 a year, then those who would advocate dramatically reduced consumption as an across-the-board prescription for Americans have to explain how families with one or two or even three children are going to live gracefully at significantly lower levels of consumption—say, at $35,000 a year for a family of four.

In the discussion that follows, I am primarily concerned with getting a clearer picture of what economic life is like for "mainstream" America. This is really the area that is in dispute. Most people will agree that it is significantly harder for those with low incomes and for the poor. And similarly, most will agree that there are some people at the top of the income spectrum who consume far more than anyone needs to.

Getting a clear vision on this is not easy. While looking at today's consumption expenditures for the average American family does suggest that we are not wildly "overconsuming," a seemingly very different picture of American consumption emerges when we look back in time. For instance, as the table below shows, if we look at real per capita consumption expenditures over the past four decades, we find a 2000 level that is over twice that of 1960—and a more than threefold increase since 1929.[35]

PER CAPITA PERSONAL CONSUMPTION EXPENDITURES IN CONSTANT [INFLATION ADJUSTED] 1996 DOLLARS	
1929	$5,134
1940	5,486
1950	7,192
1960	8,358
1970	11,300
1980	14,021
1990	17,899
2000	22,152

Similarly, if we look at median family income for married couples (with and without children) over the years, we see a pattern of significant growth. Measured in 2000 dollars (dollars with the purchasing power of a dollar in 2000), the pretax income of such families went from $20,480 in 1947 to $59,184 in 2000.[36]

The historical picture suggests enormous increases in consumption, increases of such magnitude that it seems obvious that we would have been better off if we had exchanged some of this increase for more leisure (or more inherently rewarding work). Thus, look at the consumption level of $8,358 for 1960 and that of $22,152 for 2000. This represents an increase of 150 percent. But things were not so bad in 1960. Wouldn't we all be happier today if, rather than having more than doubled consumption expenditures since 1960, we had split the difference—say, increasing consumption by only 75 percent and having three-day weekends or a six-hour day? Haven't we made a fundamental mistake in opting so strongly for increased consumption?[37, 38, 39]

We are faced, then, with two seemingly disparate pictures. On the one hand, over the broad historical period it is undeniable that there has been marked growth in consumption. But when we look at where we are now, we find that for the typical family with children, consumption levels seem rather modest.

How are we to explain the coexistence of these two facts: that consumption levels have risen greatly, and that the level of consumption of the average family seems rather modest? One explanation we have already encountered. In this view, our consumption levels only "seem" modest, when in fact they are not. Rather, it is maintained, we have undergone an escalation in our norms of decency and thus in our sense of what constitutes a necessity. Because this is a collective social phenomenon, even when we are looking at other people's spending we don't see how they can do with less, even though what the average person has would have seemed more than abundant from an earlier vantage point.

On this line of thought, this "psychological inflation" of our individual and collective sense of necessity extends the realm of "must have it" in two different ways. First, we feel today that we cannot do without a multitude of goods and services which previously didn't even exist (such as answering machines, air-conditioning, computer games, home videos, and microwave ovens). Second, with respect to those things that we did have before, we now feel it a necessity to have better quality or greater quantity. We "need" homes with larger rooms, more closet space, and with at least two bathrooms; we "need" to be able to eat out more frequently and wear nicer clothes. Moreover, as everyone else's income rises, we feel that ours must rise, too, just so we can maintain our relative standing. As the economy grows, we feel we need more and more.

There is no doubt that escalation in our sense of necessity exists, and that finding ways to hold this in check must be part of an agenda for controlling ever-rising levels of consumption. However, I don't think this is the big picture. Rather, I believe that much of the rise in income and consumption has merely gone toward meeting the same needs we have always had (e.g., safe housing, transportation, child care). Such needs have absorbed income growth in part because previously they were only partially met for most people. But, more interestingly, I will argue, *as a result of a multitude of social transformations, the real cost of meeting core economic needs has grown substantially.* If this is true, it will go a long way to reconciling the two pictures. We do indeed consume more, but that's because it used to cost less to satisfy our core needs than it does today.

CORE ECONOMIC NEEDS

Economists, in their professional work, typically avoid using the concept of needs, preferring instead to think in terms of preferences, desires, and utility. There is a general sense that there is no objective way of distinguishing between what people need and what they want. "One person's luxury is another's necessity," and so forth.

Making these distinctions is not always easy, but far too much has been made of such difficulties. On a conceptual level, needs can be distinguished from wants in a variety of ways.

One distinguishing feature is that we learn about wants and needs differently. Generally speaking (the unconscious aside) people know what they want; often, however, they don't know what they need. For instance, it wasn't until the nineteenth century that the need for various vitamins was established, and we are still in the process of determining whether or not people need vitamins E and K, and if so, in what quantities.

In order to establish such needs, scientific inquiry is brought to bear to determine what happens to a person if deprived of these vitamins for prolonged periods. Of course, no such inquiry is necessary to determine whether or not a person wants to take these vitamins. Often people want things that not only are unnecessary, but that are actually harmful to them. And often enough they fail to want and to understand what it is that they do need.

The concept of need is logically tied to the notion of well-being. Physical needs are those things that are required for physical well-being. Psychological needs are those required for psychological or emotional well-being. Insofar as we have competing conceptions of well-being, it is possible that we would also have competing answers to what an individual needs. Thus, disagreement over what people actually need emerges from two sources. First, there may be disagreement over causal connections, over what will happen if a putative need is not satisfied (e.g., does the absence of physical contact actually impair the health of infants?). Second, even if people agree on the

causal linkages, they may disagree on whether the effect of not satisfying a putative need counts as a loss of well-being, or inadequacy of health.
Thus, two psychologists may agree that lack of effusive praise may result in
a child who isn't totally self-confident, but disagree over whether that is a
bad thing.

Despite these areas of potential disagreement there is a common general
formula: to say that a person has a need for something implies that he will
suffer some harm or loss of well-being if he does not have it. No such implication follows from saying that someone wants something. Although there
are some valid problems in interpreting the concept of needs, for present
purposes most of this is beside the point, simply because we can arrive at a
substantial consensus on what our core economic needs are.

In the 1970s "basic needs problems"—such as infant mortality, illiteracy,
stunted physical growth, and disease—came to occupy a central place in
thinking about the problems of Third World economies. At that time the
U.S. Congress enacted what was known as "The New Directions" legislation, which established by law that the alleviation of these basic needs problems in Third World countries was the central objective of U.S. development
assistance.

It is possible to take a similar, "needs-oriented" approach to our own economic life and identify a set of key needs that people bring to economic life,
and that potentially can be addressed through economic life. There is no single way to do this. Depending on how such needs are identified, there is
either a greater or lesser degree of consensus. For example, we may all agree
that people have a need for ample food and shelter, but may disagree as to
whether all people have a need for self-fulfillment through creative work.

Here then are a set of core economic needs that I believe to be generally
applicable and broadly noncontroversial:

1. Housing. Need for safe, minimally attractive housing, located a
   reasonable distance from work.
2. Transportation. Need for safe public or private transportation
   that allows family members to travel relatively quickly among
   the central points of everyday life (e.g., from home to work, to
   schools, to stores, and to communal activity).
3. Food. Need for ample, healthy, reasonably diverse, and enjoy-
   able food.
4. Health care. Need for effective treatment of health problems.

5. Clothing. Need for clothing that is adequate to climate conditions and the different contexts of ordinary life.
6. Education. Need for effective and safe schooling for one's children.
7. Economic security. Need for protection against large increases in the cost of meeting the other needs (e.g., as triggered by major illnesses), as well as protection against decline or loss of income stream.

This does not constitute an exhaustive set of our core economic needs. For instance, I have not included a need for access to the central forms of communication with others in our society, such as having a telephone, because this constitutes only a small portion of household expenses. Nor am I maintaining that these exact formulations are precise and perfectly specified notions. They are, however, good enough to allow us to undertake a common sense look at our money problems.

As can be seen, there is nothing particularly elevated about these needs. They correspond to what most people would accept as necessary expenses. If those who view our present consumption levels as emerging from runaway desires and a false escalation of "need" are correct, then the satisfaction of these needs should account for only a limited portion of the income of the average family. Moreover, as consumption expenditures have risen over time (after adjusting for inflation), a significantly smaller and smaller percentage of our income should have sufficed to meet such needs. The reality, I will argue, is quite the contrary. *Even at present "high" levels of consumption, many of these needs are still not met, and the effort to satisfy these needs accounts for most of the consumption expenditures of most of the population.*[40]

HOW MUCH DOES IT COST TO MEET CORE NEEDS IN AMERICA?

When economists inquire into the changing cost of meeting core needs, they typically approach these issues by focusing on a *fixed* basket of needed goods and services. The need is identified with the items in the market basket, the necessities. This, however, is a mistake. Exactly what goods and services are required to meet a given need is not something that is fixed. The physical goods and services are only the means of meeting the need. Which goods and services will perform this function, however, changes all the time. The fact that the composition of the basket of necessities is changing is the major cause of changes in "need required income" (NRI), which is the amount of money required to meet core economic needs.

This is a very important distinction. It is not that new needs are being dreamed up. The needs remain the same, but the commodity specification, the goods and services required to meet long-standing needs, changes rapidly. For instance, workers have always had a need to get from home to work. This is a constant, a general feature of social life. When they worked on farms, they walked to work. All they required by way of commodities was a pair of boots. Today, almost all employees require public or private transport, and the money to pay for it.

Let us then explore the changing cost of meeting core needs:

Housing

In this area, NRI has grown considerably, and yet the need remains unsatisfied for many people. That is, many Americans, for all they may spend, simply do not have safe housing a reasonable distance from work, say, within a twenty-minute drive.[41]

The explanation for the growth of NRI (in real terms) lies largely in two phenomena. The most direct factor, without probing why this itself occurred, is simply that the cost of single-family homes has risen far more than the general rate of inflation. Between 1970 and 1998 the median sales price of existing homes rose from $23,000 to $128,400[42]; adjusted for inflation, this represents an increase of 43 percent. However, this statistic glosses over substantial regional differences. In the West, the real increases in housing prices for existing homes was 73 percent, while in the Northeast, the Midwest and the South the real increases were 35–45%.

Compare, then, two hypothetical families of modest means; one entered the housing market in 1970 and one entered in 1998. Assume they lived in an area where prices rose 60 percent in real terms. If mortgage payments constituted 25 percent of the household expenditures, there would be an increase in NRI of 15 percent from just this factor alone. To put this in perspective, note that from 1970 to 1998 real median family income rose only 29 percent.[43] Indeed, the situation is actually much starker if we look at median income levels of young households. Between 1970 and 1998 the real median income of families with householders aged twenty-five to thirty-four years rose only 13%. In the age range thirty-five to forty-five it rose less than 1% a year between 1970 and 2000.[44] For such families, the rise in NRI for housing explains a great deal about their sense of income pressure. For some groups this one factor alone absorbed virtually all of the income growth they might have had over the last twenty-five years.

A second factor in the growth of NRI for housing is the continuing decline in personal safety, resulting in greater demand for housing in safe neighborhoods. Thus, even in regions where aggregate housing costs have remained stable, *safe* housing has become progressively more expensive. To maintain a fixed level of safety people have had to move to progressively more expensive neighborhoods. The same is true of housing in locations where schools are safe and educationally sound. Because such housing is simply out of reach for many Americans, as high as they are, the high prices of homes in such neighborhoods do not fully reflect existing need. If middle- and low-income people had *more* money, they would increase the bidding war for housing that satisfies their needs. The problem could be termed "an inadequacy of supply." But when we see that the shortage is not of physically adequate housing, but of safe housing which is close to work and has good public schools, we see that this "supply problem" isn't going to be solved by home builders.

The extent of both the crime and schooling problems varies considerably between different regions and within regions. Where I live, in Maryland, near the District of Columbia there is a marked difference between neighborhoods. Within the Washington beltway, to live in a neighborhood where there is very little crime and top-quality public schools, one has to live where houses cost upward of $300,000. Indeed, median prices in the best school districts are closer to $400,000. Costs are lower if one moves farther out from the city, but then the extent to which one is failing to satisfy the need for housing a reasonable distance from work increases significantly.

Assume that the needs of safety, school quality, and proximity to work can only be satisfied in a neighborhood where houses cost $300,000. Using the 3:1 rule of thumb employed by real estate agents, an income of at least $100,000 would be required to live in that neighborhood. This rules out more than three-quarters of two-parent families and more than 85 percent of households. If we considered a $400,000 house, then no more than 5 percent of the population could qualify for it income-wise. Of course, in my area, and perhaps in yours, we hardly need any statistics to know this. Everyone knows that only a limited number of people can afford homes that are relatively close to the city, in safe neighborhoods, and in districts with top-notch public schools.

So, just looking at needs for housing, meaning not just the house but the distance to work and the quality of neighborhood and the schools, a good case can be made that the average American family, rather than successfully meeting its needs with a smaller and smaller percentage of its income, doesn't meet its needs at all. Of course, if we're middle class, we get by. We make some adjustments, some compromises. Either we live farther out where it is cheaper; or we live where the schools are okay, but not great; or we live where it's not exactly "unsafe," but you can't just send the kids out to play, especially once it gets dark. But this isn't an escalation in our norms of "decency." If anything, it's a slippage of standards and expectations.

For others, for those with lower incomes—well, they just have to live in neighborhoods where life expectancy is significantly lower. For instance, inside Washington, D.C., outside the white neighborhoods, life expectancy for men is under sixty years, not too different from the average life expectancy for men in most African countries.[45]

Transportation

For most Americans, transportation needs are relatively well satisfied, but only at a markedly higher cost than in earlier years. Since the 1930s, the percentage of total consumption devoted to transportation has more than doubled for all income classes.[46] Given that real per capita consumer expenditures rose by over 250 percent in the same period, we have something in the neighborhood of a 500 percent rise (in real terms) in the amount that families are spending on transportation.[47] There is good reason to think that most of this represents an increase in NRI, not the growth of luxury.

The significance of these increases in the cost of meeting transportation needs is enormous. Typically American families are devoting 19 percent of their household budget to transportation. One way of thinking about this is to say that each year, we work from January 1 through March 10 just to cover the costs of transportation needs. Years ago such needs were covered within the first few weeks of the year.

We all know what happened. First one automobile, and then a second automobile, became a necessity. This occurred not because of an inflated sense of necessity, but rather because of underlying changes in our socioeconomic life. The shift to the suburbs, motivated in large part by the search for safe neighborhoods and decent public schools, has made the private automobile a necessity, and the emergence of the two-income family has tended to make two cars a necessity. This trend has been reinforced by the decline of neighborhood stores (instead we have to drive to malls five miles from home) and the shift of communal activities (especially for children) from the immediate neighborhood to formal locations beyond walking distance. Thus, we have the Saturday- and Sunday-morning phenomenon of "soccer moms" (and dads).

To put it differently, in the early decades of the century people had the very same need for transportation that they have now, but they could and did satisfy this need without automobiles. Today, in most parts of the country, outside some urban areas such as New York and San Francisco, a family without an automobile would be far more restricted in its activities than in times past. Thus, higher real income is required to meet the core need for transportation; the "social efficiency of money" has declined.

Consider as an example a two-parent family in 1991. On the average that family spent $2,429 per year for each car it owned, when upkeep is added to a percentage of the cost of the car.[48] Between 1960 and 1991, median income for married couple families rose $16,153.[49] If consumption expenditures are assumed to be 85 percent of income, then they rose $13,730. If we assume that over those years, as women entered the labor markets, as families moved to the suburbs and so forth, annual transportation NRI went up one car's worth, or $2,429, then about 18 percent of the total consumption growth in that thirty-one-year period was absorbed by an increase in the cost of meeting transportation needs.

Of course there are families with more cars than they need, and there are families with very expensive cars. But this is not the dominant picture. Most families have what they need, but it has cost them substantially to get it.

Food

Though there are too many American families whose need for ample, nutritious food is not satisfied, for most Americans this need is reasonably well met. Moreover, the income needed to satisfy our need for food does not appear to have increased (in real terms) over the decades. In percentage terms, there has been a major decline in the extent of total consumer expenditures allocated to food. Between 1935 and 2000, its share fell by more than half—from roughly one-third of household expenditures to less than one-sixth. At the beginning of the twentieth century, almost 43 percent of the expenditures of urban earners went for food.[50]

In real terms, despite more dining out, per capita expenditures for food increased only about 16 percent between 1950 and 2000.[51] This suggests that in real terms there has been virtually no increase in the income required to satisfy the core food need, and possibly there has even been some decline.

Health Care

The very concept of need is logically related to questions of health. For instance, it is because the failure to meet minimum caloric and nutrient requirements results in significant health damage (e.g., stunted growth, malnutrition, disease) that we are able to specify minimal daily caloric and nutrient needs.

While it is a bit vacuous to speak of the need for cures for currently untreatable diseases, if there is an effective treatment of some significant health problem, then by definition a person with that problem has a need for that treatment. Here the need is derivative from a need for health itself, and is thus relative to the existence of effective treatments for health problems. In addition to the need for health care, people have a need for health care security—an assurance that if they develop a health problem, they will have effective care without destruction of the family finances.

Interestingly, unlike some other categories of need, the health area is one in which a household's expenditures capture only a limited part of what is expended nationally to meet the need. For many people, in addition to household out-of-pocket medical expenditures and expenditures for medical insurance, much of the cost of health care is met through employer contributions to medical insurance and government expenditures.

While we have all read about the vast growth in national expenditures for health care and medical insurance, to an important extent this has not been fully reflected in a growth of need-required household income. In real terms, the per capita level of total national health expenditures (public, business, and personal) almost tripled between 1970 and 1994. Yet as a society, we have been relatively successful in shielding the personal checkbook from this explosion. Adjusting for inflation, per capita expenditures on the household level for medical care and insurance rose by roughly 91 percent between 1970 and 1994.[52]

Over the long haul, health expenditures on the household level have risen roughly in line with the general growth of household income. Thus as a percentage of household expenditures, health expenditures have been relatively constant. In the period 1935–1936 they constituted 4.4 percent of household consumption, in 1988–1989 they constituted 5.7 percent, and in 2000, 5.3 percent.[53] Interestingly, health expenditures on the household level decline as a percentage of total consumption as we consider households in higher income brackets. Part of the explanation for this is that as income levels rise, so does the adequacy of employer-financed health insurance.

It is unlikely that an inflation of our sense of what counts as a necessity has been a major factor here. If a patient has magnetic resonance imaging to examine a possible tumor, it is not because he is seeking to keep up with the Joneses or because he has developed a taste for luxury.

In the health area, unlike other areas, the growth of need-required income is potentially open-ended so long as there is an expansion in effective, but expensive, technologies. The underlying reason for this is the simple fact of the human condition—death and disease will continue to be with us, and we will have need of whatever works to postpone death and reduce the severity of disease. Unlike spending in other areas (such as transportation), where increased consumption (the second car that allows the second wage earner to get to work and keeps people from being trapped in distant suburbs) represents little if any gain in well-being, spending for more effective health care does represent true progress.

Perhaps there have been some few areas within the health sector in which there has been inflation in our sense of decency—one might argue that orthodontia and cosmetic surgery are examples. But for the most part, we can't explain higher health costs in terms of inflated standards of care on the part of the consumer. While there may have been an expansion of "unnecessary" treatments and tests, the patient is rarely in a position to evaluate "necessity" if a doctor suggests a test. As far as the psychology of consumption is concerned, our need is for the income to cover the procedures doctors say are important.

Clothing

Over the last ninety years, spending for clothing and related services has shown a marked decline as a percentage of consumer expenditures. From a high point of 17.6 percent in 1917–1918, it declined to a 10.3 percent in the early 1960s, and has fallen since then to between 5 and 6 percent. In real terms, per capita spending for clothing fell between 1960 and 1988. Yet there is little basis for believing that clothing needs are less adequately met today than thirty years ago. Thus, it seems clear that in this area, at least, we have not seen any increase in NRI. Nor does there seem to have been any inflation in people's sense of how much money (in real terms) they "must have" for clothing, even when we look at the possibility of inflated standards of decency and growth of NRI combined.

This is interesting, because clothing, above all else, seems most powerfully in the grip of changing fashions and desires shaped by advertising. If one expected to find a powerful escalator of inflated desires, an escalator that makes people feel a need for more and more, it would be in this area. But apparently no such escalation has occurred. And if fashion, emulation, and advertising, all of which greatly affect *what* we wear, have relatively little impact in getting us to increase total clothing expenditures, then perhaps the critics are wrong. Perhaps advertising fails as a force to make us buy more, and only succeeds in getting us to buy this brand rather than that brand, this style rather than that style. If so, then it doesn't primarily induce new needs, but rather shifts the specification of what satisfies the same need.

Education

I have formulated the core need in this area in terms of the household's need for effective, safe schooling for children. The term "effective," of course, says nothing about what the goals of schooling should be. Within our society, there is no consensus on this question, and none should be expected, given that ultimately the answer turns on what one means by the good life, the good society, and the developed human being.

At the same time, because of the way "success" at school flows into and determines outcomes in the larger socioeconomic competition of our society, parents typically want their children to go to schools that will equip them to do well in the larger competition. This is not all that parents want, and rightly so. We might want our children to receive an education that will enable them to be effective citizens. We may want schooling that enables them to participate richly within their cultural heritage. Or more generally we might want them to be opened to all that is wonderful about the human experience.

What is interesting here, however, is that whatever the definition of effective schooling, it seems clear that, as a general proposition, that need is not being met throughout our society. Insofar as we are talking about equipping children to do well within the larger socioeconomic competition, the schools tend to reinforce rather than neutralize the differences in economic and social advantage of family circumstance and background. Moreover, as there are only a limited number of "places" within our society that combine interesting work, high social status, and high income, it is necessarily the case that not everyone can succeed in these terms, and the better any one school gets in advancing children toward those goals, the more it lowers, in relative terms, the ability of other schools to advance the life chances of its students.

With respect to educational goals that are not part of a zero-sum competition—for instance, that children should emerge from school as creative participants within a rich intellectual and cultural heritage—this happens for only a very small percentage of students. Thus, a starting point for thinking about whether expenditures for schooling exceed the level required for meeting core educational needs is the realization that those needs, at present, are not being met. This, of course, is not to suggest that simply spending more money would make an important difference. The point is merely to set any reflection on why people think they need more money than they have, within the recognition that they may understandably want (or should want) things for their children that they are presently not getting.

For the most part, our society finances schooling collectively, providing free public schools through the high school level. This was not always the case, and it is possible that this commitment will erode in the future. But what it has meant is that with the exception of preschool and college, the costs of schools have not fallen directly on the household budget. Typically, these expenses are paid locally, often financed through property taxes. For the individual household, only a minor part of consumer expenditures is directed toward meeting its educational needs. Even though households pay the bulk of property taxes, the household doesn't pay them *in order to* satisfy the household's educational needs; it pays them whether or not there are children in school.

If the public schools were successfully meeting educational needs, and meeting them through the college level, the system of public finance and free schools would be an excellent example of how a society can make simple living feasible, how it can make it possible to live the good life with only modest means. Indeed, I am convinced that if we had confidence that our children's educational needs would be well attended to regardless of our income level, we would care much less about how much we earn. I know I would.

Given the fact that public schools often fail to provide safe, effective schooling, and because some private schools do a better job, we can say that families need income sufficient to send their children to private schools, or alternatively, they need the income to live where there are good public schools. For families with children, when parents have the means to live where there are excellent public schools, this is a major factor that enters into their choice of neighborhood. But for the most part, people lack the means. Indeed, this is necessarily so. If everyone tried to move into those few excellent school districts, the housing prices would rise to levels that again make them unavailable to most people. That's how markets ration scarce resources; since there aren't enough to go around, price rises until demand falls to the level of supply.

To some extent, this has already happened; houses in good school districts already sell at a premium. Most people don't think of living there, because they know they can't afford it. In the main, people just lower their expectations, or more frequently, they form only limited expectations both for their children and their schools. The same applies to private schooling. Private schools offer parents the opportunity, for $12,000 to $15,000 a year, of giving their children a better schooling experience. Certainly one can find *some* private schools that are better (no matter how you define "better") than most public schools. But this has not resulted in any vast increase in education-related expenses on the household level. The reason is simple: while the need is there, and the "consumer service" is there, people just can't afford it.

One area in which there has been explosive growth in education-related expenditures, and in NRI, is day care and prekindergarten schooling. This is directly related to the fuller entry of women into the paid labor force and is a clear example of the way in which a significant part of our higher incomes and consumption levels go to fulfill needs that were previously filled by different social mechanisms.[54]

Between 1970 and 1995 the percentage of three- and four-year-olds enrolled in nursery schools rose from 20.5 percent to 49 percent.[55] The increase was greatest among three-year-olds—from 12.9 percent in 1970 to 35.9 percent in 1995, an increase of 178 percent. *Between 1960 and 1996 the labor force participation rate of married women with children under six rose from 18.6 percent to almost 63 percent.*[56] Between 1975 and 1996 the labor force *participation rate for married women with a child one year old or younger rose from 31 percent to 59 percent.*[57]

However, while there has been a vast increase in the need for child care, only a relatively small segment of the population meets this need by purchasing child care services. While the percentage of children in organized child care facilities has more than doubled since 1977, in 1991 these children accounted for only 23 percent of the children under five of employed mothers.[58] Today the number is somewhat higher but still limited.

The fact that most of the children of working mothers are not in organized day care explains why child care expenses, which are staggering for families that incur them, do not clearly emerge in the aggregate statistics. Typical costs of day care in major cities in 1997 were $140 per week, or roughly $7,000 per year. Before-tax median income in 1997 for married couple families with the wife working full time was $65,473.[59] Assuming annual expenditures of $52,378, the day care bill for these families would constitute 13 percent of total expenditures. The $7,000 component of NRI incurred by families who pay for day care can also be put in perspective if we compare median income of married couple families where the mother was *not* in the labor force in 1970, with married couple families with the mother *in* the labor force in 1995. In 1995 dollars, the difference in median income between these two different situations twenty-five years apart is a gain of about $21,500. If we assume that the 1995 family used day care, while the 1970 family did not, roughly one-third of the income gain associated with the entry of the women into the labor force and two and a half decades of income growth was absorbed by the day care expenditure.[60]

Higher education is the other major schooling expense that falls on the household budget. Here, too, there has been significant growth of NRI. In part this is because of an increase in the amount of schooling young people need in order to compete for employment. In addition, NRI has gone up because of the steep rise in tuition costs. In 1975 the annual cost of college tuition in four-year private schools was 19.1 percent of median family income. In 1999 it was equivalent to 37 percent of median family income.[61]

The fact that I view the need in this area as stretching not only through college but beyond might be cited as a clear instance of escalating standards. Certainly there is overcredentialization—people having to have higher levels of schooling than the substantive aspects of their work would mandate. But if there is an inflation of standards here, it is not on the part of the consuming households. For them the need is the long-standing one; their children need that schooling which will enable them to do well in the larger socioeconomic competition.

Parents see their responsibility, and a good part of their own identity and fulfillment, as bound up with how successful their children will be. When the disparities between socioeconomic winners and losers are very great, as they are in our society, the consequences of not receiving effective schooling are enormous. It is also true, however, that the magnitude of socioeconomic disparities and the relative scarcity of good jobs ensures that most people will not be successful; in principle, schools cannot equip most people to be winners in a competition with many contestants and few prizes.

This fact, however, results in more intense competition and in greater educational expenditures. In recent years, for instance, the elite colleges have experienced a very significant increase in applications, and are rejecting ever higher percentages of those who apply. As a result of the increased competition, a new specialty has emerged—the "educational consultant," whose job it is to both mold the high school student into the perfect applicant and to market him to the consultant's contacts at desirable colleges. The charge for this new service is $1,000 a year.[62] Similarly, as competition intensifies, the need for more extensive schooling increases, thus pushing up educational costs.

What has happened is that the society has changed. The commodity specification in terms of years of schooling required in order to do well in the competition has increased. Indeed, today, without some graduate education, it is increasingly difficult to get a good job. If a good job is understood in relative terms, then even with high expenditures, as a whole, the society makes no progress toward actually satisfying this need to be at the top rather than the bottom.

Economic Security

A key element of our security needs is protection against a sharp increase in NRI itself. A serious health problem that requires expensive treatment is the most salient example of this; the household expenses associated with protecting against such eventualities are included in the health care expenditures discussed previously.

Generally economic security issues have to do with protection against a severe *drop* in the income stream. This typically emerges from loss or relinquishment of one's job as a result of getting sick, getting old, or getting fired.

Economic insecurity associated with possible loss of employment resulting from adverse economic conditions or corporate downsizing has become more pervasive in recent years. There are, of course, government programs designed to mitigate the associated loss of income, but these programs provide only limited protection. For most Americans the need for protection in this area is simply unmet. As a result, increasing numbers of people live in a state of heightened anxiety.

Because there is no form of private insurance that protects the individual against this loss, and thus no obvious purchase individuals can make to offset it, the need for economic security does not clearly translate into higher expenditures. Indirectly, however, there are a variety of things individuals might do to mitigate income insecurity associated with potential job loss. One strategy is to increase personal savings. Most people are unable to employ this strategy because they simply don't have sufficient income to make a difference. Insofar as the probability of job loss has risen, then the income needed to protect against future drops in the income stream increases as well. And if the savings necessary to provide security are enormous, then the increase in NRI will be similarly enormous.

Another strategy is to seek employment in occupations that are less vulnerable to economic contraction and dislocation. For those already in the labor force, this strategy requires devoting income to retraining costs; for parents with children and for young adults, it requires paying for an education that provides access to professions that have more secure income streams. In both cases, we confront a rise in NRI, and insofar as people adopt such security strategies, the higher spending may show up indirectly in educational and housing expenditures, not to speak of the sacrifices in self-fulfillment when security becomes a dominant factor in choice of occupation.

Perhaps the greatest source of economic insecurity is associated with a potentially devastating decline in income when one approaches old age. Household expenditures (contributions) to retirement plans are the typical private-sector approach to meeting this security need. Multiple factors, including an increase in life span and greater uncertainty regarding the viability of government programs such as Social Security, serve to increase NRI. As in the area of health care, there are substantial numbers of Americans for whom this security need is unmet. Thus, increases in household expenditures for income insurance associated with retirement tell only part of the story with respect to the growth of NRI.

The data on expenditures for personal insurance and pensions (which

includes life insurance, Social Secu
contributions to IRAs, etc.) shows tl
is a very sharp increase in spending
with incomes between $15,000 and
only 5 percent of total expenditures.
between $50,000 and $60,000, and rea
over $70,000—roughly what such (
food combined.[63]

How are we to understand this vi
as income levels rise? If we had seen
tures for clothing, we would have in
cretionary spending on the part of those better off. Yet here, I would suggest
that just the opposite is true. The fact that people who have more money
spend higher percentages on security suggests that economic security is an
unmet need for most people. One of the first things people do when they
have the means is to spend to increase security. For instance, of the $28,308
more that consumers in the highest quintile spend beyond that spent by consumers in the next highest quintile, $6,132 (21.6 percent) goes for personal
insurance and pensions.

NRI grows in the area of income security as a direct result of it already
growing in other areas. For example, if an individual is purchasing income
protection for an income stream adequate to meet his needs, then as the
latter increases, he has more to protect and the costs of the insurance rise
accordingly.

A general picture emerges. Yes, Americans over the years have increased
consumption expenditures quite considerably. Much of this increase in
household expenditure has gone to meet fundamental needs, either because
needs were previously unmet, or because in real terms the cost of meeting
these needs has increased dramatically.

This is a quite different picture than that commonly portrayed with respect
to our affluent society. For most Americans their subjective experience—
that they always need more money than they have—is not to be explained by
inflation in their appetites or their standards of decency (e.g., "I must have
more square feet, a newer car, better furniture, new gadgets, or I'll just die"),
but rather by socioeconomic conditions that have resulted in unmet need or
in increased cost of meeting long-existing needs. This is true of housing,

on, and income security. Collectively these increases
...ed about money despite income growth.
...de with an example which reinforces this picture from a
...le. Between 1970 and 1995 the income of married couple
...se by 21 percent. There are two main reasons for the growth of
... for these families. First is the entry of women into the labor market;
...970, 40 percent of women in married couples were employed; by 1995,
...his had risen to 60 percent. And second, over this period the income of
women has risen considerably faster than that of men. Indeed, income
of married couple families in which the wife was not employed declined by
6 percent over this period.[64]

Let us then consider a married couple in which the wife decides to take
full-time paid employment. Assume that she earns $26,026 (median income
for full-time female employees in 1997), and that on this marginal increment
to the family income there is a combined federal and state income tax of 20
percent, and a Social Security tax of 7 percent. This leaves potentially $18,998
for increased consumption. Of this amount, some will be spent for existing
unmet needs, and some will be truly discretionary. But first, some must be
spent for the increase in NRI associated with the change from a one-career to
a two-career family. How great is this increase in NRI? Well, it depends on
the family situation. But let us assume that in this family the wife's decision
necessitates going from one car to two, and day care expenses for one child.
Consider:

Day care	$7,000
Annual cost of second car	2,500
Additional cost of lunch out	1,000
Additional cost of ordering food in, or going out to dinner one night a week	1,000
Cost of having once-a-week cleaning of home	2,500
Additional annual expense of work clothes	500
Total additional costs	$14,500

Increase in NRI as a percentage of increment in disposable income = 76%

What's left is only $4,498; of the $26,026 earned, this is only 17 percent. The
great rise in income has disappeared into thin air.

In this not atypical example, almost all of the increased consumption generated by the wife's decision to seek paid employment (the single most important factor behind increased family income) goes toward meeting necessities incurred by the decision itself. Yes, income and consumption are up substantially. Yet the family continues to feel pressed economically and now, with both parents working, is under far greater time pressure as well. This is not intended to be an argument against dual-career families, but to point out how misleading statistics may be in a period of transition from one-career to two-career families.

It also helps to explain a fascinating statistic—that more than 60 percent of Americans believe that the change in the "relationship between men and women" has made it "harder for families to earn enough money to live comfortably."[65]

BEAUTY AND THE NEED FOR MONEY

In the foregoing sections, I have limited the discussion to seven core economic needs. Although it is true, as various religious and philosophic traditions have espoused, that it is possible to develop a conception of identity and an outlook on existence in which even these basics are viewed as superfluous, such psychological gymnastics suffer from two problems. First, they can result in an emotionally constricted form of life that is far from ideal for most people. Second, because they call for a vast degree of personal transformation, they are, realistically speaking, unattainable by most people, and even if attained, do not last from one generation to another.

What I have tried to capture in the seven needs just discussed is the central economic core of need, which is both motivationally powerful and recognized as legitimate by most people within our society. I believe these needs would also be widely, though perhaps not universally, recognized by most peoples in other cultures and at other times—though, obviously, with different commodity specifications.

Insofar as this is correct, the satisfaction of these core needs is required on any conception of simple living that seeks to be broadly relevant to the perspectives and limitations of real people. In Part II of this book I will introduce and explore a particular conception of simple living termed "graceful simplicity." Graceful simplicity is distinguished in part by the centrality it gives to aesthetic values. To translate this into the present concerns is to ask about beauty and money—how much money do we need in order to have beauty in our lives? Assuming that, in addition to the core needs discussed, there is, in some sense, a need for beauty, to what extent is that need fulfilled, and what has happened over time to the amount of money required to satisfy it?

This is a much more difficult area to ponder than core needs for food or clothing. For instance, are we talking about beautiful homes with beautiful furnishings, or are we talking about access to beautiful music and art? Or are we talking about living in a beautiful city, or having access to the beauties of nature? Or all of these?

A few reflections on the place of beauty within the economics of graceful simplicity may be helpful:

- Beauty must not be thought of as residing solely or even primarily within things. There is the beauty that is the architecture of time; it requires slowing down and doing things right, and it may call for less income and more time, rather than the reverse.

- A life of graceful simplicity does not require that our homes be museums; it does not require that every artifact of daily use be striking. At the same time, from the point of view of gracefulness, a life that is aesthetically impoverished is abhorrent.

- One dimension of graceful living is the awakening of aesthetic appreciation, and with that will come a selectivity that often, without any additional cost, results in the attainment of things of beauty. Anyone who has wandered through flea markets and garage sales and thrift shops knows that there are great things to be found—beautiful objects, not noticed or not valued by others.

- Things of beauty exercise a special power—they radiate within their space—and as they draw us into their orbit they close our consciousness to that which is outside. Thus, it is not necessary that all our possessions be beautiful, only that some things are.

- One of the inexpensive sources of beauty is our own creative ability. In part, this is a matter of tapping into our own latent abilities to take a beautiful photograph, to sculpt, to draw, or to play an instrument. These to some extent involve mastery of technique. But, within the household, we are constantly engaged with the issue of design and arrangement—whether it be the utensils, the tools, the furniture, the towels—what we find in every space is that beauty resides not just in the objects, but in how they are arranged with one another. Perhaps this is better understood by thinking about marketplaces. If one has traveled in Third World countries and gone into marketplaces, sometimes one is stopped short by a staggeringly beautiful display, formed with fifty loaves of bread, or with several kilos of nuts, or with fifteen cooking pans, or with a few dozen shirts.

• The beauty in our private spaces, inside our homes, is accessible only to ourselves and our friends. But perhaps of more significance is the aesthetic quality of public space, be it the architecture of houses, yards, and gardens; the pavement of the streets; the shops; the trees; the skyline; or access to the sunset. In economists' terms, these are public goods, in the sense that the enjoyment of them by one person does not diminish their availability to others. They are not, in the ordinary sense, consumed.

An enormous part of the need for beauty in our lives can be supplied through the aesthetic quality of the outside space. It is available when one lives in a beautiful city, or when one lives in a beautiful natural environment—be it near the shore, in the mountains, or on the banks of a river. There is an aesthetic abundance that surrounds us in all of these places, a wealth that we have, merely by virtue of our being there rather than somewhere else.

It is the creation and destruction of this public beauty, whether man-made or natural, that is most significant. No fortune within the home can compensate for not being able to walk outside, for being unable to bear to look outside, for having nothing interesting to see when walking to the store. On the other hand, it is remarkable how little we feel we need when we are in a beautiful place. Indeed, rather than retreating to our private spaces, we rush to be outside. How much of our expenditures on our homes, then, represents this failure, this aesthetic inadequacy of public space?

What has happened over time? Does it take more or less money to satisfy our need for beauty? It is hard to draw up an accurate balance sheet. There are some areas, such as music, in which there really have been enormous technological advances. Today, at relatively little cost, one can hear the world's best music played by the best musicians on compact disks with very high sound quality.

But this, it seems to me, is more the exception.

- The "efficiency" of supermarkets, malls, and, now, warehouse shopping has not only driven out the small shop, but has robbed us of the chance to walk along an interesting street or to have a friendship with a local shopkeeper.
- Chain stores rather than individual proprietors have driven out the individual display, the originality and idiosyncrasy that offers opportunities for surprise and discovery.
- Fear of crime has deprived many of us of access to the beauty of the moon and stars; it has made us afraid to take a solitary walk, or run, in the park.
- Much of our urban world is unremittingly ugly, and suburbanization has made it extremely hard even to reach the countryside.
- Even the possibility of aesthetic delight in our food has suffered. A good bakery, a fine tomato, a nectarine that explodes with sweetness—these are hard to find. If we know where to get them, running from one specialty store to another, we pay extra, in time and money, for what was once an inherent part of a loaf of bread and a piece of fruit.

From what I can tell, for many the need for beauty is unfulfilled. For the few who can satisfy it, beauty comes at very high cost—living in expensive cities and neighborhoods, taking vacations to beautiful places: Paris, Martha's Vineyard, Hawaii, Greece. Such escape is very expensive. Necessarily these can be solutions for only a few: the presence of many will itself destroy the aesthetic; and at any rate, a vacation is an escape, not a way of life.

We pay a complex price for our modern world. The world we have lost was in many ways more interesting, more diverse, and often more beautiful than the world we have created. To be aware of these differences becomes sentimentality only if we make the leap to a general idealization of the past. But it is a kind of blindness if our fear of being accused of sentimentality prevents us from seeing what has been lost.

Consider just one example: pavement. Goodness knows there are many arguments for pavement. Once one gets started paving things over, there are powerful arguments for asphalt over cobblestones. Yet, if one has a chance to walk down an unpaved road, there is no telling what one will find. Perhaps an interesting stone, perhaps a mysterious animal hole that was not there last week, perhaps the erosion caused by last night's storm. What dirt roads lack is "all-the-sameness," and with "all-the-sameness" comes predictability; predictability makes it easier to go fast. So if you're in the business of getting from place to place, then asphalt is the way to go. But if you're not quite sure of the point of the destination, and not quite sure of the point of being there sooner rather than later, then pavement is the enemy, and paving over the world is madness.

There have been trade-offs, and sometimes we made them quite poorly. This is especially true with things of beauty. It seems to me that beauty has been lost because we lack the language for asserting its value. Thus, we sacrificed too much. We compensate for this aesthetic impoverishment with diverse consumption expenditures, but the road toward a simpler life is one that allows us to regain the aesthetics of public space.

More generally we need societies in which the level of NRI is low, or, to put it differently, a society in which the efficiency of need satisfaction per unit of income is high. It is the background efficiency of the society that determines how much money the individual household needs.

In the Third World context the rationale for great social efficiency is simple and powerful—it allows the satisfaction of basic needs at low levels of income. Thus, some live who would otherwise die. But we may also seek a society with low levels of NRI for a different kind of reason: because it facilitates a distinctly valuable form of life.

In a high-productivity society, if the amount of money a family needs to meet its core economic needs is rather modest, this opens the possibility of simple living. First it allows people to put in less time on the job. Therefore, in a socially efficient society, a two-career family might be able to meet core needs with two twenty-hour jobs rather than with two forty-hour jobs. This would be a blessing. It would enable us to restore some peace and harmony to our hectic, harried existence.

Second, a society with low levels of NRI is one in which we are largely freed from the economic realm. If our needs are met with limited income, we are freed from the money side of life. In choosing jobs we can focus more fully on the nonpecuniary aspects of a good job; if needs are met, we can afford to experiment, to make changes in mid-career, to rethink a life plan, to reeducate, to take a bold plunge toward that thing we always wanted to do. If needs can be met at low levels of NRI, then there is less to be anxious about if we suffer a drop in the income stream, if we lose our jobs, or if we walk away from producing or selling goods and services that do not conform to our values.

In a nineteenth-century essay on gracefulness, Herbert Spencer, searching for a definition of gracefulness, reached the conclusion that any action "is most gracefully achieved when achieved through the least expenditure of force ... [that] grace, as applied to motion, describes motion that is effected with an economy of muscular powers."[66] Using that definitional approach, we might say that an economic system operates most gracefully when it satisfies the needs of the population with the least expenditure of income. The social efficiency of money, the ratio of need satisfaction to income, is a measure of such gracefulness, and it tells us the extent to which a society makes simple living feasible. When it is high, then with modest incomes needs can be met; when it is low, needs can be met only if income is high.

In short, a high-productivity society with low levels of NRI is a society that makes possible lives that are less pressured, more centered on friends and family and on activities of inherent value and fuller dignity. How we might begin this transition is the subject of the next chapter, "The Politics of Simplicity."

Chapter Four

THE POLITICS OF SIMPLICITY

What is a politics of simplicity?

The politics of simplicity is the politics of the Alternative American Dream. As such it offers an alternative conception of the goals of our collective efforts, a different notion of what counts as a problem, a different set of priorities, and different perspectives on where to look in search of solutions.

Placing simple living at the center of our approach to public policy represents a return to older American traditions. As noted earlier, throughout American history there has been a concern with simple living, and for the most part this was expressed politically as well as personally. In the colonial period there were laws that prohibited certain forms of conspicuous consumption. The general framework of pricing carried over the age-old notion that there were appropriate prices for goods, and that it was morally wrong to raise prices in pursuit of profits. In particular the sense of iniquity associated with raising prices was strongest when it came to the necessities of life.

Throughout our history, though simple living was abandoned as an organizing principle of political thought, this concern with the cost of necessities never completely vanished. In some parts of the country we still retain controls on the price of rental housing. With respect to education, it has long been policy throughout the United States for schooling through high school to be provided free. In some localities this has extended to college education. In New York City, although tuition remains modest, there had for many decades been no tuition charge at all, allowing those with modest resources to attend excellent schools such as City College, Brooklyn College, and Queens College. I myself went to City College.

In the area of health care, the belief that poor people should receive adequate health care continues to be operative despite those who might want to end Medicaid. Other aid programs for the poor, such as food stamps, have sought to keep costs low for basic needs. While these programs were designed to respond to poverty, and while not conceptualized in terms of simple living, they embody common ground by enabling people with limited monetary income to meet core economic needs.

Medicare (as distinct from Medicaid) is an even better example of a relevant policy fragment. This is not an antipoverty program but one that applies to all Americans when they reach sixty-five. Health care costs for the elderly are singled out as a special realm of necessity that will not be allowed to impose too great a financial cost upon individuals who have reached that point in life when both costs and vulnerability may be high. Because it focuses only on the realm of health care, and only for those at the typical age of retirement, it has rarely been connected in people's minds with simple living, but were it to be conceived more generally the linkage would be obvious.

For decades, a losing battle was waged to "save the family farm." Irrespective of the congressional politics, there was a good deal of public support for such programs because the small farm was visualized as a uniquely valuable mode of simple living that should not be allowed to go out of existence. Such concern with farm life and an awareness of the threats to it emerged early in the eighteenth century, and were central to Jefferson's vision of an economic structure in which the viability of an agrarian-based democracy would be assured.

With respect to mandatory leisure time and other restrictions on work, America has also had a long tradition. Laws requiring the closure of business on Sunday were common until only a few decades ago. These emerged from a commitment to maintaining the Sabbath, which itself was part of the Puritan conception of simple living. This Sabbath commitment remained even when much else of the Puritan orientation was abandoned.

Starting in the nineteenth century, major struggles occurred over the length of the standard workday. These culminated in legislation first establishing the ten-hour day and then the eight-hour day. At the same time it should be said that only to a limited extent did these policies emanate from a desire to bring about simple living; rather they were more centrally concerned with worker health and well-being and with spreading the available work.

At certain points American political leaders explicitly sought to urge simple living on the American people. In 1901 a French clergyman named Charles Wagner wrote a widely read book on simple living entitled *The Simple Life*. It was a bestseller in the United States, and Theodore Roosevelt had the author to the White House. The president's recognition of Wagner brought him to the wider attention of Americans with the statement that there was to his knowledge "no other book . . . which contains so much that we of America ought to take to our hearts."[67] Jimmy Carter similarly hosted E. F. Schumacher, the author of *Small Is Beautiful*, at the White House, and urged us to turn from our materialist ways.

Today the self-conscious pursuit of simple living operates only on the individual level. The problem with this individualistic approach is not that it emphasizes the individual rather than the social dimension. Emphasis on the role of the individual must always be a part of simple living. The problem is that there is hardly any political dimension to the movement at all. This represents a retreat from politics, reflecting the general frustration with the political realm, perhaps even the belief that to act collectively to improve our society is a waste of time and that the only path that yields any progress is to deal with one's own life.

DO WE NEED A POLITICS OF SIMPLICITY?

Given that most Americans want simpler lives, do we actually need a politics of simplicity? That is to say, do we need to approach simple living through collective action and governmental policies?

In arguing for a politics of simplicity, two factors stand out. The first is the result of the examination undertaken in the previous chapter of the need for money. If, in fact, it had turned out that middle-class Americans have more money than they need, the issue would look very different. Under those circumstances, attaining simple living would largely be a matter of freeing ourselves from the illusion that we really need all that we have and more. Once freed from this illusion, we could reduce the amount of time that we work, and, with our expanding leisure, slow down and enjoy what's really important in life. This is how much of the current simple-living literature approaches the issue.

Even in that scenario, however, it's not quite so easy. For instance, our economic culture and structures don't make it easy to reduce work time; instead, in a variety of ways they penalize and discriminate against so-called "part-time" workers. But putting that aside, the fact of the matter is that for most Americans legitimate economic needs are just barely met or not met at all. Under these circumstances, achieving a simple life is something that most people cannot accomplish alone.

As we saw earlier when considering the potential for becoming financially independent at an early age (e.g., not having to work for a living when you are thirty-five or forty), there are some people for whom this is possible. For instance, a young professional couple with no children and with an annual income of $100,000 can, over ten years of modest consumption, build up an investment portfolio that will allow them to retire (or partially retire) on a modest income. One reason we need a politics of simplicity is simply that such strategies don't speak to the life situation of most people.

Of course, as noted earlier, it is always possible to take a radical position on what we need or on the existence of great potentialities for personal transformation. It has always been possible for some people to achieve valid forms of simple living on almost no money. Throughout the world there are religious orders in which people take a vow of poverty, and succeed in living lives of value on only a limited fraction of what we typically view as a minimally necessary income. But in the real world such solutions are simply beyond what is possible for most people. They involve too many trade-offs and require too great a degree of self-transformation. In short, they do not offer a route to a simpler life that most people are prepared to take.

So the first answer to "Why a politics of simple living?" is that we need to do certain things together. If we don't act together, we will never get there. That said, it must be reemphasized that the personal dimension is ultimately the heart of the matter; the life we have is the life we construct for ourselves. No set of social policies can create the good life for people. The good life is not a matter of existing within a set of beneficent social conditions; it is a particular human life that is lived well.

There is a second answer to why we need a politics of simplicity, and it is equally powerful: we can't avoid the fact that public policy makes simple living either more or less feasible. What I termed "the social efficiency of money"—the extent to which a given amount of personal income satisfies core needs—is changing constantly, often as a result of government policies.

Here are two examples where government has been hostile to simple living:

- *Taxes:* Our approach to taxation makes us accountants of our lives. We are pushed to live as record keepers. The kind of choice we are offered is this: either be aware of how tax law changes affect you and take advantage of them, or suffer the consequences. Why should we have to know what a flexible spending account is, or a medical spending account? Or how they differ? What kind of life is it when we have to spend our time wrestling with the distinctions between regular IRAs and Roth IRAs and education IRAs and 401ks? This pressure to so clutter our desks and, worse, our consciousness was never part of anyone's vision of the good life.

Robert Frost said it best in "The Hardship of Accounting":

> Never ask of money spent
> Where the spender thinks it went.
> No one was ever meant
> To remember or invent
> What he did with every cent.[68]

We are suffering indeed from the hardships of accounting, and it is time to put an end to it.

- *Highway construction/lack of commitment to public transportation:* The federal government built the American highway system. Without it we could not have developed into the automobile-dependent culture we have become. As a result of the abandonment of a genuine commitment to public transportation (for instance, the sort found in some European countries), we have vastly increased our need for income through our dependence on cars, and we have inflicted upon ourselves all the attendant destruction of our public space, be it in the form of air pollution or the aesthetic pollution of never-ending commercial strips along our pathways. We have transformed housing patterns and given rise to long commutes and the tension of traffic jams, road rage, and the risk of accident.

But this merely scratches the surface. With respect to everything that government does, one can ask whether the impact on simple living is hostile, beneficial, or neutral. One could argue that every government expenditure requires taxation, and taxation means that people have less disposable income to devote to satisfying their needs. That of course is only part of the story. Some government expenditures support highly efficient mechanisms for meeting our needs, so the net effect is positive. Moreover, for every expenditure and every form of taxation we can ask whose needs are being addressed, and whose income is being taxed. A highly progressive tax system that takes only a small percentage of income from people with modest means, and substantially taxes those with very high incomes, is more supportive of simple living than one that taxes everyone an equal percentage.

Public policies affect the extent to which modest incomes are sufficient to satisfy needs and, more generally, affect the broader tenor of our social life. This is true whether we are talking about tax deductions for private school tuition and tariffs on imported clothing or broader matters affecting the level of crime in urban environments or the extent to which our jobs are vulnerable to shifts in the world economy. Moreover, these effects may be quite complex, going in several directions at once, and they may make life simpler for some and far more demanding for others.

In short, government walks with a big foot. It can contribute importantly toward the possibility of simple living, or make achieving it that much harder. But either way, its impact is too great to be ignored. A politics of simplicity seeks to bring to greater awareness the costs and potentials inherent in the policy choices we make. And it seeks to pull together the multiple influences of disparate polices in an effort to reveal their larger meaning. Are they, can they, be crafted in such a way as to facilitate simple living rather than making it even more difficult to attain?

WHAT KIND OF POLITICS OF SIMPLICITY?

There is no single politics of simplicity. First, as we have seen, there is wide diversity in what is meant by simple living. Thus, diverse political programs and outlooks are possible, all under the rubric of simplicity. Simple living as understood by the Puritans wasn't quite what Thoreau had in mind.

Second, a political orientation consists of much more than the vision of the good life that underlies policy proposals. Often enough people across the political spectrum can agree on broadly articulated objectives such as national security, prosperity, or even the eradication of poverty. But what distinguishes one outlook from another frequently depends on how people respond to alternative means proposed to accomplish these objectives.

In pursuit of simple living, how are we to understand the appropriate role of the state? What limitations should be put on that role in promoting a particular kind of life? Should people be prevented from consuming in certain ways? Should they be prevented from working as much as they want? Should the state be in the business of subsidizing basic-needs satisfaction or in regulating prices? Under what circumstances should it interfere with markets?

What becomes immediately obvious is that it is possible to have a conservative politics of simplicity as well as a progressive politics of simplicity, even if they fully agree (which they would probably not) on what forms of simple living were to be promoted. At this stage avoiding too sharp a focus on specific proposals is important. There is a danger in being prematurely programmatic. It is far more important to make the more fundamental transformation: a shift in how we think of economic life, a shift in how we understand the place of the economic within the life of the good society.

Yet it is not easy to hold back on specifics. We Americans are very practical people, and the most natural way for us to understand an abstract idea, an outlook, or an ideology, is to ask, "What does it come down to? What are they for? What do they propose? What are their answers?" In what follows I will give some answers, but let me stress that any specifics of policy that I identify are of far less significance than the general shift in orientation. I put them forward as approaches and dimensions, not as agenda items.

One preliminary point should be made. The two American Dreams—the dream of making it, of money and status—and the Alternative Dream—a life that is materially modest but rich in other dimensions—have an important area of overlap that identifies them both as particularly American dreams. They overlap in their shared attachment to individual freedom, to pluralism, to the right to be different, the right to march to a different drummer.

The politics I am urging does not advocate one cookie-cutter version of the good life. And while I am partial to what I term "graceful simplicity" being concerned with an aesthetic of both time and space, emphasizing beauty in our multiple environments, there is plenty of room for lives of simplicity that differ among themselves quite radically in their central values, concerns, and pastimes. One may live simply and gracefully with very different points of focus—art, religion, friends, family, sports, service, politics, or knowledge.

What I envision is a society in which there will be a great diversity of commitments, one in which people will be deeply involved in very different life activities and life spaces. What they will have in common, however, is having been freed from the dominant engagement in getting and spending. A politics of simplicity seeks a world that is not hectic, not filled with anxiety. It is a world in which people have sufficient time to do things slowly and to do them right, whether what they are doing is building and enjoying a friendship, working on a sculpture, or studying scripture.

Moreover, it should also be clear that I am calling for a politics of simplicity that seeks not to compel simple living, but to facilitate it. It seeks to make it easier for people who want to live lives of simplicity to do so, but it does not seek to prevent people from living lives of opulence and consumption, nor to prevent them from running themselves ragged in their hectic pursuits. At the same time, it recognizes that because social institutions and government policies are never neutral, no neat line between compelling and merely facilitating can be found. We are always tilting one way or another. Let us tilt toward simplicity.

TOWARD A NEW CENTRAL ECONOMIC PARADIGM

At one time, concentration on the fundamental questions of life was thought essential to any reflective social politics. At a time before there was a distinction between economics and political theory, Aristotle put it thus:

> A person who is going to make a fruitful inquiry into the question of the best political arrangement must first set out clearly what the most choiceworthy life is. For if that is unclear, the best political arrangement must also be unclear.[69]

The point of economic and political institutions and policies is to make possible the good human life. It is against this criterion that institutions are to be evaluated.[70]

Often enough, the biggest questions we have to answer are never asked.

Because of their magnitude, because of their extensive implications, it is often hard to see that there can be major alternatives to the way things are and the way we typically think about the world.

The single biggest social policy question confronting us today remains the same question asked 2,300 years ago: "What is the purpose of economic activity?" Today this is a question rarely posed. Yet, while rarely asked, there is an implicit understanding of the good life and its relation to economic activity that underlies modern consumerism. Thus we have the following:

THE DOMINANT ECONOMIC PARADIGM

- The good life is to be found in the satisfaction of our desires, in particular desires that can be satisfied through consumption.
- The economy contributes to the good life by providing consumers with the goods and services they desire.
- Work (along with land, capital, and information) is an input within the productive process, as well as the central means through which people earn the income that allows them to purchase the goods and services produced.
- Successful performance of the economy is best understood as the sustained expansion of goods and services (i.e., economic growth).
- Efficiency is primarily a matter of achieving maximum outputs (goods and services) with any level of resource input.

This vision, if it ever served us well, is today exhausted. It leaves us adrift in a changing world, hoping that "more and faster" adds up to better. What we need is a new outlook, one that in some ways returns to a more ancient vision. The perspective of simple living offers this alternative paradigm for thinking about the purpose of economic life:

THE SIMPLE LIVING PARADIGM

- The good life is a form of simple living. It is found primarily in meaningful activity and the simple pleasures of friends and family. It requires an abundance of time to do things right.
- The economy contributes to a good life by providing goods and services to meet core needs, by offering meaningful forms of activity, and by providing economic security. Once core needs

have been met, the consumption of goods and services is of secondary importance.

- Work is itself a central arena in which the good life is either found or lost. Work is not a mere means to income or productive output; at its best it is an opportunity for people to engage their highest qualities and creativities in ways that are of value to others. The kinds of work opportunities a society has to offer are its real outputs, the forms of life it makes available.

- Economic performance should be evaluated not in terms of economic growth but by looking at the levels of need satisfaction, levels of leisure, levels of security, and quality of work roles.

- Efficiency is primarily a matter of achieving high levels of need satisfaction at low levels of labor time or at low levels of income.

Put in different terms, a politics of simplicity responds to Aristotle's question by saying that the good life is found as a form of simple living and then turns to both government and the economy and says, "Your purpose is to facilitate the attainment of such lives, to create an environment that is supportive of simple living."

A politics of simplicity recognizes that the real work of creating a meaningful life has to be done by people themselves, with their friends and in communities of common values. At the same time, it looks to the society as a whole, to our national economic and social policies, and says that they play a role of tremendous importance in creating the background environment within which such projects will either succeed or fail.

Making this shift to a different lens, to a different way of looking at economic life, to a different set of criteria for evaluating economic performance, is the single biggest element of a politics of simplicity. In many ways it turns conventional thinking on its head. It says that what are normally viewed as inputs or by-products of economic activity, namely the forms of human activity and interaction that are generated by economic activity ("work" and "jobs" and "social roles"), are its real outputs, and that what is typically viewed as economic outputs, the goods and services received from the economy, are really inputs into life. They are the means that sustain us physically as we seek to find lives of inherent value and significance.

In making this shift to a different economic paradigm it is important to see that a politics of simplicity is not antitechnology. The primary problem that we as a society face with respect to technological change has to do with the benefits of technological innovation, both in deciding which kinds of benefits to choose and in determining who is to receive them. This is best illustrated with an example.

Today there are many who fear the impact of new technologies, and there is a growing list of writers who have warned that technological changes on the horizon may threaten the jobs of just about anyone. Let us assume that this is the case; let us assume:

THE WORKER'S WORST NIGHTMARE

Five years from now, a Silicon Valley company succeeds in perfecting robot technology. They can create for each individual an exact robot duplicate. And they can produce this robot at very little cost. Through the Internet they then offer every employer in the country an exact replacement of any worker on the payroll. Because they can do so quite cheaply, they undercut the wage demands of each and every worker. No company has any incentive to hire a human.

Wages fall, but even when wages fall, humans are not hired because their wage demands are always higher than what it costs to buy and maintain the robot copy. Ultimately, even a willingness to accept starvation wages is insufficient to motivate hiring humans, because the replacement cost of the robots is less than what it takes to keep a human being alive. The outcome, then, is that, except for a select few, we are all unemployed and we all starve.

This is the worker's worst nightmare, and it seems that the devil is in the technology. But actually the technology is quite neutral. Imagine the very same technological story with one small change: rather than the robots being owned by the California company, each worker is the sole owner of his own robot duplicate. Under these conditions, with respect to any work that is not inherently rewarding, you have the option of sending your robot duplicate to work, instead of going yourself. You can create your own leisure. You can do this for a day, a week, a year, or a lifetime. In short, this very same technology is the fulfillment of an ancient fantasy. It liberates each and every one of us from labor that is not inherently valuable and frees us to devote our lives to that which will give them meaning.

Thus a politics of simplicity is not against technological change; it is not against productivity growth. Put in the service of the good life, productivity growth can be liberating. A politics of simplicity can embrace and encourage innovation. The key issues are the composition and distribution of rewards and decision-making power. Will productivity gains result in more leisure or more income? Who decides? To the extent that it is income, to whom does it go? In short, who will own the robots?

THE CENTRAL CONCERNS AND PERSPECTIVES OF THE POLITICS OF SIMPLICITY

The politics of simplicity works outward from its conception of the good life. Its central starting point is an understanding of the problems that confront ordinary people trying to find their way toward a more satisfying existence:

* There isn't enough leisure time.
* Work itself isn't inherently meaningful.
* Economic life is a source of anxiety and uncertainty.
* Income for many is not sufficient to meet legitimate needs.
* There is little beauty in our lives.
* The risks of making radical changes are too high.

Here we have the central themes of the politics of simplicity: time, work, money, beauty, and security.

TIME AND LEISURE

For most working Americans there never seems to be time to truly enjoy that which is most valuable. Between the demands of work and home and, ironically, leisure time itself, most of us feel harassed and harried. Reducing the hours of work used to be at the core of the definition of economic progress, and for much of the nineteenth century and the early decades of the twentieth century, workers struggled first to achieve the ten-hour day and then the eight-hour day. In the 1930s there was an effort to establish the thirty-hour week, but for over half a century, reducing hours has not been a central concern.

The dominant economic paradigm looks to productivity increases as the source of expanded economic well-being. The last one hundred years, though to a diminishing degree in recent years, have witnessed steady increases in the amount of output produced through an hour of work. But productivity growth need not be transformed into expanded output. It is equally possible to hold total output fixed and work fewer hours. Productivity growth represents an opportunity for either increased output or increased leisure or a mix of the two. In earlier periods we both reduced work time and increased total output per worker. In recent decades we have "chosen" only increased output.

Aggregate statistics show that since the 1950s per capita consumption in the United States has more than doubled. While this does not apply to all income groups, and reflects far less of a gain in truly discretionary income than might be thought, it still amounts to an appreciable expansion, especially during the 1950s and 1960s. During this period, for many, leisure declined or remained stagnant. Without ever having explicitly chosen to do so, we have ended up with the wrong choice; at least some of the productivity growth that enabled higher incomes and consumption should have gone instead to expanding leisure time.

What has been true of productivity growth has also been true of family decisions about how much time to put into paid employment—the market did not really offer families the options they might have preferred. In the last few decades, when married women entered the labor force in large numbers, most families didn't have an option of two good twenty-five-hour jobs. Being serious about your worklife and career meant working full-time. Men couldn't cut back their hours, and women didn't have a live option of part-time careers. The decision facing the family was a choice between having either one or two parents working a forty-hour job, and many families chose two. As a result, the increase in time pressure has been enormous. A politics of simplicity seeks to expand real options for careers built on a full spectrum of workweeks, whether fifteen, twenty-five, or thirty-five hours, without loss of security, benefits, or opportunities for advancement.

Few individuals actually have the opportunity to choose leisure rather than income growth, and expanding such choices is important. As an isolated individual, it is not easy to choose leisure rather than income growth. When, bucking the dominant trend, a given family chooses time rather than money, it forgoes consumption and finds that, relative to others, its socioeconomic standing has declined. To characterize this as a matter of not keeping up with the upwardly mobile Joneses shows little understanding of what is involved. To choose otherwise is to risk slipping out of the socioeconomic community that has provided one's sense of place; it may mean not being able to live in the neighborhood where one has lived, or it may mean that one's children can't fully interact with the other kids.

We need to address these decisions collectively. Just as we have legislation on the forty-hour week, so, too, should we consider legislation requiring three-day weekends, reduced daily hours, and guaranteed extended vacations. On one level, expanding leisure time is the easiest policy change to make. In principle, one piece of legislation could dramatically transform life in America.

In 1933 a bill that would have created the thirty-hour week, consisting of five days of six hours, passed the Senate, but not the House.[71] We need to pick up where we left off. One way to proceed is to take note of the fact that because of national holidays, we presently have about ten three-day weekends already. Rather than moving all at once to the four-day week, we could move incrementally, expanding the number of three-day weekends each year. There are fast ways and slow ways to do this. I would suggest we start with the goal of adding another sixteen three-day weekends. This, when combined with the existing ten, would allow us to have a three-day weekend every other week.

Making this initial transition would reduce annual work time approximately 7 percent. It is unlikely that it would reduce output by the same amount. Indeed, there are many situations in which the output lost would be made up by higher output on workdays. But even assuming that there was a 7 percent loss of output, there are three options for dealing with it. The loss could be absorbed by workers in terms of lower pay; the loss could be absorbed by companies in terms of lower profits; or the loss could be offset over time by productivity gains.

Given that corporate profits have in recent years increased at a faster pace than wages, a reasonable case could be made to let the bulk of the cost come out of profits. Alternatively, since productivity growth (output per hour of labor) in recent experience is increasing at about 1 percent per year, this shift to a three-day weekend every other week could itself be phased in over a seven-year period, adding two or three extra holidays per year, without affecting either profits or wages.

This would represent a very good beginning, and one that would be of real significance. However, it would not be quite so easy to move toward truly far-reaching changes in time on the job. For instance, if we sought to bring about a shift in the work time of the dual-career family from two forty-hour jobs to two twenty-five-hour jobs, this would represent a decline from eighty hours of paid time to fifty hours of paid time, a drop of 38 percent. Is it possible to bring about this kind of transformation?

MONEY: REDUCING THE LEVEL OF NRI

I have discussed the cost of meeting core economic needs, but fundamentally the issue is not the monetary costs but the time costs. Simple living is living that is rich in time; this in turn requires that the time spent on purely instrumental activities (e.g., work that is not inherently fulfilling) undertaken to meet core needs must not be excessive. Ideally, a graceful life is completely free from such necessity, but such a goal is both largely out of reach and beyond what is required.

From the point of view of the consumer, the amount of time that must be devoted to earning enough to meet core needs depends both on one's wage rate and the total cost of meeting those needs. Dividing the total cost of meeting core needs (plus taxes) by the wage rate identifies the required labor time (e.g., $50,000 divided by $10/hour equals 5,000 hours required for meeting needs, divided by $50/hour equals 1,000 hours of required time).

Since changes in real wage rates are generally reflective of productivity, the underlying variables are the cost of meeting core needs and changes in labor productivity. If the real cost of satisfying needs remains fixed, need-required labor time will decline as productivity increases, provided that productivity growth is taken in the form of higher wages. But, as noted earlier, whenever there is productivity growth, a society has a choice. Should the benefits of productivity growth be taken in the form of higher incomes or in the form of expanded leisure? Yet, without really deciding, without even recognizing that this is a fundamental decision for us to make, our overall system tends toward income expansion rather than leisure expansion. A politics of simplicity seeks to make this a matter of deliberate political decision. Substantively, it comes down strongly on the side of increasing leisure.

If we are successful in using productivity increases to reduce labor time, then income remains fixed. If needs are already satisfied, then this is not a great problem, but I argued in the previous chapter that, for many, core needs are unsatisfied and that, for many, it is a struggle to make ends meet. How, then, does a politics of simplicity respond to the financial pressure of the ordinary household?

Though higher wages remain critical for people at the bottom of the income spectrum, as a general objective, the politics of simplicity looks toward increased social efficiency rather than increased income as the means to better satisfy core needs. Why does it cost so much to meet core needs? And what can be done about it? As we saw in the previous chapter, there is no simple story with respect to the costs of meeting needs. In some areas they have been stable; in other areas they have increased enormously, far faster than income growth.

Looking backward, two areas stand out as problems that have thwarted movement toward simple living: housing costs and transportation costs. Together these two occupy roughly 50 percent of the typical household budget. Given that most Americans' needs for food and clothing are relatively well satisfied at historically low percentages of personal income, 12 percent and 5 percent respectively, had we managed to hold housing and transportation costs steady, we would have made substantial progress in opening up the possibility of simple living for moderate-income families.

What happened with transportation is particularly unfortunate. It could have been avoided had there been clarity with respect to the appropriate goals of transportation policy. For instance, we would be living in quite a different world had it been a goal of national policy not to evolve into an intensely automobile-dependent society. Instead, over the last half century, as first one car and then two cars became a necessity for most families, the percentage of household expenditures for transportation has more than doubled. Today, as we have seen, the average husband-and-wife consumer unit (with or without children) spends almost $8,000 annually on transportation, or roughly one-fifth of their total spending. Put in different terms, we might say that, of the five days we work, one day is for transportation expenses. That is a tremendous price to pay in terms of wedding individuals to a work-and-spend cycle, a tremendous price to pay for the absence of good public transport and the collapse of the urban environment.

A politics of simplicity would make lowering the amount of money required to meet transportation costs a central objective. This might involve policies in many sectors, be they public transportation, housing development, or urban revitalization. Central to this aim would be avoiding or overcoming automobile dependency. In our present situation it is worth a serious effort to ascertain the extent to which our dependence on cars might be reversed. Even if we assume that two-car dependency cannot be reversed, it would be worth an effort to see if it could be made significantly less costly than it is today.

We should seek the emergence of a new kind of automobile. It would be one deliberately designed for the simple life. This new model would be safe, reasonably priced, fuel efficient, and capable of being repaired by anyone handy with tools. It would be built to last indefinitely, with each long-lasting component capable of being replaced, and with all of its parts permanently available. This vision of the vehicle is not outside the realm of the technologically possible, and there are multiple policy tools government could use to encourage its development. Indeed, many transportation experts believe that the next generation of cars will be vastly more fuel efficient, capable of attaining eighty or one hundred miles to the gallon. With doubled or tripled fuel efficiency, doubled life spans, and less costly repairs, a new car like this would represent a significant reduction in transportation costs.

Even more fundamental than the transportation sector are the problems we face with respect to housing. Here, the goal is to facilitate the simple life, making it possible for people to have decent housing with modest incomes. The housing objective should not be understood in purely physical terms, but in terms of safe, perhaps even beautiful, neighborhoods with good schools. Of course, the topics of housings, crime, and schools are standard issues on any political outlook. A politics of simple living brings to these familiar areas of policy interest a different perception of the problem and a new criterion for solutions.

At this stage a politics of simplicity is not about answers so much as it is about how to define problems, about opening up new perspectives on old problems, and seeing new meanings in long-standing debates. One of the hard lessons of the last several decades is that solutions to public problems do not come easily. But, rather than being dogmatic about solutions, we should be experimental. John Dewey once referred to the individual states as "48 laboratories." That's not a bad way of thinking. We do not yet know how to solve the housing-crime-schools matrix of unmet social need in this country.

We do know that when we try to solve it by earning enough to escape from it, two things occur. First, we are wedding ourselves to income levels and lifestyles that squeeze out the possibilities of a simpler life. And second, we are finding solutions that work for the few but cannot work for the majority of citizens. We can't all escape from ourselves.

Thus, a politics-of-simplicity approach to the housing-crime-schools problem would emphasize the mobilization of energy and resources to transform the neighborhoods we presently live in, rather than the facilitation of upper-middle-class escape (e.g., through tax breaks for higher housing purchases, or private schools). An easy first step is beautification, with the addition of flowers and trees, trash removal, painting and polishing. Part of what a politics of simplicity brings to such problems is a perspective that redefines what's at stake. These are not discrete "issues" or "social problems"; instead these are the central obstacles that block the path to simpler, more coherent, and more vigorous lives.

FREE HIGHER EDUCATION

I noted earlier that New York City once provided free college education at several excellent schools. One might have thought that this would become the pattern for the country as a whole. We long ago instituted free public education through the high school years, and we might have chosen to extend this to the college years. Instead we moved in the other direction, and today, to my knowledge, there are no free public colleges in the United States.

We still make a substantial effort to ease the burden of college education with an extensive system of public colleges (e.g., state universities), and more than three-quarters of all our college students nationwide are enrolled in these institutions rather than in private colleges. The great attraction of the public colleges is that they are much less expensive, tuition being roughly 25 percent of what is charged by private colleges. In addition, we have a complex system of student loans, grants, work-study programs, tax deductions, and tax credits. All of this contributes to college's accessibility to those with moderate means—though in some instances these policies have also made it easier for colleges to increase tuition charges, knowing students will be able to get funding from these other sources. Responding to the pressures of college financing is part of mainstream politics, and, regularly, various political leaders propose further supplements to this quilt of programs.

A politics of simplicity would take a somewhat different approach. First, it would redefine the issue. It would place the overall goal of simple living at the center, rather than considering the issue in the more restricted terms of how families can cover the costs of college. It would seek an approach to higher education that would make it possible for people to make their long-term employment choices and make their long-term leisure versus income choices without having to worry about how they will pay for their children's college expenses ten or twenty years down the line.

A central part of this new vision would involve moving away from the quilt of constantly changing programs to the institutionalization of free public colleges and universities. What is remarkable is that this objective is readily within our grasp. In 1994–1995 the total amount that all public institutions of higher education took in through tuition and fees came to only $22 billion. In other words, roughly speaking, we could eliminate all tuition and fees for most college and postgraduate education for this amount.[72] To put this number in perspective, in 1995 the United States had a Gross Domestic Product of over $7 trillion. We could move to free tuition in public colleges for less than one-third of 1 percent of our total output. If the economy grows at 3 percent a year, the annual expansion of the economy is over $200 billion. Thus for 10 percent of just one year's expansion of the economy, we could radically change this central aspect of financial worry on the household level. If families believed that their children's access to college education was secured, this would be an invitation for alternative solutions to the work/time/money conundrum.

INCOME: A SIMPLE LIVING PROPOSAL

Consider the following imaginary proposal:

> Suppose our society said to all: "Go out and find your dream job. Or, go out and become self-employed in a realm that calls to you. Or, just go home and spend more time with your family and friends. So long as you are prepared to live on modest means, you need not fear for a living. If you do not earn enough for your family to meet their core economic needs (modestly understood),

sufficiency will be provided. The society will provide you with a supplement to the income you earn."

Were we to have the ability to do this, and were we to take such a step, the terms of reference in America would be transformed. Overnight we would enable millions of people to rethink their entire life plan. Rather than viewing economic activity as instrumental, as the source for the income that allows them to purchase the goods and services of middle-class life, everything would be turned on its head. Economic activity, for those who chose to take this route, could be limited to activities that in themselves gave meaning and excitement and enrichment to life. Money and consumption would be seen as the limited inputs that would allow us to get on with the real "business" of life. For others, those who were fortunate enough to already have rewarding work, this would be an opportunity to restore some balance to their lives. High-pressure couples might opt for two part-time jobs so that they might spend more time together, more time with their kids and friends, more time reading or playing ball.

Millions of people might take advantage of such an offer. Some would be dropouts from the corporate world; some would be young people for whom such options would cause them to radically rethink why they were going to college and what they really wanted to study. In some ways it would be like waking up and discovering that a rich aunt, whom you had never known, had suddenly died and left you a modest trust fund. It would never allow you to live opulently, but it would allow you to get by economically for the rest of your life, in any form of activity you chose to pursue, even at reduced hours.

While a proposal such as this does not fully address all the requisites for simple living, it would be a remarkable step forward, and one that would open the possibility of a fulfilling but economically modest life for millions. Even for those who would choose not to go this route, it would offer a permanent option of dropping out of the life they were living. One could no longer reasonably feel trapped within a work life that was not fulfilling.

But what fantasy. How could we as a society possibly pay for such a program? Where in the world would the tax revenues come from? And how can one imagine, in the current political climate, that anything vaguely resembling such 1960s utopianism could come to pass?

Well, perhaps this is imaginary, but consider this: we already have in place a government program that, though conceived for different purposes, is quite like what I am describing. It's called the Earned Income Tax Credit (EIC). It focuses primarily on families with children, and you must be working to be eligible for it. It operates quite simply. Like everyone else, you fill out your tax return at tax time. But if you are earning only a very modest income, you are allowed to subtract from your tax liability this particular credit (the earned income credit) in addition to your various deductions and credits. The amount you can deduct from the taxes you owe depends on how much you are earning and how many children you have. For 1998 there is a maximum of $3,756 per family. So if you are eligible for the maximum credit, you can reduce the taxes you owe by $3,756.

Now here's the interesting part. Generally speaking, families with very low incomes don't pay any income tax because their income is so low that they have no tax liability. Thus, under ordinary circumstances, a tax credit is of no value to them, their liability already being zero. But the EIC is what's called a "refundable credit." If your tax liability is zero, the government sends you a check for the amount of the credit. For 1997 the cost of the credit program was roughly $27 billion, and almost all of this was paid out in the form of cash payments in excess of tax liability. Approximately 19 million households, roughly one out of every five, benefits from this credit.

Families, including single-parent families, with two children reach the maximum credit at income levels of $9,390 (in 1998). Thus, the refundable credit of $3,756 represents a tax-exempt supplement equal to 40 percent of their income. Eligibility for the credit phases out at much higher income levels, with families receiving the credit up to an income level of about $30,000. Of course, long before this point the percentage increase in income provided by the credit declines to very limited levels, although at incomes of $20,000 the credit is still providing a 10 percent boost in income for those with two children.

If we think of "the middle class" as consisting of everyone except the very rich and those in the lowest 20 percent of the income spectrum, then in its present form, the credit makes little impact on middle-class life. As a result, it is largely unknown to most Americans. At present, the program is designed to alleviate poverty and to provide a boost to low-income working families. Very few families take advantage of it as part of a voluntary decision to live a simpler, better life at lower levels of earned income. Yet, structurally, it offers a way to have this very impact.

Because a credit of this sort can get very expensive, very quickly, there are real limits as to what is possible. One could, however, imagine some significant changes. Suppose the EIC was replaced with a "simple-living tax credit" that was much larger. For instance, the simple living credit might be equal to 50 percent of earned income up to a maximum credit of $10,000, which would be reached at the $20,000 income level. Starting at the $30,000 level, the credit would phase down, reaching zero at $60,000. A comparison of the existing EIC and the proposed simple living tax credit for a family with two children is as follows:*

	Existing EIC	Simple Living Credit
Credit percentage at max	40% of income	50% of income
Maximum creditable earning	$9,390	$20,000
Maximum credit amount	$3,756	$10,000
Income at which phase-out starts	$12,260	$30,000
Income above which credit disappears	$30,095	$60,000
Estimated cost	$26.9 billion	$150 billion

When combined with the effect of existing federal and state income tax and Social Security payments, the simple living credit would create some very interesting options for people thinking about cutting back (or thinking about switching to lower-paying but more rewarding work). Here is an example for a hypothetical family considering switching from full-time work to a thirty-hour week (either for one $60,000 wage earner, or two $30,000 wage earners):

	Option 1	Option 2
Work time	40 hours a week	30 hours a week
Pretax income	$60,000	$45,000
After-tax income	$44,500	$39,800

*Data on existing EIC from "The Earned Income Tax Credit: Benefit Amounts" by James R. Storey and Melinda T. Gish, Congressional Research Service Report for Congress, The Library of Congress, January 12, 1998. Figures are for 1998.

Thus families earning $60,000 by a willingness to lower after-tax income by $4,700 would be able to reduce work time by 25 percent—an enormous reduction equivalent to the six-hour day or three months' vacation, opening up vast new life possibilities.

Within the present mind-set critics would see this negatively as creating a situation in which people had a strong disincentive to work full-time; but from the point of view of simple living, we can view it as making it easier for people to expand their leisure time (or take lower-paying but more interesting work). For families seeking to move away from the two full-time wage earner model, this would become a major part of the equation. And for low-income families unable to meet core needs, it would provide a transformative boost in income for those who continued to work five days a week.

Of course this is something of a fantasy. The costs of a change of this sort might run to an extra $125 billion or higher. Today there is no possibility of some such "Simple Living Facilitation Act." Aside from the costs, it must be remembered that the EIC was enacted into law in the 1970s as a "work bonus" program for low-income families. The aim was to provide extra income to working people with low incomes, quite different from providing a way for people who are working full time to work less. A simple living credit of the sort I am proposing would tend to break down the distinctions between working poor and middle class—it would say that for both populations our economy is not functioning well. For both populations, it would look toward simple living as a more desirable alternative, and it would say that for both populations, the high cost of living remains an obstacle. For some, the program would primarily expand after-tax income; for others, it would hold it constant or reduce it marginally while permitting a decrease in work time.

A shift of this sort would require a fundamental change in our understanding of the purpose of economic life. Under present circumstances, some would object, saying that this program was intended for the working poor, and that people who would voluntarily choose a simple lifestyle and draw on the credit to support them were exploiting the system. Within the framework of our current understanding, the critics would say, "Why should people who are working full-time have to work harder just to make life easier for people who don't want to pay their dues?"

What is needed, then, is a change in philosophical perspective that legitimizes the overall goal of facilitating simple living. From that perspective, these are valuable changes that open new options of a saner existence for everyone in the society.

THE POLITICS OF SIMPLICITY AND ENVIRONMENTALISM

In distinction from previous eras in American history, one of the major motivations that currently draw people toward simple living is a concern for the environment. These concerns fall under the rubrics "sources" and "sinks"— concern that we are running out of crucial resources and fear that our planet has or will soon reach the limits of its ability to absorb the multiple forms of pollution we create. Simple living, then, is conceived as living with a lighter footprint, adopting a way of life that demands less by way of nonrenewable resources and that causes reduced harmful impact on our environment.

These concerns do not necessarily translate into a case for living at a lower level of consumption expenditures. One could have the same impact by shifting consumption from environmentally problematic items to environmentally sound ones. Thus, if, instead of buying a $10,000 automobile, someone bought a $10,000 violin, he would be doing the environment a favor. Nonetheless, the general impact of lower levels of consumption, all other things being equal, is to use fewer resources and to engender less pollution. In this way, environmental concerns provide motivation for simple living.

It should also be clear that it is possible to advocate more moderate (as well as different) consumption levels, without being committed to limiting overall economic growth. Indeed, lower levels of consumption, or lower-than-expected levels of consumption, open the possibility of shifting resources to address environmental concerns, or of introducing modes of production that may be more costly but are environmentally sound. In this sense, a shift to simple living is quite like deciding to consume less as individuals so that collectively we might enjoy some form of public consumption, except that rather than enjoying a museum, we enjoy cleaner air.

Simple living, in at least some of its forms, is seen as good for the environment. But another, more intimate kind of linkage exists between this lifestyle and environmentalism. It doesn't rest on the consequences of simple living, but instead on the realization that living within a healthy and beautiful natural environment constitutes a central part of the good life itself. As long as the general environment is unhealthy or devoid of beauty, private income becomes the means of access to select environments. Just as we work to save for a vacation to the beauty of Florence, we work for vacations to places where we can taste the fresh air and see the contours of the Earth. Just as we pay to live in safer urban or suburban neighborhoods, we will pay extra to live in healthier cities. Thus, the beauty and health of the general environment sustains and fulfills simple living. Partaking in that environment is a central part of that way of life; appreciating and respecting the environment expresses the core values of simple living.

Based on these close affinities between simple living and environmentalism, a politics of simplicity can emerge as a more comprehensive approach to economic life of which environmentalism is a substantial part. This would be a healthy unification in that the simple living movement would benefit from environmentalism's orientation toward issues of public policy, and environmentalism would benefit from the broader value perspective of simple living.

SIMPLE LIVING AND HEALTH

It was previously argued that when it comes to health needs, rising levels of NRI may, in fact, be a positive sign. The reason is that, being mortals, sooner or later our need for care that will restore us to health goes unmet, and we die. Thus there is an open-ended dimension to health care needs. If there is steady technological progress in meeting our need for that which sustains life, then we may find ourselves on a perpetual escalator of costs. Yet the situation is just the opposite of Galbraith's squirrel wheel. Here, as we run faster, we may actually be making progress.

In the past, philosophy and religion offered us ways of coming to terms with what we believed to be permanent givens of the human condition. But today we are on the edge of a revolution in biotechnology that will change our understanding of what it is to be human. For example, what will happen when technology makes it possible for life spans to be extended dramatically for those with enough income? What happens if it becomes possible for life extension to keep pace with the onset of new perils, so that life is indefinitely prolonged for those who have the means to extend it?

Today, beyond certain levels of income, say about $50,000 in family income (for the United States, less in other countries), higher income results in little or no extension of life expectancy. But what happens when that changes quite radically? For instance, how does it transform the possibility of simple living when people with family incomes of $200,000 or more can live fifty years longer than those with incomes of $30,000? Does it make sense, under those conditions, to throw ourselves into the effort to earn $200,000 a year? It would certainly make more sense than it does now.

In areas such as this, we, as a society, sometimes take the approach that each member of the society has a right to certain basics, and that these should not be denied to the poor or those with low income. For example, with respect to health care and education for one's children we seek to ensure access to critical social resources, even for those with minimal income, through programs such as Medicaid and free public education.

Inevitably, if there are great leaps in medical technology, we will face a great debate over access to the new technologies. In order to preserve the possibility of simple living within an era of revolutionary new medical technologies, one option might be to deepen our commitment to the idea that access to needed health resources should not be contingent on levels of income. A politics of simplicity would advocate equality of access not just to ensure that the poor not be disadvantaged, but also to enable people of ordinary means to live lives of voluntary simplicity.

Interestingly, low-cost living might become more relevant if there is a biotechnological revolution of this sort. When it becomes clear that investment in health technologies and high-tech medical interventions can transform the normal length of human life, we will face enormous pressures to earn enough, either individually or collectively, to have these technologies. If we find ways of living well by living inexpensively, we will be freeing up resources for this that might have otherwise gone to unnecessary consumption. Thus, it may be that what awaits us is a choice between long lives of simple living, or shorter lives of high consumption. It may be that we will need to live inexpensively in other realms so that we can have the resources that enable longer lives. If we learn to live well with little, this may be a blessing. Otherwise, we may become enslaved to the cost of life extension.

INCOME SECURITY AND DIGNITY AT WORK

Along with expanding leisure and reducing NRI, simple living requires change in the area of income security and employment. No life can be graceful when it is dominated by the fear of job loss, or when the work life is devoid of dignity. Herein lies part of the crucial difference between poverty and simple living.

To make lives of simplicity more widely possible, we need an economy in which economic rights are enhanced. Most fundamentally, this includes the right to a job with income sufficient to meet core economic needs. However, a simple living movement should not be dogmatic with respect to specific programs for achieving that end, such as raising the minimal wage, expanding the EIC, increasing public sector employment, or creating incentives to induce investment in high unemployment areas. We need an overall vision of where we want to go, but openness with respect to how to get there.

Dignity at work means many things. There are work lives that are below our dignity as human beings. Yet, at the same time, people of great dignity are employed in such work because it is how they support self and family. In part, dignity has to do with power relations between worker and boss, but the issue of human dignity also has to do with the kind of work we are asked to perform. The problem is not that a specific task may be arduous, mechanical, or repetitive. In themselves such tasks raise no great problem. The issue of human dignity is engaged when an entire work life is composed of such tasks. A work life that denies our individuality, our creativity, or our moral and aesthetic sensibility is a work life that denies our dignity as human beings. It may well be, as some have argued, that the continued introduction of new technologies will have a cleansing effect, eliminating jobs that are repetitive and formulaic. If so, this is half the solution. The other half lies in good education and the creation of millions of meaningful jobs. The direction of a solution is to set people to work solving the very problems just discussed: how to meet legitimate needs.

How do we, as a society, simultaneously create meaningful work, liberate people from income pressures, and deal successfully with the problems of unsafe neighborhoods, inadequate education, and unsatisfactory housing? One approach is to look to the nonprofit sector. Already a major source of employment, nonprofits provide a rich pool of flexible, meaningful opportunities for people to work for the resolution of core social problems. Public policy has long supported nonprofits by making contributions to them tax deductible. Expanding on this idea by allowing a tax deduction for 150 percent of such contributions rather than the present 100 percent, for instance, is a simple way we can increase the flow of private giving to nonprofits, thereby increasing employment and services. An even better idea might be to shift from a tax deduction (lowering the amount of income one pays income taxes on) to a tax credit (directly reducing the tax bill paid). If these credits were made refundable (those low-income families with no income taxes to pay would receive a rebate from the government), we would democratize the support of nonprofits. Those with the greatest needs would vote with their contributions on just which organizations should prosper. The broader idea is to attack the central problems of unmet need, and at the same time create meaningful jobs that do so.

The policy framework for moving toward an economy of creative work requires a holistic transformation in our approach to economic life. Such a transformation would give us new and different categories and criteria for assessing policy and for deciding how we, as a people, want to divide our national income between private and public spending. Proposals for removing the worst aspects of the worst jobs must be seen not as the final modifications that will perfect the current system, but as the tidying up we do as we move on to something much more interesting. An ultimate goal of this transformation is to elevate large components of our work to the level of a "calling"—work that fits so powerfully with who you are that you cannot conceive of doing something else.[73] Such a powerful change would do nothing short of transforming our culture. John Dewey said that the happiest day of his life was the day he discovered that it was possible to make a living doing what he most loved to do. Imagine if we all felt that way about the positions we currently hold.

What we would create, then, is an economy that seeks to expand the supply of meaningful and challenging jobs, while progressively reducing, sharing, or eliminating jobs that are not inherently satisfying. Such an economy would seek primarily to ensure that all members of the society have the opportunity to pursue their calling in some part of their work life. In this way, the financial independence objective can join with a politics of simplicity. Rather than seeking the complete elimination of paid employment, we might seek a different pattern of work. Frithjof Bergmann of the University of Michigan has suggested a one-third, one-third, one-third model in which our time would be devoted equally between paid employment of the standard kind, participation in an activity (whether paid or not) of central vitality, and engagement (perhaps with others) in some form of self-provision. On an individual level we can create such a life by cutting back on expenditures and developing some flow of investment income that will supplement our wages. But on a social level we would be greatly served in these efforts by policies that will ensure equal pay for equal work for part-time employees; the removal of policies that make it arduous and costly for companies to hire part-time workers at equal pay; laws ensuring full benefit packages for part-timers; and programs to assist people in the processes of self-discovery that will enable them to recraft their work lives.

Along these lines we might consider a proposal for work sabbaticals that former congressman Donald Fraser introduced as legislation back in the 1970s. I was on his staff at the time, but this wasn't my idea. The work sabbaticals proposal focused on the fact that the Social Security system gives people an option of retiring at age sixty-five or at age sixty-two with reduced benefits during those three years. Rather than reserving the three-year option for the end of the work life, Fraser proposed letting everyone take one of those three years every ten years. Given this opportunity, we would be partially supported to do something radically different, such as starting a new enterprise, building a nonprofit, going back to school, pursuing a long-lost hobby, or just taking it easy once in a while.

A redefinition of economic output that says work roles are equal in importance to work products implies a radical redirection of technology. The old utopians believed that once workers were no longer made to bear the brunt of the social cost of technological transformation, automation would be a blessing that eliminated the worst kinds of work. Today, however, there is a need for technologies that will re-create the work experience itself. That is to say, we need tools that allow the individual to impart his sensibilities, values, and ideas into the work product, and not just machines that restrict the qualitative range of labor inputs.[74]

A radical transformation of the supply side or qualitative nature of work activity requires an equally powerful transformation on the demand side. Generally, we can say that moving toward a work-focused conception of the good life requires the aesthetic enrichment of everyday existence. For instance, cooking and everything associated with restaurants has a different meaning in France than it does in the United States. The reason that quality cooking is a central part of the work life of those employed in French restaurants, and that French chefs are regarded as members of a profession, is that the French consumer of food is very different from his American counterpart—more discerning, more selective. In order to change the modes of production and service delivery so as to allow for such an individual aesthetic input into goods and services, we must expand the consumer's aesthetic interest in the goods and services themselves. We cannot have an economy that employs people in making beautifully crafted goods if the consumer is incapable of appreciating them; small farmers who take pride in growing genuinely tasteful and healthful fruits and vegetables cannot maintain a viable market share if few consumers care about the difference. The extent to which the labor force contains teachers and artists, poets and potters depends on the magnitude of the demand for what they produce.

Placing the inherent value of work activity at the core of our economic life is one way of moving beyond a consumption-oriented society. Yet, this alternative actually requires a new interest in what we consume. In this sense, ironically, a politics of simplicity might even be characterized as a more authentic materialism, one in which the symbolic character of what we consume would diminish while we came to care more about the taste of what we eat, and the beauty of what we purchase. Thus understood, consumption would involve an aesthetic revolution within ourselves—an awaking of aesthetic interest, a change in the way we see and hear and taste and feel. There may be some important contribution that government can make to this transformation, particularly with respect to education. But primarily what is at issue here is a cultural evolution. What a politics of simplicity offers is not policy recommendations, but rather a way of perceiving the interconnectedness between the aesthetics of consumption and meaningful work.

ELIMINATING THE WORST HASSLES OF
EVERYDAY LIFE

One of the advantages of a politics of simplicity is that it provides a vantage point for perceiving the larger meaning of issues that, in themselves, appear too trivial to warrant our attention, but when taken together bleed our spirit, deplete our energy, and deprive us of any opportunity for graceful existence. Here is an assorted list of hassles, some rather trivial alone, but collectively contributing to the continued succession of "bad days." It can be regarded as my list of personal peeves, for which the reader might readily substitute others equally infuriating:

- Traffic jams on holidays that regularly destroy what might otherwise be a particularly nice outing. How many Thanksgivings have been turned sour by an additional two hours on the way to the relatives? How many visits are cut short by the need to beat the traffic, even to the extent of getting up at five in the morning on a day one might be lolling in bed? The central culprit that causes these jams so often turns out to be the tollbooth and the simple fact that the collectors are not able to cope with the holiday traffic. How easy it would be to simply ban the collection of tolls on all holidays. Any lost revenue could be collected by making minor adjustments to tolls on regular days.

- Waiting endlessly for the opportunity to talk to a real human being in order to correct, inquire, or complain about the inadequacy of some service for which one is being charged. For instance, dealing with health insurance companies. Why not require that there be one standard nationwide form that doctors must fill out for patients? Why don't we demand that all health insurance companies retain sufficient service personnel to answer calls within three minutes? If that is asking too much, we could at least require that when they solicit new customers, health insurance companies must reveal the length of time (independently audited) it takes to get someone on the phone, as well as the frequency of challenges to their billings.

- The idiocy of lines and waiting involved in registering a new automobile when there is no reason this could not be done through the mail.

- The increasing absence of sales people in large department stores, now compounded by the practice of not even marking prices on items for sale.

- A tax system that has turned us into accountants in our everyday lives. Why not expand the personal deductions or otherwise adjust the rates so that, say, 90 percent of the public can use the short form without any penalty. Or, more radically, eliminate the personal income tax altogether, raising revenue from a national sales tax (necessities exempted) or other methods that don't impinge so diabolically upon our daily life.

A politics of simple living gives seriousness to such hassles as forms of pollution that destroy the psychological life space for graceful being. It extends our concern for the physical environment to the mental health environment of everyday life.

AGING

Given that the elderly have an equal claim to a good life, we should not assume that its elements are radically different as we age. In particular, elders, too, are in need of opportunities to both enjoy life and generously give of themselves.

However, one of the distinctive features of the contemporary world is the extreme separation of the elderly from the rest of society. From the point of view of simple living this is especially problematic. In a later chapter, I will argue that the core of each person's wealth lies in human wealth, both in their own capacities and in the access they have to the riches of other people. From that perspective, human capital is, in some respects, most extensively embodied in older people, and in the potential service that they can provide. Thus, we have a paradox in that our richest source of human services are cast aside even though we live in a world in which such services are the ultimate scarce commodity. As viewed by the elderly, it is a world in which one is treated as obsolete and useless, often when one's capabilities are most fully developed.

What are these potential services that people can provide? On one level, of course, there is no special answer here. Elderly people can provide, though typically to a quantitatively lesser degree, the full range of services they provided when they were younger. What typically happens is that work roles are designed in ways that cannot accommodate them physically. But there are also certain special services that the elderly alone can contribute. They include those having to do with human continuity—with connecting people, especially the young, with an earlier time, with a sense of the fullness of change, and a firsthand experience of worlds that no longer exist. More immediately, older people, through their very presence, teach the young about the life cycle. They are the instantiation of whether or not there will be such a thing as graceful aging and even graceful dying. To the extent that aging represents separation and ultimately disposal, the entire life cycle is infected.

The greatest mistake that we make with respect to people as they age is the lowered expectations that we impart, and that they themselves internalize. The fundamental question that the society has to answer is, "What is it to be old?" If the answer is that being old means being retired, being finished in one's contribution, being at the end of the line—then that is what people will be when they age. But, if being old means having reached a time in life when one is expected to play a certain valuable role, when one is supposed to have achieved the wisdom and perspective that comes with much living, then that, instead, is what people will be when they age. It is centrally a question of expectations for self and others.

The concept of retirement is itself an indictment of our economically centered life. On the one hand it represents being put out to pasture, no longer having a contribution to make, and thus reflects our inability to organize a society that can gain from those with a wealth of years. But additionally, retirement is seen as that point at which one can escape from the burden of work, escape into a life in which one does what is intrinsically rewarding. The fact that it all too often does mean an escape from burdensome work reveals how thoroughly the realm of work is distorted. If the people who reached the age of sixty-five were clearly in touch with who they were, aware of their own deepest values and beliefs, and had succeeded in finding or fashioning a form of life in which they could express these values, then retiring from such activity is the last thing they would want to do. What they might want, if they had found themselves working too much, with days that were too long and weekends too short, is to work somewhat less. But, then, that is what graceful simplicity tells us we all should be doing throughout those earlier years.

Here we might think about what might be called a "redistribution of leisure" rather than an expansion. While those of us working would love a break, there are many retired people who feel that they have too much time on their hands. Between 1970 and 1990, the labor force participation rate for men ages fifty-five to sixty-four fell from 83 percent to 68 percent, and for men over sixty-five it fell from 27 percent to 16 percent. One possible way to balance these extremes of work and free time is to move away from the notion of a standard "retirement age," while reducing the amount of time we each work in any given year throughout our entire work life.

We also need to rethink pensions and Social Security. Insofar as the response to a growing insecurity among middle-aged people about what lies ahead is the "everyone for themselves" approach of IRAs and 401ks, we have additional pressures to work more and earn more. A politics of plain living rejects that approach and looks for new answers. Perhaps this redistribution of leisure is part of the answer. If we had radically shorter hours and different kinds of work, few might want to retire at all and, therefore, we would eliminate the added hours and stress now associated with saving for retirement.

One of the most problematic aspects of aging is not just one's own impending death, but also the deaths of one's friends and loved ones. Given that our greatest wealth consists of these relationships, old people become impoverished through the deaths of those they have long known. That they also become increasingly isolated from the living and the healthy adds the final blow to their impoverishment. It is sometimes pointed out that the reason people in poor countries have so many children is that children provide a form of social security for the elderly. But this must be understood in nonpecuniary terms as well. The fuller security that we need to have as we age and when we come to face death is to be secure in the belief that we will not be alone. There is nothing particularly "natural" in the way our society has evolved, with people so thoroughly segregated by age group. In a search for more socially efficient ways of dealing with the problem of insecurity that accompanies aging, a politics of simplicity might then offer a new objective: how do we reestablish patterns of life so as to reintegrate elderly people back into the lives and even housing patterns of younger generations?

BEAUTY

A politics of simplicity, especially one that emphasizes graceful existence, gives centrality to the issue of beauty. The issue is not about "the arts"—it is primarily about the aesthetic of our public space and the beauty of the world of things we construct. As such, it is about the pavement on the streets, the design of street lamps, trees in our neighborhoods, flowers in front of our houses, the building materials we prefer, the houses we buy, the bottles we drink from, the hairbrushes we use, and the dishes we eat from. From the point of view of simple living, the public spaces and the face that private space presents to public view are particularly important. One of the advantages of a society in which a significant part of the average person's economic well-being comes from participation in public goods rather than in private ones is that each individual's own economic well-being is less directly connected to the ups and downs of his/her income. So, if one lives in a healthful, beautiful city, rich with public space, then as an individual one is freer to work less and earn less, because in the surrounding public space one finds less of a difference between the well-being of the rich and the poor.

We have been hearing about the perverseness of a "tax and spend" mentality for so long that we hardly consider that there is no general answer as to whether government is taxing and spending too much or too little. For instance, when it comes to spending for museums and parks and general beautification, are we better off transferring spending (through taxation) from private consumption to public consumption? If "better off" is understood in terms of being closer to a graceful existence, then a strong case can be made for vastly increasing certain kinds of public consumption.

In considering the aesthetics of economic life, as elsewhere, there is the danger that well-intentioned policy can conflict with individual freedoms. In America we have no concept of aesthetic pollution; we have no concept of the violation of the perceptual space of others. Rather, within rather broad bounds, we act as if we have a God-given right to establish as much aesthetic blight as we desire. One might reasonably be wary about any proposal to use government to limit or restrict such "freedom."

But we need to reach some better balance between the liberty to generate ugliness and our need for beautiful spaces and beautiful things—our right to not be visually assaulted. Certainly much can be done in those aspects of public space that are financed through public spending. As a society we are not totally devoid of aesthetic sense. We do have laws that establish historic preservation zones and sites. We need to build on this, however. Perhaps if we had established old trees as historic sites several decades ago, suburban tracts and parking centers would not look as they do. At the very least, there would be some shade for our cars while we go inside to load up. Perhaps if we had established commercial neighborhoods as protected zones, we could have limited the construction of the malls and superstores that have contributed so much to the utter boredom of a stroll. But in a free society, government can go only so far. It cannot substitute for a generally high level of aesthetic consciousness and valuation on the part of the citizenry. I have already referred to graceful simplicity as a form of authentic materialism, but how can this be brought about? How can we become consumers who would see and prefer the beautiful to the mundane?

Here we are talking about appreciativeness, about bringing to life an appreciation of the beautiful. Is this an impossible task? I think not. But it does require exposure to the beautiful. In cultures of beauty, beauty is more readily valued without making special efforts to awaken its appreciation. Oddly enough in our culture the one area in which great pains are taken to construct a particular sense of beauty is the area of physical beauty. We see everywhere how advertisers and commercial enterprises strive mightily to alter and shape our sense of what is beautiful. What this tells us quite clearly is that once beauty is perceived, it becomes a powerful market force. Thus, what we need is a general arousal of our latent aesthetic sense. Here, one of the roles of a politics of graceful simplicity is simply to give voice and legitimization to matters of beauty in public discourse.

One example of how several of these matters come together can be found in the area of transportation. We need to meld a philosophy of slowing down to one of creating beauty. To do so we must couple leisure expansion with aesthetic rejuvenation. In particular, we must create a system of rail transport that will be a thing of beauty in itself. Going from one place to another on this network should not be viewed as a cost of time, but rather as an activity of intrinsic worth. For this, however, every aspect of transportation policy would need to be revamped, including what there is to see out of the window, and what there is to eat on the train.

This, of course, is not a matter of having a few good policy ideas. Rather, it would represent a cultural transformation in our attitude toward time. It would be building into daily life some of what we fantasize when we dream of a Caribbean cruise.

CRIME

Simple living may or may not have anything new to propose about how to deal with crime, but it does offer a somewhat different characterization of why crime is a problem. At the heart of the matter is fear and the loss of public space. There is no gracefulness in being afraid to walk to the store at night, no gracefulness in being afraid to let the children play in the park. When we lose access to public spaces, we are separated from our wealth as effectively as if we had actually been held at gunpoint. We have already been robbed when we have lost the nighttime, when we have lost the opportunity to be outside when the sun goes down. We have already been mugged when we are afraid to be by ourselves sitting by a stream or watching the sunset.

In some of the poorest cities in the world there is little crime. When this is so, people have access to enormously valuable public goods simply by virtue of being free to look up and see the moon and stars while holding hands, or to sit out in the cool of the summer night until one or two in the morning, in conversation with friends and neighbors. My father's generation did this in a secluded corner of the Bronx, but few would dare it today.

As was discussed earlier, the high level of crime in America has imposed burdens on all of us. It has driven up the cost of housing in safe neighbor-hoods; it has given us a need for private schools; and it has imposed long commutes on those who made their escape. For those who cannot escape, for those condemned to live amid gangs and drugs, all pretense of the riches of a simple life, through frugality and inner capital, remains a sham. Thus, in a politics of simplicity reducing crime—in particular, violent, stranger-to-stranger crime—is especially important.

I have no magic solution that will dramatically reduce street crime, but the recent positive trends, largely caused by demographic changes, should awaken us to a greater sense of what is possible. We really can have a society in which it is genuinely safe to be outside, anywhere. The perspective of sim-plicity points in the direction of thinking holistically about the total concep-tion of life that animates a person. Insofar as graceful simplicity represents a powerful model of the good life, and one that can be attained without opu-lence, it may have something to offer to the fragmented world out of which much street crime emerges. It may be that public policy should give some priority to facilitating lives of graceful simplicity in just those communities that are most ravaged by crime. This would require a multifaceted effort to provide meaningful service, public beauty, and education for simple living in these neighborhoods. It would not take as its goal that people successfully transition into our larger society; rather it would facilitate the emergence of something different and more interesting.

Rather than assuming that the only alternative to poverty is escaping into middle-class life, it might prove both more viable and ultimately more ful-filling to move from poverty to simple living. Once physical needs are met, this is a matter of overcoming intellectual, social, spiritual, and aesthetic impoverishment. In this, all communities have untapped riches to draw upon. Even in poor communities a rich potential exists for people to provide personal service to one another. Thus one can imagine patterns of consump-tion that are rather meager with respect to goods which one buys from out-side the community, but are startlingly abundant in the exchange of services within the community—whether it be entertainment, home-based restau-rants, religious instruction, music lessons, storytelling, athletic training, child care, home visitations for the sick and elderly, tutoring, chess clubs, local the-ater, art classes, dance troupes, and so forth. What is needed are processes that energize people, allowing them to see that it is within their power to cre-ate not just the pale shadow of middle-class life, but something that in many ways is more vibrant.

EDUCATION FOR SIMPLE LIVING

Simple living involves knowing how to live well in time. It requires knowledge of what is important in life, and understanding how to appreciate that which is given to us, be it another person or a spring day. It calls us to become centered and often independent of the judgments of others.

Clearly our schools do not equip children to live lives of simplicity and to resist the hectic, frenetic alternatives that pull at them. One might say that such is not the job of the schools, that this is the work of the family or of religious education. But the idea that the schools can somehow be neutral between different ways to live is a myth. It rests on thinking of schools as abstractions rather than as real-life places that children attend for seven or eight hours a day, for twelve or sixteen or twenty years. So much of what goes on in schools is instrumental and directed at equipping students to succeed or, at least, to find their place within our socioeconomic order. Therefore, schools inevitably are transmission belts for the values and perspectives that sustain the dominant way of life.

In our competitive social world where there is a powerful semiconsensus on what success means and a limited number of successful life places, parents look to their child's school years and school performance as decisive factors in determining how he/she will fare in life. The schools, aware of the key role that they play in society's central game, see themselves in a similar fashion. Given this, how can it be otherwise than that the entire schooling experience, including that part which occurs within the home, will both implicitly and explicitly endorse the central terms of that competition. In particular, what is affirmed is the dominant conception of the good life that is operative within the social competition.

Yet, at the same time, what happens in schools is complex and multi-dimensional. Insofar as people break free from opulence-based versions of the American Dream and find their way back to the simple living version of that dream, it is often things that happened in school that enable them to shift direction. Rather than lambasting schools, it is useful then to consider those things that sometimes happen in schools that do contribute to a person's ability to form a life of graceful simplicity.

In educating for simple living, three building blocks stand out: fostering a love of books, developing a stronger aesthetic sensibility, and enhancing our ability to create things of beauty.

A LOVE OF BOOKS

I put this first for several reasons. If one loves books, if one loves to read, if in a family people read to each other, then a foundation has already been laid for a simple life of great pleasure at little expense. Entering this world— provided that one has learned to love what is within it, and has developed the appreciative skills required to fully participate in it—is to have the key to the central repository of human wealth. Reading good books can serve as the central emblem of a life of simplicity. If one wants to look for a single operative criterion of whether schools are succeeding or failing in their central task (as understood from the perspective of the simple life), then look to whether they have helped to develop a love of reading in the children who attend them.

AN AESTHETIC SENSIBILITY

The presence and appreciation of beauty is central to the good life. At their best, schools offer an alternative to the larger society, as intentionally crafted environments designed to affect the development of children in beneficial ways that will not be forthcoming from the general social environment. Thus, within a culture in which there is limited beauty and limited aesthetic sensibility, it becomes especially important for the school curriculum to focus on beauty and creativity. For some, schools are the first and perhaps only place where children are exposed to the finest in art, music, sculpture, and poetry. Yet, as we all know, exposure to and the development of an aesthetic sensibility are not one and the same. Often enough appreciation courses can be deadly—and it remains a central challenge to educators to master their craft in this area.

AN ABILITY TO CREATE THINGS OF BEAUTY

Central to the development of an aesthetic sensibility is the nurturing of one's own creative abilities. Within the broad rubric of arts and crafts, ranging from fine arts and music to carpentry and even cooking, it is not asking too much of schools to require that all students emerge having attained some degree of excellence in at least one form of creative endeavor.

Being able to produce something of beauty is among the greatest of capabilities. With it one can always contribute to the richness of the lives of others; one can always be deserving of the esteem and respect of others; one can always undertake activities of unique joyousness; one is provided with something of a vaccine against a shoddy materialism. With this ability one becomes a participant in the development of a general economic demand for things of beauty and thus a participant in the central mechanism that will enrich our entire society.

The choice of school curriculum is always a matter of trade-offs, for there is only so much time in the school day. If I am urging something as contrary to current practice as preparing skilled artists, or woodworkers, or cooks, then what in the school curriculum would I cut back on in order to expand the development of creative capabilities? This is an extremely difficult question to answer. My own view is that we have swung too far in the direction of what started as an effort to keep up with the Soviets when Sputnik was launched in the 1960s, and what we emphasize today in the effort to stay a technological step ahead of the Japanese. If I had to choose between giving greater emphasis to math and science or greater emphasis to the arts and humanities, I would choose the latter. To those who worry about international competitiveness, it is worth considering that for the overwhelming bulk of the population, marginal differences in their scientific and mathematical prowess may make little difference in determining whether American science and engineering make cutting-edge breakthroughs.

The broader point here is not these specifics. It is simply that when you ask the average parent what they wish for their children in life, they mostly say that they want them to be happy. If we accept this as legitimate, even if not complete, the central question that faces us is whether we believe that happiness is to be attained through successfully navigating our existing socioeconomic competition, or whether we believe it is to be found in better equipping children to find happiness in a qualitatively rich form of simple living.

What is telling of our need to approach these questions together politically is that all too often we can see the limitations of the existing framework, but we're not prepared to send our own children down any path other than the ones most conventionally understood as leading to success. In part, this may be a lack of courage, but it also emerges from the genuine concern that the price may be too high for our children if, as isolated individuals, we and they break with the mainstream. A politics of simplicity will empower us to deeply rethink schooling and to act boldly.

JUSTICE, GRASPING, AND GRACEFULNESS

In Boston, in the seventeenth century, a merchant named Robert Keane was tried and found guilty of having charged his customers excessively. In sermons delivered after the trial it was pointed out that what Keane falsely believed was that "a man might sell as dear as he can, and buy as cheap as he can."[75] His sin, his graspingness, was in fact what today many would regard as nothing more than seizing a golden opportunity to make a buck. Indeed, there are many who believe that this is the proper way for economic agents to behave, and that it is in virtue of their doing so that markets perform their desired economic functions—e.g., signaling that there is a shortage in some area and inducing greater production. It is thus that market economies achieve their so-called "efficiency."

Robert Keane was tried for raising his prices. And raising prices is indeed one of the ways in which people break the harmony of the world. This, of course, gets serious when we have spirals of runaway inflation, with everyone trying to lay off price increases on someone else. The idea of a "just price" is perhaps nothing more than the result of confused thinking, but we can indeed value and achieve a world of greater stability.

Historically, the medieval espousal of graceful acceptance of what is rested upon the idea of a preordained order established by God, and it was not the place of any man to challenge that, either in his own life or in his designs for society as a whole. While such a basis for social or personal acquiescence is long past, what is worth recognizing is that at the core of this idea was not fear of God, but rather acceptance of the rightness of the way things were. God's plan was brought into the story in order to give credibility to the otherwise unbelievable notion that the existing order was indeed just. This neat mutual support between religion and power is, fortunately, largely in the past. The important lesson here for achieving a more graceful and harmonic society is that a valid social order needs to be based on a generally shared conception of justice.

At present, if we were to seek to articulate how Americans understand the terms of our socioeconomic relationship, we might characterize it as one of modestly constrained competition. While we do have a social safety net for the "deserving" poor, our framework is that this is an opportunity society. Our economic life is about making it, and about *fairness* within that competition. As such, it is a framework that endorses as valid the dominant vision of success and that accepts the social implications of the competition. It views all this as largely cost-free, not seeing within this any distortion of either character or life itself.

A politics of simplicity, however, comes to economic life with a somewhat different vision. As did Aristotle, it says that there is indeed a limit beyond which we should not go, and that to do so is to distort ourselves and our lives. It offers a different understanding of how much is enough, one quite at odds with the desire to get rich. Furthermore, it says that our competitive struggle for those limited numbers of successful places in the social order is self-destructive. It argues that of material riches, we should have what we need, but no more, and that we should adopt ideals that potentially can be achieved by all, rather than by only a few.

Out of this orientation, it is possible to articulate an alternative to the "fair competition" vision of the opportunity-to-make-it society. The elements of a simple living framework for our collective life might be these:

- We seek such forms of social provision and policy as make it possible to achieve high levels of need satisfaction on modest levels of personal income.
- We require all to work who are able, and we guarantee that there will be jobs for all.
- We set as our goal a "simple-living wage" such that, at that minimum wage, and with more efficient use of income for need satisfaction, a two-parent family with children can meet their core economic needs with neither parent working more than twenty-five hours a week.[76]

This is a liberating framework. It is one that makes it possible for those who want to, to pursue lives of simplicity. It is one that will allow those born into the middle class to reconsider whether they want to reproduce the lives of their parents. It will provide those of us who are older with sufficient security that we might undertake the risks of attempting to reformulate our lives. And because it addresses the needs of rich and poor alike, this is not a framework for welfare programs, but for our general social well-being.

AMERICA'S SELF-PERCEPTION

On the most basic level a politics of simplicity represents a way of perceiving; it means seeing things from within the realization that the good life resides in the achievement of gracefulness in all of its dimensions.

What happens to the American self-perception if we look at the world in that way? What happens to us as Americans if we see other peoples from that perspective?

Americans, even when they explicitly withdrew from the world in the early colonial years, have always understood themselves in relation to it. It has been a given of the American self-perception that what we have in America is largely better than what exists elsewhere. Ironically, this is as true today, when boosters proclaim the high standard of living in the United States, as it was in the early years of the American experiment when we saw ourselves as undertaking an escape from the venality of commercial civilization to build a city on a hill. We Americans have always seen our social world as better than what exists elsewhere.

Not every country sees itself this way. Indeed, many in the world share this perception of America, and many have come to America to have for themselves that good life they could not attain at home. Nor should this self-perception be tossed off lightly as some boorish tendency toward self-aggrandizement. In important ways life in America is vastly superior to that found in many other countries. In particular this must be said of our general ability to satisfy our most basic physical needs—we may have varieties of malnutrition, but we don't have mass starvation. America has been spared the horrors that have occurred in Nazi Germany, Cambodia, China, the Soviet Union, El Salvador, and Guatemala, even if we have our own wretched legacy of slavery and the quasi-genocide of Native Americans.

But if we restrict ourselves to the matter of graceful existence, it is something again to consider how the United States compares to other countries. If one were to focus on the upper middle class we would find far more graceful existence in Third World countries than here. The reason, however, is that when there is extreme poverty, it is possible to purchase personal services for next to nothing. Thus, in poor countries, as was once true in the United States, it is possible for middle-class families to have servants—and thus certain forms of gracefulness. But the absence of servants in American life must count for us, not against it. The question of gracefulness must be posed in terms of the life of all, not merely a few. How does America compare to other countries as a place where valid but simple lives are widely feasible?

No summary judgments are possible here. If one sought to build a comparative international index of the extent to which different countries facilitate lives of simplicity, we might ask questions such as these:

+ How long do people have to work to meet core needs?
+ How odious is the work of most people?
+ How beautiful are the cities?
+ How stimulating to the eyes and ears and nose is it to walk through an urban shopping area, or a rural market?
+ How tasty is the food?
+ How beautiful is the natural environment?
+ How rich is the texture of human relations?
+ How tight are the bonds between young and old?
+ How much time is there to spend with friends?
+ How much beauty is to be found in the objects of everyday life?
+ How quickly can one reach the countryside?
+ How free is one to walk the streets without fear?
+ How relaxed is the general pace of life?

What such an index would confirm is that, when it comes to achieving lives of graceful simplicity, there is no clear distinction to be made between the so-called developed and developing countries. Once we are past issues that bear on the link between economics and health (e.g., availability of food and clean water) there is no simple story to be told about "the great ascent" that we have made and that others have yet to take.

At bottom, wrestling with the implications of this conclusion is the core goal of a politics of simplicity—to reconnect our political discourse and collective action with a deeper understanding of what is really important.

INTERLUDE

Chapter Five

HOW DID WE GET WHERE WE ARE?

In the preceding chapters I contrasted, in various ways, two ways of thinking about life, whether it be one's own life or our collective social life. There are various ways of conceptualizing this great divide. We may contrast, as Aristotle did, two different ways of thinking about money or external goods. Or we may look at the American experience and find two alternative versions of the American Dream, one that focuses on riches, and one that sees simple living as the entry point to the good life. Or, as in the last chapter, we may contrast two different paradigms of economic activity, one that stresses the expansion of material goods, the other that emphasizes the importance of meaningful activity, whether paid or unpaid. Behind all this lurks a fundamental value question: how are we to understand the good life?

These same value quandaries appear in another guise—how are we to understand what happens in history? Is history a story of human progress? Is it a story of human decline? Is it just a matter of ups and downs, not going anywhere? For over 2,000 years, the answers to such questions have shaped Western civilization's varying self-perception. In part, this is a matter of facts, a matter of beliefs about what will happen and about what has happened. But most centrally the disagreements have been about "what really matters, and what does not." Things occur in the world, but they do not come with labels on them that say "this is important" or "this is better than that." It is only against the backdrop of our values that we can develop a conception of what happens in time. As we shall see, the history of the notion that mankind makes progress is itself a history of the abandonment of some values in favor of others.

An inquiry into the history of the idea of progress shows how unusual it is to think about the economy as we do—as an independent realm to be evaluated in terms of the magnitude of its output rather than in terms of its contribution to a larger vision of life. Further, an inquiry into the history of the idea of progress shows that the issue we are concerned with, the value of simple living, has been a recurring theme in the effort to understand "what happens" in history. This should come as no surprise, for the idea of simple living is an ancient ideal and it has often represented a challenge to dominant values.

From the point of view of graceful simplicity, an inquiry of this sort is particularly illuminating. It shows that to a considerable extent the debates in the past over whether mankind makes progress in history were debates over the relative beauty of the art and literature of different historic periods. Yet when those debates ended and there emerged something of a consensus that adhered to a belief in progress, it was not because agreement was reached on the relative merits of ancient and modern arts. Rather, what happened was a shift in the implicit definition of progress, beauty, and creative power once central concerns had been relegated to the periphery. In short, the emergence of the idea of progress reflected the dominance of new values. In particular, it represented the emergence of the modern way of thinking about economic life.

THE LOVE OF BOOKS

I have suggested that a love of books is the hallmark of whether our schools are preparing children for living the good life. And in reading a good book, either to oneself or with others, whether with friends or children, one finds proof that the sources of both pleasure and growth are as abundant as fruit in an orchard.

When we think of history as the story of human progress, especially when we think of it as involving the progressive evolution of human sensibilities and relationships, then inevitably we postulate a radical gap between ourselves and those who lived long ago. Yet consider as a corrective this ancient passage from *The Instruction of Duauf*, to which Toynbee calls our attention.

I believe it the most ancient affirmation of the wisdom of building one's life around books.

Duauf, an Egyptian scribe, is writing for his son, Pepi, having installed him in the School of Books:

> I have seen him that is beaten, him that is beaten: thou art to set thine heart on books.
>
> I have beheld him that is set free from forced labor: behold, nothing surpasseth books. . . .
>
> Would that I might make thee love books more than thy mother; would that I might bring their beauty before thy face. It is greater than any calling. . . .
>
> Every artisan that wieldeth the chisel, he is wearier than him that delveth. . . .
>
> The stone-mason seeketh for work in all manner of hard stone. When he hath finished it his arms are destroyed and he is weary. . . .
>
> The field worker, his reckoning endureth for ever . . . he too is wearier than can be told, and he fareth as one fareth among lions. . . .
>
> The weaver in the workshop, he fareth more ill than any woman. His thighs are upon his belly, and he breatheth no air. . . .
>
> Let me tell thee, further, how it fareth with the fisherman. Is not his work upon the river, where it is mixed with the crocodiles? . . .
>
> Behold, there is no calling that is without a director except (that of) the scribe, and he is the director. . . .[77]

On one level this passage is a parent's advice to a son. As such it is advice that we have heard before. Essentially Duauf the Egyptian is telling his son to "stay in school!" While this is sound advice in our contemporary world, what is most remarkable is that Duauf gave this advice to his son over 4,000 years ago. One thousand years after it was written, around the time of King David and Solomon, well before the Bible was written down, this text was being used by Egyptian schoolboys in their copy books.

How startling it is! Duauf speaks to the practical issue of human capital formation, the relationship between education and vocational life. With considerable poignancy Duauf reflects on the difficult conditions faced by laborers throughout the social order. He speaks not only of physical exhaustion but of freedom within the workplace: "There is no calling that is without a director except that of the scribe." There is even, perhaps, a fleeting recognition of the difficult condition of women ("The weaver in the workshop, he fareth more ill than any woman. His thighs are on his belly, and he breathest no air.")

What does it tell us about history that this exchange between father and son, with these sensibilities, occurred almost 4,000 years ago? It is not easy to fit this ancient text into our modernistic vision. It reveals an ancient history to one of the common dilemmas of life—"What will I do when I grow up?" And it bears witness to human relationships and human sensibilities that mock our distinctions between modern and traditional societies. It suggests to us that much of life has always been and will continue to be about the basic relationships and common problems.

There is something else in this passage. Duauf tells his son to "set thine heart on books," and he says, "Would that I might make thee love books more than thy mother; would that I might bring their beauty before thy face."

In holding up the standard of "love . . . more than thy mother," the passage attests to the bond between child and mother. But against this most fundamental standard of love, Duauf interposes books. Books, too, are a matter of the heart; they are the objects of love, a love that might appropriately surpass even the love for thy mother. Perhaps Duauf senses that books themselves are our mothers, giving birth to our ever-renewed selves. Books, he tells us, are things of beauty. But not necessarily beauty that is immediately visible. Duauf says of this beauty, "Would that I might bring [it] before thy face." The appreciation of their beauty requires instruction.

What we have in this passage is Duauf's love for his son, his love for books, and his effort to bring about a love-marriage between these two objects of his love. This is to be a marriage that will be valid in itself. Like all marriages, it is one that will take cognizance of the realities of economic life—there is a practical side to loving books. Specifically, for Duauf's son, there is his potential career as a scribe. How are we to fit this image in among our other images of ancient Egypt as a past world, a world of idol worship and pyramid building? From his relationship with his son, from his mixed role as affectionate father and practical guide, from his own love of books, it is clear that the world in which Duauf lived turns around remarkably fixed points of human experience. How, by the way, are we to explain Duauf's love of books? Perhaps we have yet to understand what books were and meant in ancient Egypt. Often enough we think that "back then" what was recorded was only a listing of the triumphs of the Pharaoh, or of the financial records of the Pharaoh's ministers. But for us, the "book" of ancient Egypt that *we* can love the most is itself Duauf's instruction—preserved in clay tablets as a text for schoolchildren to copy. It is this writing of Duauf himself that, for us, is the book that opens up the inner world of ordinary people at the time of the Pharaohs, opens up their beauty, their love, and their anxieties.

THE PROBLEM OF HOMER

In our rush toward the future and our indifference toward the past we are all victims of the idea of progress. This is a Western idea, and any understanding of it should start with Homer. It is not that Homer wrote about progress, though it is possible to read *The Odyssey* from that perspective. It is rather that the phenomenon of Homer has always represented a problem for the idea of progress. This was true in the fifth century B.C.; it was true in the seventeenth and eighteenth centuries; it is true today.

Homer did not write. He was a poet in an oral tradition. The tales he told had been told for several hundred years. But it was his account that was written down and preserved. Possibly *The Iliad* and *The Odyssey* were the works of two different authors; we do not know for sure. But it is the Homer of *The Iliad* who is most problematic.

The Iliad is the earliest known work in Western literature. It was written down in the eighth century B.C.E. In sheer volume it is impressive, an epic poem of 600 pages. It is the story of the Trojan War. Thus, our first story is a war story. Yet it is not what one might expect. It opens nine years into the war. There is no Trojan horse in the story; there is no account of Achilles' death, no mention of his vulnerable heel, and there is no account of the fall of Troy. It is a slice of experience at a critical point during the war.

It is most essentially a human story. There are no faceless, nameless masses of soldiers. Each death, and there are many, is unique. Each is of an individual human being who is individually connected to other human beings, be they Greek or Trojan.

Perhaps *The Iliad* should be seen as the story of Hector. Hector is the great

Trojan warrior, brother of Paris, whose thoughtless kidnapping of Helen
started the conflict. The doomed Hector must fight Achilles, who is half god.
Hector curses his thoughtless brother:

> "As for me, I go
>   for Paris, to arouse him, if he listens.
>   If only earth would swallow him here and now!
> What an affliction the Olympian
>   brought up for us in him—a curse for Priam
>   and Priam's children! Could I see that man
>   dwindle into Death's night, I'd feel my soul
>   relieved of its distress!"[78]

Hector has a wife and child. He knows that he is fated to die in this sense-
less war. He speaks with his wife, fearing that she will end up a slave in a
Greek household. And she replies:

> "Oh, my wild one, your bravery will be
>   your own undoing. No pity for our child,
>   poor little one, or me in my sad lot—
>   soon to be deprived of you! Soon, soon
>   Akhains as one man will set upon you
>   and cut you down! Better for me, without you,
>   to take cold earth for mantle. No more comfort,
>   no other warmth, after you meet your doom
>   but heartbreak only."[79]

When the time comes, Hector's great courage fails him. He flees from
Achilles, and three times around Troy they run. But Achilles is known as
the great runner; he cannot be escaped any more than death itself. Finally,
Hector turns. He will stand and fight. In short order, he is mortally wounded.
As he is dying Hector speaks to Achilles:

> "I beg you by your soul and by your parents,
>   do not let the dogs feed on me
>   in your encampment by the ships. Accept
>   the bronze and gold my father will provide

> as gifts, my father and her ladyship
> my mother. Let them have my body back,
> so that our men and women may accord me
> decency of fire when I am dead."[80]

Achilles refuses, thus adding to Hector's total loss—"Dogs and birds will have you, every scrap."[81] But when old Priam, Hector's father, journeys alone to Achilles' camp, he is allowed to claim his son's body.

The Iliad is a story about human dignity. It is also about mortality and about being caught within the larger fatality of history and duty. Even in translation, it is beautiful poetry.

For centuries the study of Homer was at the center of education for ancient Greeks. Professionals who traveled from city to city recited Homer. It was believed that "Homer enshrined all wisdom and all knowledge. . . . Homer held and nourished the minds and imaginations of Greeks for generation after generation—of artists, thinkers and ordinary simple men alike. . . . Aeschylus was said to have described his own work, modestly, as 'sliced from Homer's banquet.' "[82] In the fifth century B.C.E., amid perhaps the greatest flourishing of the human spirit, some, increasingly aware of how much they had progressed over the past, found in the greatness of this older poet a problem for their self-image, and they turned against Homer. The poet Timotheus proclaimed, "I do not sing ancient melodies, my own are better by far."[83]

This was not the last time Homer served as the benchmark of human excellence. In the seventeenth century, 2,500 years after *The Iliad*, many had a similarly difficult time understanding their place in history without first settling whether they had surpassed Homer. In our own time, a full 2,800 years later, Simone Weil could say of *The Iliad*, "Nothing that the peoples of Europe have produced is worth the first known poem to have appeared among them."[84]

This, then, is the problem of Homer. It is so good! Being so, it casts in doubt the claim that we have made progress. Nor is this just a matter of Homer's individual genius, great though it was. For he arose out of a tradition; it was to Greek sensibilities that his poetry was directed, and it was Homer, above all others, to whom the Greeks responded. They were thus capable of recognizing Homer's genius and appreciating *The Iliad*. So the problem of Homer is really the historical problem. Given the heights that

were achieved by individuals and cultures at the dawn of Western civilization, how are we to accurately orient ourselves toward the great expanse of
human experience and change that followed?

MUSINGS ON THE HISTORY OF
THE IDEA OF PROGRESS

When historians inquire into the history of the "idea of progress," they are
arguing about the history of a specific set of beliefs about progress. They
are interested in when those beliefs first arose, in who held them, in what
those beliefs expressed, and in the consequences of those beliefs having
been held.

What are the beliefs that constitute the idea of progress? The historian
George Hildebrand has identified three elements:

+ "The belief that history follows a continuous, necessary and
  orderly course."
+ "The belief that this course is the effect of a regularly operating
  causal law."
+ "The belief that the course of change has brought and will continue to bring improvement in the condition of mankind."[85]

There is considerable debate as to whether or not there was, in this sense,
an idea of progress prior to the seventeenth and eighteenth centuries. Some
writers such as Robert Nisbet find the idea of progress in virtually every era
of Western history with the exception of the Renaissance. The absence of this
concept in the Renaissance can perhaps be understood as following from the
rediscovery of the classical world, and in the light of that rediscovery, a perception of the vast period in between as a period of decline and stagnation.[86]

Other historians argue that the ancient and medieval world lacked a
full sense of the idea of progress. They emphasize several ways in which
the dominant outlook of other periods varied from the key elements identified above.

It is pointed out that:

• The Greeks typically believed that there had been some earlier
  Golden Age from which mankind declined.

- When the Greeks focused sharply on the progress that had occurred, they did not anticipate that it would continue indefinitely, but rather imagined that they were near the end of the process.
- The Christian view of history centered around acts of divine intervention rather than the operation of causal laws, and even when it celebrated scientific and technological change, it anticipated that the world would end in the not-too-distant future.

We can accept these points; yet, what is remarkable is how much of a "progressive mentality" there has been, reaching as far back in Western thought as we can go. Most important is that, for over 2,500 years, the West has been change-oriented. It has been aware of the fact that important processes of deep social change occur over time.

We tend to think of our current period, whether this be the last hundred years, or the last two or three hundred, as a unique period of change and awareness of change. Yet something of this sort must also have been true among the ancient Greeks and possibly the Romans. Consider the following passages from Thucydides' *History of the Peloponnesian War*. They are extraordinarily rich in what they reveal about the awareness of multiple levels of rapid transformation. Thucydides is providing background about Greece:

> The country now called Hellas had no settled population in ancient times; . . . There was no commerce, and no safe communication either by land or sea; the use they made of their land was limited to the production of necessities; they had no surplus left over for capital and no regular system of agriculture.[87]

Thus, the first thing we learn about is economic change. This passage suggests an implicit theory of economic growth. The ancient peoples produced (either by necessity or design) only what they needed. There was no economic surplus that could be devoted to capital for greater productivity.

> In these early times, as communication by sea became easier, so piracy became a common profession both among the Hellenes and among the barbarians who lived on the coast and in the islands. . . . At this time, such a profession, so far from being regarded as disgraceful was considered quite honorable. It is an attitude that can

be illustrated even today by some of the inhabitants of the main-
land among whom successful piracy is regarded as something to
be proud of.

Thus, Thucydides tells us that the moral ideas of people change over time.
What is now viewed as disgraceful was once viewed as honorable. Some of
the old customs and attitudes, though no longer dominant, are still visible in
Thucydides' world.

Among these people the custom of carrying arms still survives
from the old days of robbery. Since houses were unprotected and
communications unsafe it was the normal thing to carry arms on
all occasions, and this was a general custom throughout the whole
of Hellas as it is now among foreigners. The fact that the people I
have mentioned still live in this way is evidence that this was once
the general rule among all the Hellenes.

Though Thucydides does not say it outright, there seems an implicit view
that it is not merely that there is change in our moral ideas and practices,
but that such change moves in one direction, and is a change for the better.

The Athenians were the first to give up the habit of carrying
weapons and to adopt a way of living that was more relaxed and
more luxurious. In fact the elder men of the rich families who had
these luxurious tastes only recently gave up wearing linen under-
garments and tying their hair behind their heads in a knot. . . . It
was the Spartans who first began to dress simply and in accor-
dance with our modern taste, with the rich leading a life that was
as much as possible like that of the ordinary people. They, too,
were the first to play games naked, to take off their clothes openly,
and to rub themselves down with olive oil after their exercise. In
ancient times even at the Olympic Games the athletes used to wear
coverings for their loins, and indeed this practice was still in existence not very many years ago. Even today many foreigners, especially in Asia, wear these loincloths for boxing matches and
wrestling bouts. Indeed, one could point to a number of other
instances where the manners of the ancient Hellenic world are
very similar to the manners of foreigners today.

In this last reference to ways in which the manners of foreigners are similar to those of the ancient Hellenic world, we have a vision not unlike contemporary views that see the world as divided into the developed and the less-developed countries, with "our country" representing the apex of development.

Thucydides displays not merely an awareness of change, but a tremendously broad sense of the elements that undergo transformation. These include the physical form of cities, level of technology, modes of political organization, forms of economic activity, agricultural practices, level of material well-being, moral attitudes (e.g., toward piracy), attitudes toward nudity and sports, modes of dress, and even hairstyles. The fact that Thucydides moves so easily from discussing whether men wear underwear to how they build their warships suggests that for him all aspects of human life were part of one broad process of transformation.

He presents changes as one-directional. He gives no indication that any of them have ever been reversed, nor does Thucydides express any expectation that they will be. Rather, he talks of the Hellenes as having been "the first" to make certain changes. He apparently expects that other societies will eventually undergo similar transformations. Thus, implicitly, there is a vision of a single pattern of change through which all societies move.

It is true, of course, that many believed that they had declined from a Golden Age. There were those who believed in the continuous recurrence of historical cycles, yet they, too, believed that there were long periods of time within which mankind gradually gained critical inventions, techniques, and institutions: the plough, use of fire, navigation, law giving, mathematics, metallurgy, and cities.

In Thucydides the picture that emerges, then, is one of vast change in almost all aspects of life, change that is pushed by technological innovation, and that ultimately will carry all of mankind with it. Thus, there is nothing uniquely modern about a modern self-consciousness. We are not the first to see ourselves as modern, in self-conscious contrast to a more ancient past out of which we have progressed. Rather, this way of thinking about history goes back to our earliest reflections on history. Though, just as today, there were those in the ancient world who challenged whether all this change constituted any real progress.

PROGRESS AND KNOWLEDGE

In ancient days, as in the current century, a more convincing case could be made that there was progress in some areas rather than others. Like today, our knowledge of the world, if not our wisdom, appeared a cumulative matter that grew as it was passed on to the next generation. The first full and clear statement of the continued progress of knowledge into the indefinite future is to be found in the writings of the Roman Stoic philosopher Seneca, who wrote:

> There are many peoples today who are ignorant of the causes of eclipses of the moon, and it has only recently been demonstrated among ourselves. The day will come when time and human diligence will clear up problems which are now obscure. We divide the few years of our lives unequally between study and vice, and it will therefore be the work of many generations to explain such phenomena as comets. One day our posterity will marvel at our ignorance of causes so clear to them.
>
>   How many new animals have we first come to know in the present age? In time to come men will know much that is unknown to us. Many discoveries are reserved for future ages, when our memory will have faded from men's minds. We imagine ourselves initiated in the secrets of nature; we are standing on the threshold of her temple.[88]

And,

> Much remains to do; much will remain; and no one born after thousands of centuries will be deprived of the chance of adding something.[89]

What distinguishes Seneca's vision is that, unlike the seventeenth- and eighteenth-century apostles of progress, in Seneca, and in the intervening centuries, there is no broad assumption that progress with respect to knowledge means an increase in human virtue, well-being, or happiness. Either it is thought that these are independent matters, or it is suspected that increased knowledge might itself be the cause of human unhappiness.

   In the earliest myths, be it the Garden of Eden or the Decline from the

Golden Age, it is ignorance, not knowledge, that is associated with human virtue and happiness. Knowledge is associated with the forbidden, and its acquisition is associated with theft, dishonesty, and disrespect for the gods. And thus there is a heavy price to be paid for increasing knowledge.

Seneca is despairing about human virtue and happiness. Taking issue with contemporaries who celebrate their modern world, he makes a critical distinction among kinds of knowledge, distinguishing wisdom and philosophy from ingenuity, saying:

> Posidonius says: "When men were scattered over the earth, protected by caves or by the dug-out shelter of a cliff or by the trunk of a hollow tree, it was philosophy that taught them to build houses." But I, for my part, do not hold that philosophy devised these shrewdly-contrived dwellings of ours which rise story upon story, where city crowds against city, any more than that she invented fish preserves, that are enclosed for the purposes of saving men's gluttony from having to run the risk of storms and in order that, no matter how wildly the sea is raging, luxury may have its safe harbors in which to fatten fancy breeds of fish. . . . Was it not enough for man to provide himself a roof of any chance covering and to contrive for himself some natural retreat without the help of art and without trouble? Believe me that was a happy age, before the days of architects, before the days of builders! All this sort of thing was born when luxury was being born.
>
> . . . A thatched roof once covered free men; under marble and gold dwells slavery.
>
> On another point also I differ from Posidonius, when he holds that mechanical tools were the invention of wise men . . . it was man's ingenuity, not his wisdom, that discovered all these devices.
>
> . . . The things that are indispensable require no elaborate pains for their acquisition; it is only the luxuries that call for labour. Follow nature, and you will have no need for skilled craftsmen.[90]

Here, 2,000 years ago, we have the link being made between a doctrine of progress and a philosophy of simple living. With progress in ingenuity, that is, technology, we have a variety of new products and processes. We have apartment houses and architects and aquaculture! Invention, mechanical skill, ingenuity, labor, or, to call it what it is: economic growth. All of this (for Seneca) emerges from human vice and foolishness. Before such luxury men were free and there was little need for labor. The path of wisdom and happiness lay elsewhere.

In a very severe way, Seneca advocates restricting economic activity to the satisfaction of only our most basic needs. He tells us:

> Houses, shelter, creature comforts, food, and all that has now become the source of vast trouble, were ready at hand, free to all, and obtainable for trifling pains. For the limit everywhere corresponded to the need; it is we that have made all other things valuable, we that have made them admired, we that have caused them to be sought for by extensive and manifold devices . . . that moderation which nature prescribes, which limits our desires by resources restricted to our needs, has abandoned the field. . . .[91]

Seneca's advocacy of a simple life and his despairing vision of what happens in history have a common root—his judgment about what is important. If one sees in the simple life the full resources for whatever happiness and nobility is possible for mankind, then one is not likely to see history as a story of progress.

What we do not find in Seneca's distinction between ingenuity (technology, economic growth) and wisdom is the idea that they could indeed be combined. Neither Seneca nor Aristotle envisioned technological change and the growth of productivity as opening the way for the masses of mankind to be freed from toil or freed to live a life that was economically modest but abundant in the higher aspects of life. For Seneca this would have been unnecessary because, as a Stoic, he maintained that almost nothing of a material nature was really necessary for the good life. Whereas for Aristotle, the problems of the mass of humankind simply did not arise.

HOW THEY OVERCAME HOMER

In the seventeenth century boundless confidence and pride in scientific progress expanded into the more general assertion of human progress, both that it had occurred, was occurring, and would continue to occur. These assertions were contrasted with the perspective of the Renaissance, which emphasized the greatness of the classical achievements and took pride in their rediscovery and in having regained the heights achieved centuries before. As was the case with Seneca, there were those who questioned the sweeping claims. The issue was not so much whether there would be continued progress in the future, but, rather, whether genuine progress had in fact been made. In the seventeenth century, the issue emerged as "The Quarrel Between the Moderns and the Ancients"—a phrase used to describe an ongoing intellectual exchange that lasted over a century, primarily in France and England.

This quarrel is interesting in several respects. First, for one hundred years there was an extended intellectual debate over whether mankind actually makes progress. Second, to some extent the modern idea of progress emerges out of this debate, and thus the terms of the debate reveal not just the factual conclusions of the participants but their deeper definitions and values. Finally, joining this debate allows us to again enter into the big question of what happens in history. Who was right? Were (or are) the moderns superior to the ancients?

Bury, the great historian of the idea of progress, identifies the earliest writing on the subject as that of the Italian Alessandro Tassoni, in his *Miscellaneous Thoughts* published in 1620. But Tassoni refers to "the quarrel" as a "current dispute," so its origins are obscure.[92] Tassoni, himself a poet, and knowing his enemy, leveled an attack on Homer, identifying faults in language, plot, characterization, and imagery. He concluded that modern writers were on the whole superior to the authors of the ancient classics.

Fifteen years later, in 1635, the attack on Homer was renewed, this time in France. One of the founders of the Académie Française, a dramatist named Boisrobert, speaking to that body, delivered a violent attack on the ancient poet. Indeed, it was Homer who was the ancient most frequently vilified.

A central voice in the attack on the ancients was Charles Perrault, remembered today as the author of *Cinderella* and *Sleeping Beauty*. Perrault made one particular contribution; in his account the issue shifts away from the simple comparison of modern and ancient works. He argues for the superiority of modern accomplishments on the basis of general processes which guarantee that that which is later will be superior. Thus knowledge advances with time. Perrault does not claim for the moderns themselves any inherent superiority of talent or genius. Rather he argues that nature is the same at all times. Those of the present have the same natural ability as those who came before, but being later, their works in both science and art are superior.

This line of thinking—that there are at work general processes whereby advance is assured—increasingly serves to build confidence in future progress. Indeed, a great deal of effort, especially in the nineteenth century, will focus on the identification and specification of such processes. Moreover, broadly opposed political philosophies will emerge based in part on whether these processes require for their full operation that we understand them and deliberately manipulate the world in accord with them.[93]

As Bury points out, Perrault did not extrapolate his process of progress into the indefinite future. Quite the contrary, he wrote:

> Our age had, in some sort, arrived at the summit of perfection. And since for some years the rate of the progress is much slower and appears almost insensible—as the days seem to cease lengthening when the solstice is near—it is pleasant to think that probably there are not many things for which we need envy future generations.[94]

The exposition of the fuller version of the progress of knowledge was left to Perrault's contemporary, Bernard de Fontenelle, author of *Dialogues of the Dead* and *Digression on the Ancients and the Moderns*. Like Perrault, Fontenelle argues from an exploration of the processes of change that, in physiological terms, men of his time are the same as those of ancient times. He dismisses the effects of climate as a determining factor. He infers that whatever differences exist are due to either the passage of time or social conditions.

Fontenelle saw mathematics, physics, and medicine as cumulative, and thought it a natural process that in these areas those who come later will know more. The process envisaged was not entirely linear, but involved the elimination of a multitude of false routes. Error was part of the cumulative process whereby advance was achieved. Similarly, he noted that, of necessity, those who came first would be the authors of the first discoveries. But he felt this entitled neither group to greater distinction.

Fontenelle takes a big step. He separates out from this process poetry and eloquence, arguing that they do not depend on correct reasoning and do not require a long course of experiments. In these areas he maintained that perfection might be attained in a few centuries. While the ancients might not be surpassed, they could be equaled.

With respect to the role of social circumstances, Fontenelle did not see them as playing a decisive creative or shaping role, but rather believed that they may, at points (e.g., war), provide a breach in the ongoing process. But to the process whereby knowledge expanded there was a kind of necessity. Knowledge could be slowed down or blocked, but in time it would resume.

Fontenelle thus provided the two final ingredients to the idea of the progress of knowledge: that it would proceed indefinitely into the future, and that this indefinite extension was necessarily the case. If Seneca also came to all of these conclusions, they did not take firm root in ancient times. However, with Fontenelle this concept was part of the general rationalism of the period, and it ultimately emerged as the wider idea of progress that encompassed social progress.

On this Fontenelle was also like Seneca. Neither believed in the connection between progress in knowledge and progress with respect to either human virtue or human well-being. The difference, however, is that, for Seneca, if neither human virtue nor well-being (nor, I might add, creativity and aesthetic accomplishment) progressed, then there was no progress in what is most important. In Fontenelle one finds a change in emphasis. While, like Seneca, he does not believe that there is progress in wisdom or virtue, he celebrates what does progress—scientific knowledge. The difference, it seems, is that Seneca believed that technological progress, in fact, makes us worse off. It draws us away from a more simple and free life toward a more artificial way of being.

In England, somewhat separately, the quarrel between the ancients and the moderns was also pursued. Perhaps the most enduring contribution is Jonathan Swift's *A Full and True Account of the Battle Fought Last Friday Between the Ancient and the Modern Books in St. James's Library*. Known for short as *The Battle of the Books*, it details how inside the Royal Library the books of the ancients and the moderns came to life and did battle.

That Swift would conceptualize the conflict between the ancients and the moderns as a conflict between their books is more than a hint as to where he himself comes out. If, ultimately, the issue at stake in the debates over history is "what matters," for Swift the answer is "books." Books capture the value of a civilization, and like Duauf, the ancient Egyptian scribe, Swift believes that it is books that we should love.

In a clear identification with Homer, Swift wrote the key battle scene of *The Battle of the Books* in the style of *The Iliad*. Best of all, using a touch of Homer's own style, Homer himself becomes one of Swift's characters and enters the combat to vanquish his modern challengers:

> Then Homer slew W—sl—y with a kick of his Horse's heel; He took Perrault by mighty Force out of his Saddle, then hurl'd him at Fontenelle, with the same Blow dashing out both their Brains.[95]

The Battle ends with a defender of the Moderns (Wotton) being chased (and slain) by an ally of the Ancients (Boyle) in much the same fashion as Achilles chased Hector. Swift offers this good-bye to the dispatched Wotton: "And happy and immortal shall you be, if all my Wit and Eloquence can make you."[96] And again, Swift is right; it is Swift, through his dispatch of Wotton, who has given him what immortality he has.

This final victim, William Wotton, in his *Reflections Upon Ancient and Modern Learning*, did, however, make an important contribution. He deepened the distinction between art and knowledge. In the former he places poetry, oratory, architecture, painting, and statuary. In the latter: mathematics, natural science, physiology, and their dependencies. He maintained that in some of the arts the ancients were superior to all who came after. Here he strengthens a direction that Fontenelle was moving along. This distinction was widely accepted throughout the eighteenth century as literature and art were viewed as distinct from the general progress perceived in all other areas.

This is particularly interesting because the quarrel started roughly at the opening of the seventeenth century with the attack on Homer, and it appears to close with a sharper distinction between art and science and with a full idea of the indefinite progress of science. In the eighteenth century it is on this basis that the extension is made to social progress as a whole. This foreshadows a notion of social progress that is divorced from both aesthetic and moral progress. Indeed, this is part of the general mechanism in terms of which the idea of progress is able to achieve credibility: *the value base in terms of which progress is maintained gets narrower and narrower.* Now, rather than arguing that Homer has been equaled or surpassed, the entire realm of art, literature, and general sensibility is pushed to the side as a matter that no longer counts for much. The same is true of the concern with moral virtue, the central criterion employed by Seneca.

Thus, the idea of progress becomes plausible not merely because of the scientific revolution, but because there has been a shift in the relative weight given to the alternative criteria for assessing whether there has been progress.

Specifically, the emergence of the idea of progress required stripping from our definition of what counts as "progress" the aesthetic and moral dimensions of life. Instead, what we have left is the unstoppable progress of technology and its utilization in the production of the things of economic life. Thus, to think of history as the story of the inevitable improvement in the human condition, and to think of ourselves as fortunate consumers of an ever-expanding material pie, is really to think of two sides of the same coin.

MANDEVILLE'S FABLE OF THE BEES

Aristotle, Seneca, and peoples of the quite different orientations that dominated both the Middle Ages and the Reformation found common ground in the impossibility of conceptualizing human progress primarily in technological and economic terms, divorced from matters of human personality, character, and behavior. Whether it was a matter of ancient virtues of creativity, of artistic and literary perfection, or of piety, honesty, and religious virtue, there was little worth celebrating in economic expansion per se.

The opposite perspective emerges most powerfully in the beginning of the eighteenth century, crystallized in the works of Bernard Mandeville. In 1705, halfway between the 150 years that separate the landing of the Puritans in the New World and the publication of *The Wealth of Nations*, Bernard Mandeville published a twenty-six-page poem called "The Grumbling Hive: or, Knaves Turned Honest." In 1714, the poem reappeared as part of a much larger work entitled *The Fable of the Bees: or, Private Vices, Publick Benefits*. This larger work, which ran to several hundred pages, was a detailed explanation of the various theses maintained in the poem. Subsequent editions enlarged Mandeville's commentary on his own poem.

The book created considerable scandal, and at one point was determined to be a public nuisance by the Grand Jury of Middlesex. Ultimately Mandeville's explications required an additional work: *The Fable of the Bees: Part II*.

Mandeville's poem is an attack directed at those who would live the simple

life. When Mandeville wrote his poem, the great utopian experiment in religiously based simple living, the effort to build a "New England," was not yet
one hundred years old, the Plymouth colony having been founded in 1620.

All had not gone well for the project of simple living. From the pulpits of
New England the clergy denounced a materialism that had betrayed the
pious ideals of earlier generations. Yet the impulse toward pious simplicity
was still very much alive, and the great religious awakening of the 1730s that
swept through the colonies and called people back to a simple piety was still
decades away.

Mandeville was not concerned with New England, but with England herself. He is offering a cautionary message: look what would happen here if
those seekers after the simple life of virtue were to gain the upper hand.

The basic poem appears to be a simple tale. It is the story of a flourishing
hive of bees that, not having the sense to leave well enough alone, prayed
to the God Jove that they be made virtuous. Jove answered their prayer,
but virtue proved their ruin. My primary concern in calling attention to
Mandeville is not his novel empirical thesis (that private vice is beneficial to
the public good), but rather the values and perspectives that are implicit in
his thought. As we shall see, it is in this respect that Mandeville can be
viewed as the first great voice of what is today the dominant way of thinking
about economic life.

Stripped to its essentials, Mandeville is telling us that a thriving, prosper-
ous economy is what is important and that, if it turns out that such prosperity
requires behavior and character that violate religious, moral, or spiritual
ideals, then we best not trouble ourselves about such ideals.

Mandeville is the intentional voice of the great separation of economic life
from any project of human transcendence. He differs in one main respect
from contemporary voices. He is absolutely clear-eyed about the corruption
he accepts, while in contemporary life the separation he represented has
advanced to such an extent that we do not even perceive economic life within
the larger context of our ideals for human life and character.

Like many others, his tale is that of The Fall. But it is not a fall from grace,
innocence, or purity. Mandeville's Eden has a very particular character. Consider the happy state in which his bees originally find themselves:

> A Spacious Hive well stockt with Bees,
> That liv'd in Luxury and Ease;
> And yet as fam'd for Laws and Arms,

As yielding large and early Swarms;
Was counted the great Nursery
Of Sciences and Industry.[97]

The Hive is not just man's social life, it is life within the nation-state. It is life under a particular government "fam'd for Laws and Arms." The central accomplishment of that famed country is the achievement of a life of ease and luxury. It is this that will be lost, not the spiritual innocence commonly ascribed to Paradise. The bees in Mandeville's Paradise are far from innocent.

Among the inhabitants of the Hive there were "Sharpers, Parasites, Pimps, Players, Pick Pockets, Coiners, Quacks, South-sayers." This, of course, might be true of any society; there are always those who prey on it from the outside. But Mandeville tells us that while "these were call'd Knaves, . . . the grave Industrious were the same . . . All Trades and Places knew some Cheat, No Calling was without Deceit."

He then proceeds to describe, profession by profession, the universal deceit. He describes lawyers whose art was in "raising feuds" and inflating fees, of doctors who valued "Fame and Wealth Above the drooping Patient's Health." He tells us of a clergy that allowed men to "hide their Sloth, Lust, Avarice and Pride," of a military in which while "some valiant Gen'rals fought the Foe, Others took Bribes to let them go." It is the same with public servants who robbed "the very Crown they saved"; and of judges "brib'd with Gold."

Thus, Mandeville paints a picture of an entire society that is untrue to the values inherent in their social roles. It is a picture of decadence and corruption, but of a very particular kind. It is a corruption in which the pursuit of money supplants all the values that are inherent to the activity and profession in which people are engaged. It is precisely the kind of destruction of the integrity of each realm of life that Aristotle warned of. Indeed, Aristotle even offered doctors and soldiers as examples of such corruption.

But Mandeville views it all with an easy eye. Having painted this vivid picture, he takes his novel turn, maintaining that all this is to the good:

Thus every Part was full of Vice,
Yet the whole Mass a Paradise;
Flatter'd in Peace, and fear'd in Wars,
They were th' Esteem of Foreigners,
And lavish of their Wealth and Lives,

> The Balance of all other Hives.
> Such were the Blessings of that State;
> Their Crimes conspir'd to make them Great.[98]

He then proceeds to sketch how this worked. It seems that each vice produced some benefit. Thus,

> The Root of Evil, Avarice,
> That damne'd ill-natur'd baneful Vice,
> Was Slave to Prodigality,
> That nouble Sin; whilst Luxury
> Employ'd a Million of the Poor,
> And odious Pride a Million more:
> Envy it self, and Vanity,
> Were Ministers of Industry;
> Their darling Folly, Fickleness,
> In Diet, Furniture and Dress,
> That strange ridic'lous Vice, was made
> The very Wheel that turn'd the Trade.[99]

Mandeville's perception of "modern" life found its echoes two centuries later in Veblen and Galbraith. He zeroes right in on the issue of consumption; he looks at what lies behind consumer demand, and he finds vice and folly, vanity and envy, and even the fashion industry! Yet he embraces it all. And what is the central benefit he cites? It is the very luxuries and pleasures of economic growth that Seneca disdained when he distinguished wisdom from ingenuity:

> Thus, Vice nurs'd Ingenuity,
> Which join'd with Time and Industry,
> Had carry'd Life's Conveniencies
> Its real Pleasures, Comforts, Ease,
> To such a Height, the very Poor
> Liv'd better than the Rich before,
> And nothing could be added more.[100]

Here we have the celebration of modern economic life. It is the sharp polar opposite of the perspective voiced by Mandeville's contemporary, the

Quaker John Woolman, and sometimes it almost seems as if Mandeville and Woolman were debating before a single audience. While Woolman believed that a concern with "superfluities" turned us away from a virtuous life and was the source of injustice against the poor, slaves, and Indians, Mandeville simply affirmed that more was better. Mandeville's values are the ones that have dominated our economic thought. Since Mandeville first stated it, it has been repeated a thousand times: jobs and income, employment and higher per capita GNP. This is the bottom line.

The tale continues. The bees are undone because of their pursuit of virtue. They failed to recognize "the Bounds of Bliss." They called out for honesty, and Jove, in anger, "rid the bawling Hive of Fraud."

Bit by bit disaster sets in. With a change in motivation and appetite, market demand collapses. "The Price of Land and houses falls"; "The building Trade is quite destroyed, Artificers are not employ'd."

> The slight and fickle Age is past;
> And Clothes, as well as Fashions, last.
> Weavers, that join'd rich Silk with Plate,
> And all the Trades subordinate,
> Are gone . . .[101]

> As Pride and Luxury decrease,
> So by degrees they leave the Seas,
> Not Merchants now, but Companies
> Remove whole Manufactories.
> All Arts and Craft neglected lie;
> Content, the Bane of Industry,
> Makes 'em admire their homely Store,
> And neither seek nor covet more.[102]

Ultimately, the Hive is attacked by external foes, the bees fight and are forced to retreat. Many die, and the survivors fly off to a hollow tree. Implicit in the poem is an emphasis on and an argument for enhancing the power of the nation-state. The pre-Fall Hive is "fam'd for Law and Arms," and the ultimate denouement of the virtuous Hive occurs because they are attacked from without. Thus, the economy must be thought of as within a violent competitive international arena. National defense issues are central to issues of economic life.

As a diagnostician Mandeville is fascinated by the issue of human character. And the categories he is most concerned with are those of the Christian
tradition: avarice, envy, vanity, pride, etc. But he simply is untroubled by finding that such characteristics and motives pervade human life. Mandeville
not only doubts that much progress can be made in the elimination of base
motives; he is not even attracted to such transformations. If anything, he is
amused by the human spectacle.

Moreover, it is not that there is some other set of characteristics or virtues
that he is concerned about (e.g., Aristotelian courage or Nietzschean vitality).
He simply is not seized by the project of our becoming very different than
we are. Independent of his view of the utility of vices, Mandeville would
not be concerned to eliminate them. He simply accepts human beings as
they are, no matter how they are. In this, in fact, he echoes the contemporary "value-free" economist. The latter does not make any assessment about
people's desires; he takes them as a given. In academic jargon, economic performance is to be judged in terms of the ability to move to the outermost
curve on a preference map. On the validity of preference, the economist has
no opinion qua economist. Similarly Mandeville states that he is of the "opinion that, whether men be good or bad, what they take delight in is their
pleasure ... we ought to dispute no more about Men's Pleasures than their
Tastes."[103]

The question of what it means to be "better off" is of central importance
to any critique of economics. Certainly, one major criterion for the evalua-
tion of economic circumstances and alternative economic systems is whether
or not the population, or any representative individual, is better off in one or
the other. Mandeville tells us that "the very Poor Liv'd better than the Rich
before," and we look to his explication to reveal his understanding of what it
is to have "liv'd better."

He writes:

> If we trace the most flourishing Nations in their Origin, we shall
> find that in the remote Beginnings of every Society, the richest and
> most considerable Men among them were a great while destitute
> of a great many Comforts of Life that are now enjoy'd by the
> meanest and most humble Wretches.[104]

Here his answer appears to be quite simple. One's life is better insofar as one
has more of "the Comforts of Life." In the contemporary idiom, he may be

said to hold an opulence notion of standard of living: those who have more things live at a higher standard than those with less.[105]

Mandeville goes on to explain how our notion of what constitutes a luxury is constantly changing:

> Many things which were once look'd upon as the Invention of Luxury are now allow'd even to those that are so miserably poor as to become the Objects of publick Charity, nay counted so necessary, that we think no Human Creature ought to want them.[106]

He then goes on to identify some of the remarkable luxuries that are now available to all. He calls our attention to "the most ordinary Yorkshire Cloth," saying, "What depth of Thought and Ingenuity, what Toil and Labor, and what length of Time must it have cost, before Man could learn from a Seed to raise and prepare so useful a Product as Linen."[107] And he further points out:

> The Arts of Brewing, and making Bread, have by slow degrees been brought to the Perfection they now are in, but to have invented them at once, and a priori, would have required more Knowledge and a deeper Insight into the Nature of Fermentation, than the greatest Philosopher has hitherto been endowed with; yet the Fruits of both are now enjoy'd by the meanest of our Species, and a starving Wretch knows not how to make a more humble, or a more modest Petition, than by asking for a Bit of Bread, or a Draught of Smal Beer.[108]
>
> From Caves, Huts, Hovels, Tents and Barracks, with which Mankind took up at first we are come to warm and well-wrought Houses, and the meanest habitations to be seen in Cities, are regular Buildings contriv'd by Persons skill'd in Proportions and Architecture. If the Ancient Britons and Gauls should come out of their Graves, with what Amazement wou'd they gaze on the mighty Structures everywhere rais'd for the Poor![109]

While Mandeville does not use the term "progress" to characterize the phenomenon he has focused upon, it is clear that he is offering a progressive vision of history. This last passage, in which he speaks of the great architectural achievements, is remarkably similar to one quoted earlier from

Seneca, only Seneca dismissed the value of these technological triumphs and indeed saw the process whereby what had been thought of as luxuries are later considered necessities, as part of our enslavement. For Mandeville history moves in one direction, toward what is better. It does not move in the reverse direction. It is a slow process, one that Mandeville sees as a process of human betterment. This is, of course, credible, if one accepts Mandeville's notion of what it is to be better off: to have more of what one desires from the marketplace.

From our point of view Mandeville's significance is that he perfectly captured in 1705 so much of the way in which we presently think about economic life. The central elements of his outlook are the following:

1. a lack of concern with whether higher or lower aspects of the human personality are brought to the fore in the economic realm
2. his view of the economic realm as outside moral concerns, to be evaluated on its own terms (e.g., levels of employment, income, production, consumption)
3. his view that all classes gain as a result of economic growth
4. his underlying identification of "living well" with living at a high level of material consumption
5. his refusal to base policy judgments on any view of true human happiness other than those found within the actual behavior of economic agents (desire is never in need of education, development, or refinement)
6. his vision of economic policy as situated within the world of national security and interstate competition, with these areas providing the central criteria for policy making
7. his concern with the possibility of economic collapse and unemployment, and his focus on the importance of high levels of consumer demand as necessary for economic vitality

These are all very much a part of contemporary thinking. When Mandeville was writing, they represented a dramatic break with the way the Western world had heretofore thought of the economic realm. Today, we take them for granted.

In the poem, when Mandeville maintains that the poor lived better than the rich before, it might be thought that he has introduced a new criterion that would, in fact, represent moral progress over the way Aristotle viewed the good society—namely a concern for the poor. Yet, this is not the case. His comments on how the poor live better today than in previous centuries are little more than rationalizations. Indeed, in his attitudes toward the poor he is worse than indifferent. He states, "I have laid down as Maxims never to be departed from, that the Poor should be kept strictly to Work, and that it was Prudence to relieve their Wants, but Folly to cure them."[110]

And further, in explaining his opposition to providing free schools and provisions for the children of the poor, he wrote:

> Abundance of hard and dirty Labour is to be done, and coarse Living is to be complied with: Where shall we find a better Nursery for these Necessities than the Children of the Poor? None certainly are nearer to it or fitter for it. Besides that the things I called Hardships, neither seem nor are such to those who have been brought up to 'em, and know no better. There is not a more contented People among us, than those who work the hardest and are the least acquainted with the Pomp and Delicacies of the World.[111]

Mandeville continues:

> It being granted then, that abundance of Work is to be done, the next thing which I think to be likewise undeniable is, that the more cheerfully it is done the better, as well for those that perform it as for the rest of the Society. To be happy is to be pleas'd, and the less Notion a Man has of a better way of Living, the more content he'll be with his own. . . .
>
> As by discouraging Idleness with art and Steadiness you may compel the Poor to labour without Force, so by bringing them up in Ignorance you may inure them to real Hardships without being ever sensible themselves that they are such.[112]

A few rhetorical gestures notwithstanding, it is clear that for Mandeville the poor are a lesser form of humanity. Indeed, he is happy enough for them to live out their lives in total ignorance of their conditions—essentially as work animals. For him they are a mere means to greater objectives. When he speaks of public benefits, or of a flourishing economy, his concern is with the aggregate features of the economy and the polity that it sustains.

The fact that Mandeville is essentially unmoved, either by equity concerns or by the wretchedness of the lives of those at the bottom, helps to explain why it is that he can remain content with society as he finds it. Woolman's linkage between the pursuit of superfluous consumption and poverty, slavery and injustice (even if Mandeville accepted the connection), would have left him unmoved. He does not share in the passion for social justice that has animated the reformers and revolutionaries of the last several centuries.

Yet it was just this passion for a better world for the ordinary person that was to explode at the end of the eighteenth century with the French Revolution. From the perspective of the revolution, the condition of everyman matters most of all and with a new vision of what matters comes a new way of thinking about progress and history.

No figure better exemplifies this passion and this new vision than the French mathematician, historian, and political leader, Condorcet.

CONDORCET AND THE PROGRESS OF EVERYMAN

Born into a noble family, the Marquis de Condorcet was a leading figure during the French Revolution. In 1789 he was elected to the Commune of Paris and in 1791 to the Legislative Assembly, ultimately becoming its president. Yet, in 1793, as the revolution devoured itself, Condorcet went into hiding. Over a nine-month period he developed a two-hundred-page plan for his intended great work. This *Sketch for a Historical Picture of the Progress of the Human Mind* is all we have of this vision; later that year he was arrested and died in prison at the age of fifty-one.

In Condorcet we find the idea of progress in full bloom. He expresses it thus:

> Nature has set no term to the perfection of human faculties; . . . the perfectibility of man is truly indefinite; . . . the progress of this perfectibility, from now onwards independent of any power that might wish to halt it, has no other limit than the duration of the globe upon which nature has cast us.[113]

What is particularly interesting in Condorcet is his reconceptualization of the real subject matter of history. When history is seen as political history, it is filled with particular events: wars, assassinations, coronations, declarations, and rebellions. To Condorcet this was secondary; there are certain critical events in history, even critical political events, but this is not what history is about. These events take on their importance only insofar as they bear on something else.

For Condorcet, there is really only one story. It is the story of how mankind comes into an awareness of its ability to think for itself. It is the discovery of the power we possess in our own reason, our ability to learn and assess the world, each of us relying on our own rational abilities, free from reliance upon authority.

The issue of authority is central to Condorcet's account. The theme is reminiscent of the nineteenth-century essay "The Fixation of Belief," by the American philosopher Charles Peirce. Peirce considers the different ways in which people come to have and to hold their beliefs. He contrasts the "method of authority" with "the method of science." In Condorcet's world, this ultimate releasing of mankind from authority (that is, from the intellectual control of others) is the central theme of human history. Coming to be able to think for oneself, both in virtue of freedom from the control of others and in being capable of knowledgeable reflection, constitutes mankind's attainment of maturity. This, for Condorcet, is what matters.

Along these lines it is possible to take as one's subject matter "the human mind" or "the human spirit" and to see this as something that evolves over time, at first embodied most completely in one people and then in another people, great thinker, or philosophy. Hegel in fact did something of this sort. But what is most striking about Condorcet is that rather than thinking of "the human mind" as an abstraction, he took as the central subject of history the mind or mentality of the ordinary person. Going beyond this, he set this evolution of the ways of thought of the ordinary person within the context of a political struggle between the ruled and the rulers.

The central value in terms of which Condorcet distinguishes those changes that constitute progress from those that do not is the "freedom of the mind." This, however, has to be understood as being composed not only of a freedom from intellectual tyranny, but also a positive freedom that consists of the acquisition of the methods of rational inquiry. For Condorcet this development of the mind—a freedom from superstition, a freedom from authority, and the emergence of certain mental dispositions (e.g., intellectual self-confidence, habits of rational inquiry)—is of ultimate value. Condorcet, as much as anyone before or since, conceives of progress and of the history of mankind in terms of a movement toward enlightenment, understood in both its psychological and social dimensions.

Given what we said earlier about the centrality of books to the vision of progress (are those of the ancients superior to those of the moderns?), it is interesting to note that books continue, though in a different way, to be central for Condorcet. He focuses on the invention of printing. This invention serves to mark off the seventh from the eighth stage in human history. Only the invention of the alphabet, which marks the third from the fourth stage, has an equal place. In blissful ignorance of our own century, though sounding very much like those who now sing the praises of the Internet, he wrote:

> Has not printing freed the education of the people from all political and religious shackles? It would be vain for any despotism to invade all the schools; vain for it to issue cruel edicts prescribing and dictating the errors with which men's minds were to be infected, and the truths from which they were to be safeguarded. . . . The instruction that every man is free to receive from books in silence and solicitude can never be completely corrupted. It is enough for there to exist one corner of free earth from which the press can scatter its leaves. How with the multitude of different books, with the innumerable copies of each book, of reprints that can be made available at a moment's notice, how could it be possible to bolt every door, to seal every crevice through which truth aspires to enter? For though this was difficult enough even when it was only a question of destroying a few copies of a manuscript to annihilate it for ever, . . . has it not become impossible today when it would be necessary to maintain an absolutely ceaseless vigilance and an unresting activity?[114]

Thus, whether as the intrinsic touchstones of progress, or as the guarantor of intellectual liberation, books were again affirmed in their import. While enlightenment is at the core of Condorcet's conception of progress, it remained for Condorcet only part of the story. At the same time, he cites an increase in ordinary people's happiness as the criterion of progress. Here, as before, he is exceptionally clear in directing our focus toward those invisible millions upon millions who constitute the bulk of humanity. Indeed, he tells us that what actually happens to these people is the real touchstone of progress and the subject of history.

I will quote this at length, as it represents a genuine turning point in human understanding:

> Such are the subjects that ought to enter into a historical sketch of the progress of the human mind. In presenting it, we shall endeavor above all to exhibit the influence of this progress on the opinions and the welfare of the great mass of the people, in the different nations, at the different stages of their political existence. . . .[115]

> Up till now, the history of politics, like that of philosophy or of science, has been the history of only a few individuals: that which really constitutes the human race, the vast mass of families living for the most part on the fruits of their labor, has been forgotten, and even of those who follow public professions, and work not for themselves but for society, who are engaged in teaching, ruling, protecting or healing others, it is only the leaders who have held the eye of the historian. . . .

> It is this most obscure and neglected chapter of the history of the human race, for which we can gather so little material from records that must occupy the foreground of our picture. And whether we are concerned with a discovery, an important theory, a new legal system, or a political revolution, we shall endeavor to determine its consequences for the majority in each society. For it is there that one finds the true subject matter of philosophy, for all intermediate consequences may be ignored except in so far as they eventually influence the greater mass of the human race.

> It is only when we come to this final link in the chain that our contemplation of historical events and the reflections that occur to us are of true utility. Only then can we appreciate men's true claims to fame, and can take real pleasure in the progress of their reason; only then can we truly judge the perfection of the human race.

The idea that everything must be considered in relation to this single point of reference is dictated both by justice and by reason.[116, 117]

This is a great contribution. Both in its sophistication and its morality it truly represents progress over previous centuries of discourse. Here Condorcet not only puts forward a new conception of history, but a new standard in terms of which to decide whether history can be viewed as the story of progress: the condition of the common person.

But what does Condorcet mean by improvements in the condition of the common person? On the one hand he has this rich notion of enlightenment. On the other hand, when he speaks of human happiness and of those things that will advance it, he operates on a very basic and practical level. His predictions for progress in the future, which are in many instances prescient, include:

- voluntary birth control, based on "a duty towards those who are not yet . . . not to give them existence but to give them happiness"[118]
- "New instruments, machines and looms" that "add to man's strength and can improve at once the quality and the accuracy of his productions, and *can diminish the time and labour that has to be expended on them* [precisely what Aristotle did not understand— JMS]. The obstacles still in the way of this progress will disappear, accidents will be foreseen and prevented, the insanitary conditions that are due to the work itself or to the climate will be eliminated."[119]
- increased agricultural productivity
- social insurance, guaranteeing people in old age a "means of livelihood produced partly by their own savings and partly by the savings of others who make the same outlay, but die before they need to reap the reward"[120]
- an indefinite expansion of the life span through improved health and "the end of infectious and hereditary diseases and illnesses brought on by climate, food, or working conditions"[121]

What we find here are many of the elements that are emphasized in the politics of simplicity—a reduction in the arduousness of work, increases in the amount of leisure, increasing economic security, and improved health. Essentially, Condorcet is fleshing out how one would think of economic progress if one took it from the point of view of the life of the common person. Not as Mandeville asserted in terms of greater and greater luxury, but in terms of finally satisfying the core economic needs of everyman.

Condorcet himself was a transitional figure, and the values that he used in defining progress still included the older criterion—the moral perfectability of mankind. But this, as well as Condorcet's rich notion of enlightenment, did not endure. What did continue, however, was the notion that in deciding whether or not mankind has made progress, one should look at the conditions of ordinary people. Here, however, Condorcet's concrete approach to material well-being, in terms of health, food, security, leisure, and quality of work, never took hold.

Instead, what emerged was a cross between Mandeville's value-free endorsement of whatever the market produces and Condorcet's concern for everyman. In contemporary terms, this is growth with equity. For economists it is a rise in per capita GNP coupled with a concern for the Gini coefficient (which measures the degree of inequality of income). In short it is an embrace of the ever-expanding cornucopia of consumption, but with a concern that everyone gets a share.

The French social theorist Sorel maintained that the idea of progress was the ideology of the middle class. The values it ultimately embodies are those that Seneca rejected; they are the values associated with having more things, with expanded production, consumption, and acquisition. In short, they are the values associated with economic growth; the values of the economically rising class, the bourgeoisie. No one argued for progress on the grounds that there had been an expansion of the older values of the nobility: chivalry, military prowess, and personal fidelity. Nor was there progress to be found in terms of the Stoic values of inner freedom, self-understanding, wisdom, and peace. Nor was progress successfully argued on aesthetic grounds. Rather, the quarrel between the ancients and the moderns conceded that, in these terms, there may not have been progress. No, progress is evidenced first, as always, in the progress of knowledge and secondarily in the progress of technology and economic growth. So, one might say that the idea of progress is essentially a vision of history as seen through the values of a rising and democratizing middle-class consumer.

Whatever the limitations of this conception of progress, what it represents is an assertion of the importance of what happens to the middle class. And as almost everyone came to think of themselves as middle class, it represented a triumph of equality. Ultimately progress comes to be defined in terms of the well-being of individuals and, at least in theory, all individuals count and count of equal significance.

Today, we can dispense with the grand idea of progress, with the belief that history has been, and will continue to be, the story of progress. As a view of history this is both impoverished and naive. What we cannot dispense with, however, is a definition of progress. Ultimately this is a matter of values, and is at the heart of any politics. For a politics of simplicity, a good starting point is the definition implicit in Condorcet: an emphasis on the ordinary person, yet a concern with the extraordinary potentials of the human mind. This includes an awareness of the aesthetic realm coupled with a concern for the practical facts of economic life. This concern is with the material world, but rather than accepting unending acquisitiveness, it focuses on meeting core needs, increasing leisure, and reducing the arduousness of work. With this, an essential recognition of the importance of freedom is understood, in part, as each person's ability to think through for himself/herself the deepest questions of life and history and then to live accordingly.

TOWARD A MORE ADEQUATE DEFINITION OF PROGRESS

Interestingly, while the term "progress" does not play an important role in contemporary economics, the one area in economics in which there is considerable debate and innovation with respect to such matters is in what is called "development economics." Unfortunately this is generally understood as the economics of poor countries, but the issues apply to the rich countries as well. Here it is the term "development" that is the central issue.

In discussions of the Third World, the term is used with respect to a wide variety of subjects. Thus, we speak of economies as being undeveloped; we speak of political development; we speak of less-developed countries, of developing nations, and of underdeveloped societies. A comprehensive theory of development should offer an account of the relationship between these different applications.

Rather than focusing on economies, nations, or countries as that which gets developed, we might focus on societies, and say that a developed economy is one that sustains a developed society. But what is it for a society to be developed? Is this, also, the most basic notion of development? I think not. Instead, following Condorcet, we might say that societies are developed insofar as they give rise to human beings who are developed. It is the notion of the developed human being that is our central concept.

Insofar as there are a multiplicity of alternative conceptions of a developed human being, there will be a multiplicity of notions of a developed society and quite possibly of a developed economy. The immediate question has to do with how one is to link an appraisal of societies to judgments about the kind of human beings they give rise to. One perspective emphasizes the heights of human development. Here one would look primarily for greatness or its absence. Surveying world history from this perspective is the kind of enterprise that was undertaken by those caught up in the debate between the ancients and the moderns. When we do this, we find remarkable differences. There are certain periods in which the human spirit seems to flourish, in which a kind of brilliance and power of intellect and sensibility stand out. In Western history we typically identify the classical period in ancient Greece and the Italian Renaissance as two outstanding periods of human development.

From this perspective development is not linear and progressive; it comes and goes. Thus mankind's cumulative accomplishments are of less importance, and those who argued for the ancients had a plausible case. One can quite reasonably argue that the heights of human development were attained over 2,000 years ago; that in ancient Greece there was more creativity and human energy and a sharper sensibility and aesthetic awareness than at any time since. Their great thinkers were bolder and wittier than ours, their command of language and rhetoric more skillful. Their artistic creations were unparalleled, their skill and imagination rarely seen in human history. By contrast we appear confused, coarse, uncertain, mechanical, depressed, and misguided.

Against such a perspective, what have we to offer to suggest that, say, twentieth- (or twenty-first-) century America represents a more developed society than Athens of the fifth century B.C.E.? Our list might look something like this:

1. We know vastly more. The Greeks lived in considerable ignorance about the nature of the human and physical world. We have all the benefits of 2,500 years of discovery.

2. Our average level of consumption is considerably higher. True, one might doubt that the rich today live much more luxuriously than the ancient rich, but on the average we are considerably better off.

3. Their society depended on a slave class and an agrarian class that did not significantly partake in most of those things we celebrate with respect to ancient Greece, whereas over 50 percent of our high school graduates attend college.

4. The condition of women—half of the population—is radically different now. In ancient Athens women were under the control and tutelage of men. They were married as children to mature males and rarely left the household compound. In general, they did not partake in the vast creativity and democracy of Athens.

5. In terms of health and life span, we are considerably better off. True, the oldest today are much the same age as the oldest then, but our average life span is over seventy years, while theirs was probably more like twenty, with large numbers of children dying in infancy.

6. Presumably, the vast majority of the Greeks who had to work, worked much harder and longer than we have to. We have the advantage of our vast capital and technological base that not only provides us with more output, but requires less labor input.

What is interesting is that the case is not all that overwhelming. It is a strange mixture of considerations. Some seem very important; others less so. What emerges more than anything else, however, is that our claim to be more developed stands primarily on the breadth of human development achieved rather than on the height. Broad social injustices toward slaves, women, and underclasses have been considerably overcome. Our highest peaks of education, consumption, psychic health, ease of life, and political participation may have been equaled or surpassed by many ancient Greeks, but in our society these benefits are more widespread.

The issue goes well beyond Greece. It is unlikely that there have been any societies in which some people were not more fully developed than we are as a whole. Even in societies steeped in superstition and ignorance, societies without a written history, societies attached to human sacrifice, we will find individuals learned in their traditions, masters of their oral histories, creators of art and dance and music. We may not find other societies achieving either the heights or the breadth of human excellence found in Athens. But for whatever human attribute we value, be it intelligence, wit, creativity, craft, physical attainments, compassion, or moral breadth, we will always be able to find individuals who put us to shame. There are essentially two things that we do not find. One is accurate information (or knowledge, if you will), and the other is the widespread distribution of physical well-being.

Our advantage with respect to knowledge comes little from ourselves; it is largely the accident of our being here rather than there. Most of us have absolutely no capacity for adding anything to the stock of what is known by mankind. Despite what Condorcet hoped, we are like most people have always been. We believe what we have been told. The difference is only that, over the centuries, mankind has made significant progress in attaining a vast stock of accurate information. Similarly, our greater incomes and wealth come not from possessing greater human capacities, but primarily because we are fortunate enough to have inherited an enormous stock of physical and intellectual capital that vastly enhances our labor productivity.

Our claim to developmental progress, then, rests on two points:

1. a vastly broader attainment of material well-being and freedom
2. our vastly more extensive and accurate information and science

The second of these is largely instrumental. The difference between people who believed the Earth was flat and those who know it is round is simply not very important. What this suggests, then, is that our claim to greater development rests primarily on the breadth of well-being. Given the horrors of human domination over others, and the terrible sufferings of starvation and early death that peoples have experienced, this is no small accomplishment. But it is only half of the story. Using both dimensions, the extent of development of various societies could be represented on a graph such as this:

Aristocratic
dimension

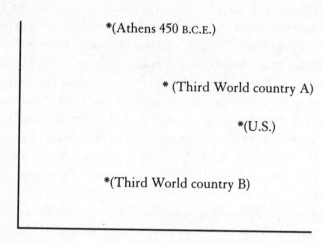

*(Athens 450 B.C.E.)

* (Third World country A)

*(U.S.)

*(Third World country B)

Egalitarian dimension

There are many ways to think of the vertical dimension. Some may consider it in terms of the spiritual level to which a society rises. Others might emphasize the moral virtues, or the aesthetics realm, or the intellectual. Taken together the two dimensions allow us to envision the developed society as an environment within which an ideal of the human person is attained both in height and in breadth—the greatest development of the greatest number.

Within this framework the case for a politics of simple living can be restated as the belief that the heights of human development are pluralistic, but that what they have in common is that they require a platform of achievement with respect to economic need. Once this platform of economic need satisfaction is achieved, however, attaining fuller development requires that people turn away from the economic realm to pursue things more important, and to exercise their higher capabilities.

What we look for in a developed economy, then, is that it provides this general platform of freedom from the economic for all persons. And it is on this platform that we individually and collectively seek a higher form of life.

PART II

TOWARD A PHILOSOPHY
OF SIMPLE LIVING

Chapter Six

GRACEFUL LIVING

For those of us in the broad middle class, it is often hard to say what is wrong with the way we live. It is not some single element, nor is it anything that we could plug in here and there and have things be radically different. It is a quality that pervades life in its entirety; my word for it is gracefulness. Within our contemporary world what is most striking is the near total absence of gracefulness.

To say that people live gracefully, or that they go through life gracefully, tells you quite a bit about what their life is like, both in its externals and in its internal experience. But there is much it doesn't tell you. For instance, it doesn't tell you what they do. Unless one thinks that it doesn't matter what people do but only how they do it, then at best gracefulness can be only part of an ideal of living. I focus on it not because it represents all that is important, but because it seems to me that which is most absent, even from the lives of those thought to be successful.

Understood as a quality of life, gracefulness is not what we readily associate with simple living. When we think of graceful living, the most natural way of picturing such a life is to see it as free of care, and to see that freedom as emerging from abundance, indeed, from overabundance, an abundance that is suffused with security and ease. The vision is not merely one of wealth but of the enjoyment of wealth, indeed, of the effortless enjoyment of wealth. It is not just money; it is money possessed and used with style—being elegantly wealthy, not just having tasteful things, but consuming them tastefully. In short, graceful living seems to imply a mastery of the art of being wealthy.

We typically associate such style not just with money, but with old money—that is with money that one is comfortable with to the point of second nature. It is money that not only serves life through the things of beauty that it provides, but does so effortlessly. Moreover, it is money that is *attained* gracefully. The magazines that picture graceful consumption rarely mention what one does to make that consumption possible. Indeed, it might break the spell if we knew. The implicit assumption, if not of inherited wealth, is that money comes easily.

It is not hard to disparage such images, but there is something terribly important to be learned about how to move gracefully in the world of things. This is not easily done; the ability to live gracefully, even for those who are rich, may require more than one generation. It may be that attaining this art of graceful living is something that is achieved over many years, and is handed down through the family—a tradition of knowing how to live and be.

Later I will argue that graceful existence does not depend upon significant material wealth, and indeed, to pursue gracefulness through material acquisition is a fool's quest. For now, however, my aim is to explore gracefulness itself. Just what is it? Whether or not an abundance of possessions is required, a graceful life is one of beauty, security, comfort, ease, and naturalness. It is a life that is free from overriding anxiety and ceaseless striving. It is largely peaceful rather than hectic. There may be adventure and challenge, but it is a life that does not suffer from constant hassle and hustle. As such, gracefulness is an achievement within the aesthetic of being. For most of us, except for rare islands in time, modern life is utterly devoid of gracefulness.

To live gracefully is to live within flowing rhythms at a human pace. It need not always be the same. There is gracefulness in fast dances and in slow dances—but most of us are not dancing at all. In a graceful life there is time to pay respect to the value of what you do, to the worth of those you care for, and to the possessions you own. Gracefulness is not possible when life is frenetic, when we are harried, or suffer from overload, time crunch, and a vast multiplicity of commitments and pressures.

When I first considered the term "graceful," in addition to its association with opulence, I had reservations because of its religious connotations. This is not a book about religion, nor is it about New Age spirituality. Saying grace and receiving grace initially seemed to be notions that have little to do with what is under discussion. In that I was wrong. Important linkages exist between grace in the religious sense and gracefulness as an aesthetic of life. Whether religion has any place in one's life or not, there are connections that are worth pondering. Consider the act of saying grace before a meal. Here the core is an attitude of thanksgiving, of appreciation. The focus is on recognizing the full value of what one has, rather than lamenting what one does not. While one can mouth the words, one cannot authentically begin a meal with a benediction of grace and at the same time maintain a sense of dissatisfaction with what one has. There is a certain peaceful contentment that is part of genuine thankfulness.

When one does approach a meal gracefully, one can look in two different directions. One can consider what one has against the "perspective of less," contrasting what one has with what others do not. This means seeing things against the backdrop of poverty, of hunger, of times and places of suffering and deprivation. Here the act of consumption is also a moment to see oneself and one's situation within the broader perspective of human experience, and so seen, to be thankful of what one has and more aware of what one has been lucky enough not to have experienced. Thus, one is thankful to have something to eat, when others have starved. And one is thankful to have friends and loved ones to share the meal with when others are lonely, and when there may come a day when those friends and loved ones are gone. This is the perspective of the commandment to remember that "we" were once slaves in Egypt.

Then there is another perspective, one that does not take its power from the contrast with deprivation and suffering, but rather seeks to put us in touch with the abundance in front of us. Here the appreciation of the food rests not on an awareness of hunger, but on how good this food is, of how remarkable a thing is the simple potato or the diverse ingredients of a salad or the crust on a good bread. And then to look around the table and take stock of those who are there, valuing them not against the possibility of loneliness but in virtue of the richness that they provide.

Here appreciativeness goes beyond thankfulness, to being open to the values that are inherent in something. This kind of appreciativeness requires a certain kind of experiencing. It is not primarily a matter of intellectual assent, but of an openness, of an accessibility to what is valuable, be it another person, a piece of music, a work of art, a spring day, or a great ball game. Often such appreciation is most present when we are young, when the world is fresh. As we age and as we get into our harnesses, our ability to take pleasure dulls. In other contexts appreciation is not automatically present but is the result of learning and exposure: for example, the appreciation of art and music, especially if it comes from other cultures.

This appreciativeness is an orientation that we bring (or more likely, fail to bring) to any of the things of ordinary life. Thus, with respect to food and meals, we may be oblivious to the difference between good cooking and bad, oblivious to the pleasure of eating off of a handsome dining table versus a card table. We may be blind to the value of those we eat with, blind to those we live with, blind to those we parent. Here we are appreciative not because we remember that we were once slaves in Egypt, but because we look at the splendor of what has been created and in imitation of the God of Genesis 1: "See that it is good."

Yet for this second kind of appreciation to be valid, there has to be something there to be appreciated. What if the tomatoes taste like rubber, the food is overcooked, the bread is dismal, the spouse is in a foul mood, and the children are obnoxious? Where is gracefulness then? What is there that is worthy of appreciation?

Thus, in this second sense, a graceful meal requires more than the appropriate attitude; it also involves the presence of a qualitative richness, what we might call "good fortune," so long as we do not view ourselves as passive with respect to whether such fortune is before us. This links to another dimension of the act of saying grace. The grace ritual requires that we take a moment before digging in, a moment of pause, a moment of quiet that gives a certain dignity to the meal. It separates it from what precedes it. In spirit, if not in practice, the initial benediction establishes a space that pervades the entire meal. When we have a meal in this way, we do not wolf down our food. We set the meal apart; the benediction allows us to break with the hectic pace of a busy day. To an extent it turns the meal into a ceremony. As such, it is not only a space worthy of appreciation, it is a space worthy of taking the time and energy to create properly.

Saying grace is not necessary for graceful living, nor as I understand it, does saying grace require any religious belief. But in its authentic form, making a place of grace out of the dinner table can be an important constitutive element of the aesthetic of life under consideration.

There is another religious connotation of grace found within some religious traditions (the idea of receiving something "by the grace of God") that may also seem at first only a different notion of grace, one that has nothing to do with the kind of graceful living under discussion. Here we are dealing with a theological doctrine that during the sixteenth and seventeenth centuries was the subject of fierce debate within Christianity. At issue was the question of how one attained salvation. Was salvation attained "through works"; that is, through living righteously in accord with religious commandments, through doing good, through attaining merit, through living a life that deserved to be saved? Or was salvation something that could not be obtained through the fulfillment of a contract? Was it the case that nothing that we could do could compel, even morally compel, God to dispense salvation? If we were to be saved it was through the free gift, through the grace of God alone.

What, if any, relationship does this religious conception of grace have to graceful living? Some of those within such religious traditions might maintain that it is only through the grace of God that we can ourselves attain a truly graceful existence. But this is not what I have in mind. Rather, it seems to me that in the religious conception it is God who is graceful. He is the dispenser, and what he gives he gives out of his grace, that is to say, he gives out of his bounty, not because he has to, not because he is morally compelled to, and not because we have earned it or covenanted for it.

Social existence is primarily a matter of giving to others and receiving from them. To live gracefully in a world of others implies gracefulness in these interactions. Yet this is what is sorely missing in our lives. On the most fundamental level we are too busy and too self-engaged to give much time or attention to others. What we do give is often limited to what we sense we are obligated to provide. Often what is done is done reluctantly, resentfully, or stingily. This stinginess runs through our relationships, be they fixed patterns of exchange or diverse social relations, be they relations between husband and wife, between parent and child, between friends, between boss and worker, between colleagues, or between telephone operator and phone caller. We don't have the time, patience, or interest for the other—often enough, even for those we call friends.

The flip side of this, however, is that people need opportunities to give of themselves. Often enough we long to be of importance to someone else. When there is no receptiveness to what we might want to give, we are bottled up, prevented from coming more fully into existence—whether by others, by the structures of interaction, or by structures of production. Thus, we may find ourselves devoid of significant opportunity, or devoid of the skills, or simply devoid of much to give. My father used to say that it was much harder for an old man to be without his wife than for an old woman to be without her husband, because a woman (but not a man) can always make herself useful to the children and grandchildren. Of course this perhaps tells us more about him personally, or about gender roles at a specific point in time, than it does of universal truths. But in a specific context, for a specific person, it may be true enough.

THE STRUCTURE OF GRACEFULNESS

It should be clear then that gracefulness is not a simple notion. We can speak of a person as graceful; we can speak of an activity as graceful. There is grace under fire, and grace under pressure. A home may be graceful, as well as a home life. There is a gracefulness that resides in a person's character independent of how he or she lives, and there is the gracefulness of specific patterns of behavior.

We might think of gracefulness as a way of being in the world. This is so, even when we think of that kind of graceful living that we associate with wealth. While our possessions themselves may indeed be objects of great beauty and elegance, merely being the possessor of them and having one's home filled with them does not make one's own life graceful. To live gracefully is to live in a certain form of interaction with the varied things of the world, be they material objects, other people, or even the environment.

In some situations what we refer to as graceful may be limited to overt behavior. For instance, one might characterize someone as having shown great grace when, under powerful emotions and disappointments, fears and anxieties, he or she succeeded in carrying off some responsibility with dignity—for instance, the candidate who makes a graceful speech conceding the election to his opponent. But beyond graceful behavior there is the deeper gracefulness of an inner peacefulness. This is a matter of a person's way of being, his way of relating to diverse events and changing circumstances. Such gracefulness is more than style and more than overt behavior. It is a way of taking in the world, of experiencing the world differently than others might experience it. This, in turn, is rooted in self-possession, in knowing who you are, and in being at peace with oneself. It goes too far to understand this as "keeping an even keel" no matter what happens, though that was the Stoic ideal. Gracefulness is not the opposite of emotionality, but it does mean a life that is free from overriding anxiety and insecurity.

Often this is a matter of proportionality, of responding to the world in relation to what is at stake. The ability to maintain gracefulness in the face of a world that frazzles others is not then a matter of surface presentation, of pretense, or of holding things back. Rather, it comes from seeing things in a perspective that others often cannot, from knowing what one's real wealth is and seeing that it is not threatened.

For the Stoics, who placed central value on this kind of inner tranquillity, this was urged as the response to every kind of situation because they urged a self-definition so restricted that one would be virtually immune to external threat. But one need not go down this road. Rather, we should recognize that gracefulness itself has its appropriate limits, and that here, too, it rests not just on our inner makeup but also on the good fortune of an external environment that is not overly hostile. Thus, a politics of simplicity might seek to facilitate gracefulness by dealing with the real-world sources of human insecurity, not merely through inner transformation.

A useful way of thinking about graceful living is to see it as an interaction between two factors: an inner capability coupled with an external environment (what I have referred to as "good fortune"). We can think of this almost as an equation:

$$(\text{Good fortune}) \times (\text{Inner Orientation}) = \text{Gracefulness}$$

If we represent gracefulness as a fixed number, then there are many different pairs of multiples that equal that number. While neither can equal zero, each can range quite widely. For any specific level of gracefulness, the more good fortune one has the less one is dependent upon having achieved a special inner orientation. And conversely, the more one has the appropriate inner orientation, the less one is dependent upon good fortune. In seeking a graceful existence, there have been those who have placed all the emphasis on one or the other aspect. Thus, one might characterize various philosophic and religious traditions (e.g., Stoicism, Buddhism, or certain forms of Christianity) as offering paths to a graceful way of being in the world (including even the ability to face death gracefully) that are independent of good fortune. At the other end of the spectrum there is the radically different outlook that seeks to dispense entirely with what we bring to each aspect of life, and sees gracefulness as something that can be attained merely through good fortune.

Where does the truth lie? It does not, perhaps, lie in a single place. Perhaps, in principle, both extremes are possible. But the extremes may also be largely irrelevant to the situations and the psychological givens of most people. In the search for gracefulness the approach of more general usefulness is one that recognizes both dimensions.

Thus, a politics of graceful simplicity is not a substitute for the development of inner capabilities; rather, it looks for those points where collective actions can serve to improve our good fortune. In doing so, it responds to the fact that so many of the situations in which we find gracefulness lacking are contexts that are related to broad social transformations. Thus, for example, achieving gracefulness is harder in our world than it was for those privileged Athenians who did so within a context of slavery, economic servitude, and the subjugation of women. Today, even when we find great inequality, we do not encounter subservience; that comes only when such distinctions are accepted as normal and proper. This refusal of people to accommodate themselves to inequality (which must be applauded) is itself a cause of many of the rough edges in our social life, be it in the interactions between racial groups, or the tensions between men and women within the household, or the upward economic drive of ordinary people who refuse to accept the idea that they are entitled to less of the good life than others.

The varied dimensions of gracefulness are not isolated elements, but interacting facets. One of the ways they come together is in a broader conception of beauty. Beauty, for instance, can of course be found in material things, but there is also an inner beauty that itself involves a simplicity and purity of motivation. This in turn is related to an underlying tranquillity and self-possession that comes from being at peace with oneself.

In trying to picture what life looks like when these multiple elements of beauty—the aesthetic of time, inner tranquillity, appreciativeness, generosity, and inner and outer harmony—are conjoined, one is tempted to say that this is a way of being not for humans, but for gods. In the extreme, perhaps this is true. But for ordinary mortals these matters of degree make an enormous difference in the tenor of life.

In what follows I want to consider three paths toward a more graceful existence. Each has a long provenance. They are: the observance of the Sabbath, the construction of utopian communities, and the attainment of wealth. I start with Sabbath observance because for many it offers the most accessible point of entry into both simple living and gracefulness.

What is the connection between the Sabbath and simple living? Well, consider that for those who are doing well, the greatest dissatisfaction with their life seems to be the constant time pressure, the constant rush, and the inability to simply relax in time. Often we feel that we cannot "afford" a true day of rest. But how is it that we do not have a four-day workweek or a six-hour workday? Why do we need two parents working full-time outside the home? How can it be that three thousand years ago, when people lived in what today would be seen as material poverty, they were able to proclaim one day of the week a day of rest? And three thousand years later, not only have we not moved beyond a two-day weekend, but we have instead turned the weekend into a space for catching up on the hundreds of tasks we were unable to do during the week? Sabbath observance, even if not fully adhered to, is still part of our culture, and a demonstration that for thousands of years, we were indeed able to "afford" a break with our business, at least for one day a week.

GRACEFUL LIVING AND THE CONCEPT OF THE SABBATH

What exactly is it to have a Sabbath, to keep the Sabbath? In his book, *The Sabbath,* Rabbi Abraham Heschel says the following:

> The meaning of the Sabbath is to celebrate time rather than space. Six days a week we live under the tyranny of things in space; on the Sabbath we try to become attuned to holiness in time. It is a day on which we are called upon to share in what is eternal in time, to turn from the results of creation to the mystery of creation; from the world of creation to the creation of the world.[122]

Heschel writes, "He who wants to enter the holiness of the day must first lay down the profanity of clattering commerce, of being yoked to toil. He must go away from the screech of dissonant days, from the nervousness and fury of acquisitiveness and the betrayal in embezzling his own life."[123]

It is critical to remember that the Sabbath is intended to be a single day standing in contrast with the rest of life. This is very different from, say, the Stoic message, which also seeks to free us from self-induced bondage, but which advances a general way of going through life. The Sabbath is an approach to one day of the week.

There is a strong dose of realism in this Judaic focus on a single day. It does not ask people to abandon the world, nor does it ask for them to engage in rarely attainable personal transcendence. Rather it established both for the individual and for the society a rule that there would be this one day off. It was "off" in a very full sense, not a switch from fieldwork or commerce to household toil. Yet, it is doable without utopian change.

There are several distinct aspects to this ancient injunction. First, it is *public* in that it involves the regulation of overt behavior and social interaction. Second, it is *private and internal* in that it requires a change in personal attitude to actually achieve the spirit of the day. Indeed, without the personal component the commandment is not truly fulfilled. Heschel writes, "Not only the hands of man celebrate the day, the tongue and the soul keep the Sabbath. One does not talk on it in the same manner in which one talks on weekdays. Even thinking of business or labor should be avoided."[124] Thus, it goes beyond the behavioral limits of policy to an inner realm. And third, it is *mandatory*: a social rule that in the Old Testament is intended as a matter of law, a rule for the entire community. Indeed, not just a law, but a basic law, the fourth of the Ten Commandments.

Viewed from the point of view of economics, observing the Sabbath represents a decision with respect to the income/leisure trade-off. Though as a social rule rather than an individual choice, it is a decision that we make collectively. Insofar as there is a trade-off between the contribution to the good life that comes from labor and commerce and that comes from withdrawing from the world of things, the Sabbath injunction says that the quality of life requires that we free ourselves from work at least some of the time. It is both an injunction in behalf of leisure, and an injunction about the use of that leisure.

The Sabbath is to be a day of rest. Exactly what rest means needs to be clarified. Heschel maintains that rest is an art. It is something to be learned, and involves a harmony of body, mind, and imagination. The restfulness of the Sabbath is not slothfulness. It requires discipline of its own sort.

On the one hand the Sabbath "is not an occasion for diversion or frivolity; not a day to shoot fireworks or to turn somersaults, but an opportunity to mend our tattered lives."[125] On the other hand, it is not a day of mortification, quite the contrary. We are told, "Sanctify the Sabbath by choice meals, by beautiful garments; delight your soul with pleasure and I will regard you for this very pleasure."[126]

This emphasis on choice meals, beautiful garments, and pleasures found with each other is a good starting point for understanding graceful simplicity. There are pleasures of the day, but they are simple pleasures. They are pleasures of meals together, of good food, of good behavior and company, of quiet time, and of attractive surroundings. Proper Sabbath observance, on this account, then involves knowing how to live, which is knowing how to take certain kinds of pleasures. It is in some ways a sophisticated, religious, once-a-week form of epicureanism. Understood as a religious injunction, the Sabbath is not an injunction to turn away from the world, but rather an injunction to turn away from an instrumental engagement in the world. Instead, it is a remarkable injunction to experience that which is intrinsically valuable. It says, at least once a week, "Thou shalt live well!" It offers an account of that living that might be called graceful, both in the attitudes of peace and thankfulness, and also in the partaking of that for which one should truly be thankful.

Heschel speaks of tranquillity, serenity, peace, and repose. He uses the Hebrew term *"menuha,"* which is often translated as "rest," saying that "to the biblical mind, menuha is the same as happiness and stillness, as peace and harmony. . . . it is the state in which there is no strife and no fighting, no fear and no distrust. The essence of good life is menuha."[127] Thus, on this account, correct Sabbath observance involves, for that one day, a graceful (i.e., tranquil, harmonious) existence. This is something that is conceived as being available to all, be they rich or poor.

On the Sabbath one is proscribed from using not just capital goods utilized in production, but also a vast array of complex consumption goods. Thus, the religiously observant do not drive, they do not use the telephone, or the home computer, or the video recorder, or the stereo. In short, while the Sabbath day can be viewed as a form of the good life, it is a form in which much of the modern mode of consumption is rejected.

Heschel writes, "In regard to external gifts, to outward possessions, there is only one proper attitude—to have them and to be able to do without them. On the Sabbath we live, as it were, independent of technical civilization: we abstain primarily from any activity that aims at remaking or reshaping the things of space."[128] If this is correct, that on the Sabbath we live independent of technical civilization, then the graceful state of mind is combined with a radical simplicity of consumption.

Yet, this seems a gross overstatement of what actually occurs on the Sabbath. Surely one lives in the same house as on any other day—and the house is the main possession of most people. True, one abstains from, say, driving a car, but one still partakes of the car in eating the food that was brought by car the day before. As for technical civilization, there are orthodox homes in which the lights go on with timers so that the individual can abstain from turning them on.

Even among the most Orthodox Jews, in actual practice, the removal from technical civilization is limited and, in part, only a symbolic removal from technical civilization. Indeed, it is hard to see how it could be otherwise. For instance, the Orthodox will not answer the phone on the Sabbath, but should the higher commandment to save life be engaged, the phone is there for a call for an ambulance and a ride to the hospital for the best health technologies available. What this means is that the security provided through these devices of technical civilization is also present throughout the Sabbath.

While the Sabbath involves some simplification, it does not make a radical break with technical civilization. It clearly is not, and perhaps could not be, a one day a week removal from technical civilization. Technical civilization is not so easy to remove oneself from. Insofar as one is a consumer of a large array of durable consumption items, it is not really possible to separate oneself from them for a given day.

THE SABBATH AND SIMPLICITY

The Sabbath exists as a commandment and as an institution for all, those of average means as well as the rich and the poor. Thus, it would seem that just as there can be graceful opulence and graceful simplicity, so, too, can there be the Sabbath of the rich and the Sabbath of the poor. Opulence is not necessary, but it is also not incompatible with authentic Sabbath observance.

The mere fact that the Sabbath commandment falls equally on all is suggestive. It tells us that (a) even for those who are lacking in material goods and can ill afford to take a day to rest, it is more important still to maintain the Sabbath, and (b) even for those who make a great contribution to the community through their work, be they rich or poor, it is more important for the community that they abstain.

Deuteronomy 5:15 states that on the Sabbath:

> Thou shalt not do any manner of work, thou nor thy son, nor thy daughter, nor thy man-servant, nor thy maid-servant, nor thine ox, nor thine ass, nor any of thy cattle, nor thy stranger that is within thy gates; that thy man-servant and thy maid-servant may rest as well as thou.

Thus it is not merely that we can do no work on the Sabbath, but in addition, we may not have others do work for us. The Sabbath is enjoined on our servants and even upon the stranger within our land.

Thus, the Sabbath injunction forbids the receiving of personal service work from others. In this critical respect the Sabbath does require limiting consumption. While the Sabbath may be spent in a fine home, and with fine food and furnishings and dress, in this one central dimension of opulence, the receiving of personal services, we are restricted. Indirectly, of course, one can still benefit from the personal services one receives on the other days; for instance the food one consumes might have been prepared the day before by the cook, if one is wealthy enough to have a cook. But at least on that day, no one actually extracts the labor power of another. The cook may have prepared the food beforehand, but at least we serve it ourselves.

From an economic point of view this restriction on receiving personal services one day a week places off limits one-seventh of the amount of labor power that any person can in general require or utilize—though it can be argued that more is then demanded on the other six days. To see the implications of this injunction, consider if it went further. Suppose that for six days of the week no one was allowed to perform personal services for others. The result of this would be a great qualitative equalization of consumption. Suppose that there was an extremely wealthy 10 percent of the population, and that each of these persons had at their disposal several servants. If suddenly their use of servants was restricted to just one day a week, this would represent a vast reduction in the disparities between the classes. True, the unspent income saved on services could be spent on goods or on seven times as many servants for just one day, but this would represent a radical change in what it was to be rich. A ban on hiring personal services significantly moves the life experience of the rich in the direction of the middle class.

Of course the Sabbath injunction does not go that far, applying to only one day. Yet even so, it represents a major assertion of an ideal of human equality, mandating that at least one-seventh of the time, no matter how wealthy we are, we will not have others serving us. Thus, on that one day, our consumption of goods and services is quite significantly reduced, of goods because certain kinds of consumption are proscribed, and of services because none are allowed to provide them.

THE SABBATH AND COVETOUSNESS

Heschel maintains that there is a critical relationship between the fourth and the tenth commandments—between keeping the Sabbath and not coveting.

He sees the Sabbath as the key to the fulfillment of the not coveting commandment, arguing that by observing the Sabbath and by developing a life that is a "pilgrimage to the seventh day," one displaces coveting the things of space for things of time. He says, "The longing for the Sabbath all days of the week . . . is a form of longing for the eternal Sabbath all the days of our lives."

Heschel calls attention to that form of the commandment which says, "Remember the Sabbath" as opposed to merely "Keep the Sabbath." The implication is that the way that we live on the Sabbath is to be remembered during the rest of the week, and is to serve as an antidote to the coveting of things, even when we are not involved in direct Sabbath observance.

Lifted out of the religious context, and stated in terms of graceful existence, this amounts to a suggestion that having actually and regularly experienced a taste of the truly good life (i.e., graceful existence), one knows that it does not depend on vast accumulation, and that this knowledge is liberating. It serves to weaken the acquisitive desires.

THE SABBATH AS AN IDEAL FOR THE ENTIRE WEEK

My interest is to explicate the notion of gracefulness, not as a way of living one day out of seven, but as a general mode of life. To this end I have focused on the Sabbath and wonder if it might not be turned into an ideal for life as a whole. To what extent can we make an architecture out of time that is quite the reverse of six plus one? Why not have one day of work and six days of rest? Or if we can afford it, why not have seven days of rest? Is the problem only that we must work more than one day, or is it that the Sabbath ideal does not make sense if extrapolated to the entire week? Does authentic Sabbath observance offer an ideal for life as a whole, toward which we should aspire, and in terms of which we can measure progress, viewing three such days as better than two, and two as better than one?

Consider the suggestion made by Thoreau:

The order of things should be somewhat reversed, the seventh should be man's day of toil, wherein to earn his living by the sweat of his brow, and the other six his Sabbath of the affections and the soul—in which to range this widespread garden.[129]

What are we to make of Thoreau's suggestion? First off, his conception of the Sabbath is not the same as Heschel's. Thoreau's focus is centered on liberation from days of toil. He is telling us that we work too much and enjoy the good life too little, and that if we were to learn to live with less we might well be able to liberate ourselves from excessive work.

If the seventh day is seen merely as the absence of toil and an opportunity for enjoyment, then perhaps this is not very complicated. But if the Sabbath is seen as Heschel understands it, then can this ideal be extrapolated to six or seven days, or is it inherently restricted to a limited portion of life?

The one-day character of the Sabbath ideal emerges when we consider this:

> The Sabbath is no time for personal anxiety or care, for any activity that might dampen the spirit of joy. The Sabbath is no time to remember sins, to confess, to repent or even to pray for relief or any thing we might need. It is a day for praise, not a day for petitions. Fasting, mourning, and demonstrations of grief are forbidden. The period of mourning is interrupted by the Sabbath. And if one visits the sick on the Sabbath one should say: "It is the Sabbath, one must not complain; you will soon be cured." One must abstain from toil and strain on the seventh day, even from strain in the service of God. . . .
> It is a sin to be sad on the Sabbath day.[130]

So understood, the Sabbath ideal cannot be extrapolated to an ideal for all seven days. Life itself is far too rich to be contained within the framework of the quiet of Sabbath observance. Where is the time for passion, for sport, for physical exertion, for struggle for social change, for heated debate, or for self-governance?

Heschel writes that the passage from Exodus 35:3, "Ye shall kindle no fire throughout your habitations on the Sabbath day," has been interpreted to mean, "Ye shall kindle no fire of controversy nor the heat of anger."[131] Thus, if it were viewed as a seven-day ideal, the emotional state of the Sabbath would at the very least represent a totally transformative psychological orientation equivalent in its denial of certain emotions to Stoicism in its most ambitious form.

If graceful living is not the Sabbath writ large, then what is its relationship to the Sabbath? Because the Sabbath is lived gracefully, it serves at least as an example of one kind of gracefulness, of how a day might be passed gracefully, even if it is not a model for all days. Even if it is not a model for all, it can be a model for more than one day. For instance, Sabbath gracefulness is not just a matter of abstention from work, but requires being at inner peace. So, too, is inner peace a general dimension of graceful existence.

Sabbath observance, while compatible with opulence, does not require it; nor does the essential quality of the Sabbath seem to be reduced in its absence. Thus, the gracefulness of Sabbath simplicity points toward the general possibility of graceful simplicity. Moreover, just as graceful existence for all is difficult to achieve if there is general opulence (and thus a need for extensive personal services and an absence of service providers), so, too, does the general requirement that all participate in the one-day gracefulness of the Sabbath result in even the rich being thrown back on the self-provision of personal service on that one day.

Finally, if graceful living is not the extrapolation of Sabbath observance to the entire week, how does the Sabbath itself, as a religious observance, fit into graceful existence? Of course, Sabbath observance is compatible with graceful living; yet one cannot say that it is required. One can imagine graceful living in which there is no special day. Nonetheless, the idea of a Sabbath, of a day that stands out as a quieter, fuller disengagement from the world, with the remaining six being themselves graceful, and vibrant, and self-justifying, does offer itself as a particularly attractive pattern of existence. Moreover, for millions of hectic contemporaries, people whose thinned family traditions still retain some contact with that Judeo-Christian-Islamic tradition that affirms the importance of the Sabbath day, getting serious about setting aside this one day for graceful existence may be the most potent point of entry into simple living.

GRACEFUL EXISTENCE AND WORKDAYS

The ancient Sabbath commandment may have been the first law in history that was prolabor. As noted earlier, after 3,500 years we have, at very best, gone from one day off to two. Except for the very young or the very old, earning a living is overwhelmingly the single activity in which we are, at any given time, most likely engaged, other than sleeping. Taken broadly, this is not just the 2,000 hours a year on the job but also years spent in preparation for the job market and countless hours each year expended in thinking about or recovering from one's work experience, as well as vast amounts of time simply preparing for work, getting there, and getting home again. All together, it is reasonable to assume that we spend one-third of our working years asleep and 50 percent of the remaining time directly or indirectly in the effort to earn a living.

What happens during these working hours often determines whether a graceful existence is possible. It is easy to see how work can function as a destroyer. Can one live gracefully if one is never free from work, if one not only goes to work all one's days, but, further, allows it to follow one home at night? Can one live gracefully if one lives in fear of loss of job and income? Can one live gracefully if work leaves one physically or mentally depleted?

For work to be part of a graceful existence it must be in respectful harmony with the other parts of life. It must not distort the entirety of the whole; it must not deplete and overwhelm the other realms; it must respect each component of life.

Work represents a great challenge to graceful living because gracefulness is an aesthetic for all of life. It is not merely for one or two days off from work, nor does it merely describe our homes as if achieving grace were a matter of graceful dining and tasteful furniture. Graceful existence involves our work, our relations with our children and our friends, even our relation to political change and struggle. Above all else, gracefulness must be found in that which we do.

With respect to work, there are two alternative strategies that are possible. The first is the strategy of escape. It views work as inherently, or at least incorrigibly, incompatible with graceful existence, and thus one should do as little of it as possible. This perspective is often extended to work inside the home as well.

In this outlook, which was discussed in chapter two under the heading "Working Less Through Financial Independence," rather than trying to make work into something that it is not, people should seek out the highest-paying employment they can attain (consistent with their values), and thereby meet their strictly limited consumption needs with the shortest work hours possible. One approach is to concentrate these discordant hours within a limited part of one's life span. Thus, rather than working until one is sixty-five and then retiring, if when young one goes after very high paying employment, reduces consumption to the bare minimum, and invests one's savings wisely, one might be able to retire at forty, or at least reduce future work time dramatically. Thus, at the expense of, say, fifteen years of the wrong kind of work, one might be able to live a life of graceful simplicity for the next forty or fifty years.

For some people, under some circumstances, this makes sense. But a variety of considerations might make someone unwilling to embark on such a strategy:

- ✦ an unwillingness or inability to undertake the radical reduction in consumption required to significantly reduce future work time
- ✦ an inability to find, or unwillingness to undertake, the truly high paying employment required by the strategy
- ✦ the danger that the psychological costs of engaging in the wrong work for a sustained period of life are simply too high
- ✦ the belief that there is a better option, that work can be found or transformed in ways that do not make it antithetical to the good life[132]

It is this last possibility that I want to examine. Thoreau said that the central issue is "how to make the getting of our living poetic!" Indeed, Thoreau warned, "if it is not poetic, it is not life but death we get."[133] From this perspective we do not try to eliminate work, but rather to find that form of work that is our poetry.

The early-twentieth-century writer Sinclair Lewis explored this theme in his novel *A Work of Art*. It was the tale of two brothers, one a painter, the other a hotel manager. As it turns out, it is the "artiste" who is the Philistine and the hotel manager whose work emerges as a grand poetic enterprise. Lewis's instruction to us is that we should not assume that only certain kinds of work, in particular certain forms of fine art, might constitute our human poetry. Yet, having internalized Lewis's lesson, it would be a mistake to imagine that you can turn just any job into poetic form.

Consider, for instance, the issue of workplace dignity. Dignity, I would argue, is a component of work that is graceful. To see this relationship between dignity and gracefulness, let us step back from the workplace for a moment.

Imagine first a young and beautiful dancer who moves gracefully across the stage; her movements are elegant and liquid. Now a second figure appears. She is an elderly woman of great dignity, also walking across the stage. She is stiff and in need of a cane. Yet she is composed and erect. As different as these two are, there is a point at which the gracefulness of the one and the dignity of the other come together. The common point is in their carriage, in their bearing. To each there is a center, a certain wholeness of self.

Inner dignity is a structural feature of the personality, a wholeness, a sense of pride in who you are, an inner compass, a set of central values and purpose, an understanding of what you will do and what you will not do, an inner peacefulness that rests in a knowledge of what is of import and what is not. These different dimensions come together in a determination or a refusal to fully subject oneself to the arbitrary will of another.

We sometimes speak of people being stripped of their dignity, and this occurs when, out of fear or under threat, they are made to do things that violate that inner compass. Individuals with inner dignity do not lightly abandon their own standards. Indeed, there are some things that some people would not do even under pain of death.

This unwillingness to bow down is a metaphor, but for what? It cannot be a simple refusal ever to compromise, for there can be no life without compromise. Indeed, every choice involves a trade-off, a decision to abandon this in order to have that. Yet to carry oneself in life with an inner dignity is to never abase oneself, to never be fully for sale. It means that there are limits.

Workplace dignity, and thus gracefulness, implies first that people come to the workplace with a sense of dignity. They know who they are; they have specific values both for themselves and their work. They are not there to punch a clock but, in some sense, as professionals who take pride in their work. It is this sense of pride and internal standards that is regulating, not the foreman, or the threat of dismissal, or the search for gain. In the work itself this pride must not be violated. One is not coerced into acting against oneself, or in compromise with oneself. One is not subject to the arbitrary rule of others. This is not to say that one must be self-employed, but rather that, if employed by others, there must be a continued respect for the worker as an autonomous contributor to a task that accords with his or her deepest values. If this does not occur, work is not free. But how many jobs actually respect that free dignity of the individual who would find and express his inner poetry?

Gracefulness within one's work life is also expressed through what I have termed generosity or "graceful giving." To give gracefully is to give unmotivated by any expectation of return, and to give unmotivated by any sense of obligation, either legal or moral. It is to give out of one's inner bounty, in celebration of one's inner riches.

Such graceful giving is sometimes thought of as reserved for certain relationships or spheres of life. Thus, within an inner circle, perhaps a circle of expanded selfhood, such as among one's children, a parent might give gracefully. Or perhaps a love relationship might be such that each partner gives to the other out of their own bounty. Or perhaps it is so with friends. So conceived, as a relationship untainted by the exchange of money, gracefulness would seem to be incompatible with paid employment.

But rather than search for realms that are pure, the more useful way to think about graceful giving is to consider *within each act* the extent to which that which is given is done unmotivated by expectation of return. For very few of us is it true that we come to the workplace unmotivated by financial reward. We must earn a living, and we do not have the luxury of being where there is no financial return.

We come to the workplace, to any workplace, with monetary return as an impetus for our being there. But the real issue is not how one gets there, but rather what occurs on a moment-by-moment basis, day in and day out, when one is there. When on the job, in the profession, behind the counter, on the phone, at the computer, or in the meeting, to what extent are one's actions permeated by a generosity of spirit, by a graceful giving of oneself to others, to a cause, or to a project? Or to what extent are one's actions typically restrained and limited, either by the structures of work and employment, or by resentment over the fundamentals of the employment relationship itself?

Whether one gives gracefully within one's work depends in part on the person himself. But it is of central importance that work often severely restricts the opportunities for graceful giving. The most fundamental reason for this is that the work environment and indeed the determination of both the intended work product and the process, except for self-employed individuals and professionals, is largely decided by others. Typically, little or no priority (or even awareness) is given to the creation of opportunities for graceful work.

What we see then is that attaining graceful existence, both outside work and within work, is no easy task. It may not be a task that can be achieved if we seek it only in our individual lives. Understood as beauty, peacefulness, appreciation, and generosity, it certainly is not a residue that emerges just from consuming less. To live gracefully and simply is to have mastered an art; to learn to do so is not easy, and rather than thinking of it as something attained or absent, gracefulness might best be thought of as a dimension that may be more or less present in our lives as individuals, as families, and as a culture.

Chapter Seven

GRACEFUL LIVING AND RETREATING FROM THE WORLD

I have used the notion of the Sabbath, and in particular Heschel's brilliant analysis of it, to provide entry into the notion of graceful existence. In that discussion I pointed out that, unlike Thoreau's aspiration, the Sabbath was intended not for seven days but for one. Sabbath observance, though it may affect all the other days, leaves much of the rest of life largely in place.

Let me now turn to a different perspective, one that also emerged in the earliest periods of Western civilization, but that, in fact, seeks a form of gracefulness as a general way of life, a seven-day affair. Here, while religion plays no part, the attainment of graceful existence requires turning away from opulence and its pursuit. More generally, it requires turning away from the central pursuits of daily life. Indeed, it seeks to find the good life by constructing a refuge from the world at large. Today many idealize the home as such a refuge, but at other times it was thought that we could find the good life by taking retreat as an entire community. This vision of life was first articulated by the Greek philosopher Epicurus.

In some ways Epicurus is a puzzle. Perhaps this is because we have so little of his actual writings. He was said to have written 300 manuscripts, which, if true, would make him among the most prolific of writers the world has witnessed. But all that remains are a few pages of aphorisms and a handful of letters. There is no doubt that he was enormously influential. Some 700 years after his death there were communities that identified themselves as Epicureans. But why was this so? Why, for instance, 200 years after his death would Lucretius write, "We must say of him he was a god, a god I say, who first disclosed that principle of life we now call wisdom and . . . rescued us from the seas that engulfed us and the thick darkness."[134] Indeed, why 2,000 years later would Thomas Jefferson write: "I too am an Epicurean. I consider the genuine (not the imputed) doctrines of Epicurus as containing everything rational in moral philosophy which Greece and Rome have left us."[135]

When Aristotle died in 322 B.C.E., Epicurus was twenty years old. While there is no record of their having met, Epicurus was no doubt familiar with the thought and writings of the great philosopher. As we have seen, Aristotle was the first to maintain the diminishing marginal utility of money. His belief was that each additional increment of money is of progressively less benefit to its possessor, and beyond a certain point, having more is of no value, and may even be harmful.

So phrased, this is a very radical thesis. It is considerably stronger than what is required as a basis for the simple life. For instance, to argue that we would be better off cutting back on work and having more time for friends and family, even at a lower income level, one need only maintain that, after basic needs are met, the value of additional money declines sharply, or that, beyond a certain limited level, the psychological, social, and physical costs of additional hours of work rise very sharply. One need not argue that additional money is of no value at all, and certainly not that more money is actually harmful. One need only argue that our overall well-being would be enhanced by gaining more free time, even if it means lower income.

Yet it seems that Epicurus, like Aristotle, believed that there were not just problems of diminishing value associated with higher levels of income (or its pursuit), but that there were dangers of a deep distortion of life and personality. He maintained that "poverty, when measured by the natural purpose of life, is great wealth, but unlimited wealth is great poverty."[136] This should not be seen as some philosophical paradox, but rather as a formulation of the very point made earlier about simple living and poverty. There are many kinds of impoverishment and many kinds of enrichment. A life that focuses on material riches runs the risk of deep impoverishment. And, while material poverty is in itself not enriching, a material simplicity is the gate through which the greater riches of life may be found.

But what are these riches? What is the form of simple living that Epicurus espoused? Both Epicurus and Aristotle rejected a life absorbed in matters of acquisition. Aristotle identified the contemplative life as the highest life for man. This has a rather passive sound to it, and might better be translated as "the life of the mind"—a life absorbed in creative thought and inquiry. Yet, in *The Politics*, when he attacked an insatiable engagement in matters of acquisition, he was clearing the way for what he referred to as the second-best life—the life of engagement in the democratic polis.

It is important to remember that the meaning of democratic citizenship in ancient Athens was radically unlike what are generally understood as the duties of citizenship today (e.g., voting once every few years). In ancient Athens citizenship involved active, extensive, and sustained participation. Every adult male was part of the Assembly, which served as the supreme law-making body and met on a monthly basis. Its actions were guided by the deliberations of a 500-person council (roughly the size of the House of Representatives), and citizens took turns spending a year on this smaller council. Thus, it was as if every citizen were to spend a year as a member of Congress. This meant that the average citizen was engaged in serious public discourse on the affairs of state on a regular basis, sometimes with significant power and sometimes with little.

To live this way required devoting a great deal of time to political life and public affairs. Consider, for instance, jury duty. For us, this occurs perhaps once or twice in our adult lives. But in Athens, juries consisted of between 101 and 1,001 persons, depending on the importance of the case.[137] This was out of a population of free male Athenians of approximately 20,000! One must have constantly been hearing and deciding disputes among one's fellows. Thus political life, so understood as a form of the good life, consists not merely of fulfilling the obligations of citizenship, but is a life of genuine engagement in the affairs and life of the community. And this takes a lot of time. Oscar Wilde once leveled an incisive criticism of socialism, saying that the basic problem was so damned many meetings. But the same can be said of genuine democratic participation.

The Athenians, of course, did not experience things this way. Politics was not something that pulled one away from life; it was life itself. For this to be true it was necessary that people had a self-identity such that they experienced self-fulfillment within that participatory life. Within this Athenian context, Epicurus took a radical stand. He did not reject engagement in the economic realm in order to clear space for engagement in the political realm. Rather, he rejected them both. He wrote, "We must release ourselves from the prison of affairs, and politics."[138] Both an engagement in economic life and an engagement in political life were seen as forms of self-enslavement.

Two desires in particular stand out as the vehicles of this bondage. In the case of economic life the desire is for greater wealth, for more and more. In the case of politics we must free ourselves from the search for what the ancients termed "honors," i.e., fame or respect in the eyes of the public. (We contemporary Americans are more likely to seek honors within our "careers.") Together these constitute the quest for riches and celebrity— what is generally thought of as "making it." We are imprisoned by these desires because they are never satisfied. One always wants more; one fears for the loss of that which one has. Thus, Epicurus wrote, "The disturbance of the soul cannot be ended nor true joy created either by the possession of the greatest wealth or by honour and respect in the eyes of the mob or by anything else that is associated with causes of unlimited desire."[139]

There are elements here that might suggest that he was a religious man— there are sayings, for instance, that sound similar to those attributed to Jesus of Nazareth. Thus, he said, "The wise man when he has accommodated himself to straits knows better how to give than to receive."[140] Yet while Epicurus was not an atheist, he was not only thoroughly hostile to religion as he found it, he viewed most religious beliefs as superstitions from which we must also be liberated. But rather than being a religious reformer, he urges us to disengage, not only from economic and political life, but from religious life as well.

His critique of religion starts from the thesis that "the blessed and immortal nature knows no trouble itself nor causes trouble to any other, so that it is never constrained by anger or favour." By "the blessed and immortal nature," he means what others refer to as "God." Thus, what he is saying is that God "knows no trouble itself nor causes trouble." Put in different terms, Epicurus is saying, "Yes there is a God, but he doesn't care what we do (he is not troubled by us), and he doesn't make trouble for us either. He does not intervene in the affairs of mankind. He does not punish mankind for anything. Being untroubled by anything, he is not affected by our doing good or bad. He neither rewards nor punishes."

This is in diametric opposition to the conception of God developed by the Israelites that, in modified form, came to be dominant within the West. Here, God not only intervenes in history, but what happens in human history and in each human life is his central concern. Much of the time he acts out of anger, but sometimes out of compassion and love. God in this conception is passionate; he is filled with emotions, and we are what he gets most emotional about. It is as if emotion itself were the primary force of existence.

The God of the Bible not only punishes and rewards, he virtually explodes. At the time of Noah he obliterates his living creations and is so stunned by what he himself has done that he places the rainbow in the sky to remind himself never to do it again. Moreover, he has a remarkably fine-grained concern for how we should live. He actually cares what we eat for lunch, for instance, that we not eat unclean animals. He cares how we act, how we treat one another, what we believe, and what we feel. In short, the entire totality of existence is pervaded not just by God's awareness but by his passionate engagement. In virtue of simply existing, in this Judeo-Christian-Islamic tradition, we are thrown into a violent drama of life. And it is within this, through doing right, that we find what peace we can.

Epicurus, in the fourth century B.C.E., was not reacting against this Judaic conception of life and existence; quite likely he had little familiarity with it. His own target was the common religious beliefs that he found among the Greeks: the multiplicity of gods, the constant and prescribed offering of sacrifices, and the fear that an irregularity might be found irritating. In great bold strokes he swept it all away as superstition. In this his outlook was similar to the eighteenth-century view called deism, which held that God created the world but was essentially a great watchmaker; once he wound it up and started the world ticking, he did nothing more. For Epicurus God does not intervene in the world. In operational terms, that is, in terms of reward and punishment, it is as though God does not exist.

But if he rejects the economic, political, and religious realms, what is left? One might think only family life. Yet Epicurus never married and had no children. He was also quite skeptical, or perhaps cynical is the better word, about love and sex. He wrote, "The pleasures of love never profited a man and he is lucky if they do him no harm," and "Remove sight, association and contact, and the passion of love is at an end."[141] Yet he was no Puritan, for he maintained, "No pleasure is a bad thing in itself. . . ."[142] And of sex, except for prudential considerations, he says, "You may indulge your inclinations as you please."[143]

In very practical terms, Epicurus is the advocate of a simple and quiet life that stays out of politics and largely outside of economic competition. It is a life in which the central human relationship is friendship. He advocates a retreat from the larger world to a world of our own creation, a world with limited concerns and anxieties. To make this possible he actually constructed a garden compound within which his disciples lived. Within the walls of a garden compound, surrounded by friends, one engages in the pleasures of the mind.

The key to being able to actually live this tranquil life is to be able to distinguish, and ultimately to eliminate, desires that are "unnatural and unnecessary." He writes, "He who has learned the limits of life, knows that that which removes the pain due to want and makes the whole of life complete is easy to obtain; so that there is no need of actions which involve competition."[144]

This phrase "learned the limits of life" is deceptively simple. For Epicurus, learning how to live is a process within a larger conception of learning. How can we know how to live if we don't understand the most fundamental features of the world we live in, for instance, whether our life span is a matter of several decades, or whether there is an afterlife in which we are rewarded and punished by the gods? Thus, an enormous amount of Epicurus' own writings and inquiries were in areas that we might assign to fields such as theoretical physics, cosmology, metaphysics, astronomy, and philosophy. For instance, he adopted and modified the atomic theory of earlier Greek philosophers who believed that ultimately the world was composed of atoms and the void, and that all that complex range of sensory experiences that we have can be explained in terms of combinations of the atoms. Epicurus' modification of this theory centered around the introduction of a realm of spontaneity in the behavior of the atoms. This, he believed, was necessary in order to allow for the existence of free will within the system. (As a historical aside, it is interesting to note that this specific aspect of Epicurus' thought was the subject of Karl Marx's doctoral dissertation.)

Thus, learning about the world is part of the process of learning who we are and of learning how to live. Ultimately this all contributes to our ability to distinguish among our own desires; of being able to see some of them as valid and some of them as emerging only from "the idle imaginings" of man; and of being able to see some of them as necessary and some of them as unnecessary. Through this process we come to take possession of ourselves; we attain the self-possessed character that is the Epicurean ideal, a state of being in which we are at peace.

Merely being within the Garden walls does not suffice. Epicurus' Garden was a Garden School. People came from the far corners of their known world to live and study there. There was no fixed tuition, no rigid curriculum, no graduation, and no preparation or training for some future social role. It was education for the sake of life itself.

Epicurus, it seems, lived in a house that was outside the Garden, while his disciples and students lived in huts within the Garden. The house has been described as the first publishing house. Both Epicurus and at least some of his central disciples were constantly involved in writing, and whatever was written had to be copied by hand to make multiple copies. This must have been a permanent labor that students and teachers of the school carried out.

In the Garden, life was very simple. They ate substantial amounts of bread and water—but they were not doing a penance. There was also wine, and vegetables that were grown in the Garden. In one letter Epicurus asks a friend to send a bit of cheese. Yet even this simple life required funds. In large part the Garden School, this alternative society, was supported by contributions from rich followers. There is a fragment of a letter to an unknown recipient that reads: "The only contribution I require is that which . . . ordered the disciples to send me, even if they are among the Hyperboreans. I wish to receive from each of you two a hundred and twenty drachmae a year and no more."[145]

This sounds very familiar. It has the ring of a fund-raising letter to two of his followers. Yet in the tone of the letter, and in the phrase "ordered the disciples to send me," there is a clear indication of lines of authority within this society of friends and of norms in terms of which one could "order" disciples and by virtue of which, without external compulsion, they would obey.

So Epicurus built a philosophy, a school, a Garden community, a brotherhood of friends—essentially, an alternative society—that lived within the larger social order and sought to duplicate and expand. In some ways this seems similar to the communities of early Christians that emerged 300 years later. Indeed if, as some suggest, the early Christians did not view Jesus as a divine being, then the similarity is even stronger. Like the Christians, the society spread through disciples and through letters that were written to be shared, copied, and saved. Like the Christians, the Epicureans always looked back toward one individual, one master, as their guide.

There are clearly aspects here that also resemble first one and then another of the utopian simple-living communes in American history. The emphasis on learning and on friendship, the participation of leading thinkers, and the absence of a religious base call to mind the Brooks Farm experiment of the 1840s. Participants in Brooks Farm said they were seeking "to secure as many hours as possible from necessary toil" so they might have the leisure "for the production of intellectual goods." One visitor wrote of Brooks Farm that it "aims to be rich, not in the metallic representation of wealth, but in wealth itself, which money should represent, namely, leisure to live in all the faculties of the soul."[146]

Brooks Farm lasted only a few years; the Shakers, imbued with a religious fervor, lasted 200 years; the Epicurean organization lasted longer still. Like the Shakers many Epicureans were celibate—they expanded and continued through new recruits and converts, not through new generations of children. Like the Shakers, they sought to quietly make converts and found successive communities. Interestingly they differed from most of the collective simple-living experiments of the nineteenth century in that the Garden community was not a commune in the sense of having combined all private property. Common property, Epicurus maintained, reflected a lack of confidence in the bonds of friendship.

The Epicureans are particularly interesting because they were not only among the earliest simple-living societies, but because they may have been the most enduring and the most influential. For the present discussion they hold a special interest because their conception of simple living is a form of gracefulness, though not the only form it can take. Gracefulness involves four elements—beauty, peacefulness, appreciativeness, and generosity of spirit. Consider these in turn.

In the fragments we have from Epicurus, beauty is not singled out for special treatment but is included within the general endorsement of pleasure. Thus, he wrote, "I know not how I can conceive the good, if I withdraw the pleasures of taste, and withdraw the pleasures of love, and withdraw the pleasures of hearing, and withdraw the pleasurable emotions cause to sight by beautiful form." Further, "Beauty and virtue and the like are to be honored, if they give pleasure; but if they do not give pleasure, we must bid them farewell."[147]

What comes through here is something that Epicurus takes totally for granted—that beauty, in general, does give pleasure, that we cannot be happy if we live in a world without beauty. Living in ancient Athens, Epicurus was part of one of the most beauty-conscious civilizations ever to have existed. Here I mean not just the beauty of art, but also the beauty of the human form, not to speak of the natural beauty of the Greek isles. Were we to transport ourselves back in time to Epicurus' world, and to his very Garden, perhaps we would be struck above all else with just how very beautiful it was.

Peacefulness understood as an inner state of self-possession, a certain inner calm and tranquillity, and an absence of anxiety seems to have been the central goal of Epicurean self-transformation. For the Epicureans the ultimate blessedness is seen as an absence of troubledness. The central problem to which the Epicurean philosophy and institutions are directed is fear, be it the fear of the gods, the fear of death, or the very real fear of the harm that others may cause us. Freeing ourselves from the multiple forms of anxiety is the central objective of his teachings and community.

Appreciativeness of what we have is also a central feature of the Epicurean outlook. It is not a matter of thanking God for good fortune—this Epicurus does not believe in, though he is prepared to thank Nature. He writes, "Thanks be to blessed Nature because she has made what is necessary easy to supply and what is not easy unnecessary."[148]

What we have lost and need to reacquire is most centrally the ability to take great pleasure in what is very simple and readily at hand. This he sees as our natural state; we have lost it through the acquisition of unnecessary, artificial, and insatiable desires. To free ourselves from these desires is the path of transformation.

We have certain natural needs. These must be satisfied, but, when they are satisfied, nothing more by way of luxury is required for us to have the greatest happiness. "The flesh cries out to be saved from hunger, thirst and cold, for if a man possess this safety and hope to possess it, he might rival even Zeus in happiness."[149]

Beyond this, what we most need is the company of others, indeed, not just their company, but genuine friendship. "Friendship goes dancing round the world proclaiming to us all to awake to the praises of a happy life."[150] And, "Of all the things which wisdom acquires to produce the blessedness of the complete life, far the greatest is the possession of friendship."[151]

Generosity of spirit is the fourth element of gracefulness; though perhaps less visible, it, too, has a place within the Epicurean framework. He writes, "The wise man when he has accommodated himself to straits, know better how to give than to receive, so great is the treasure of self-sufficiency which he has discovered."[152] Note that he does not say, "give and ye shall receive"— an injunction that can be understood as saying, "give so that you shall receive." Such would not be graceful giving but only wise investment. Understood as information about the rewards in heaven, it is just the kind of otherworldly promising that Epicurus rejects.

When Epicurus says that the wise man knows better how to give than to receive he specifies, "when he has accommodated himself to straits," meaning when he has appropriately dealt with the basic needs of nature that we all have. Epicurus is not urging self-sacrifice. Instead he says of the wise man's giving that it emerges from "the treasure of self-sufficiency"—the wise man is one who has freed himself from artificial desires and, given that the most basic needs are satisfied, he knows that he is rich. It is this knowledge that is essential to his self-sufficiency, and it is out of this richness that he is able to give gracefully, because he seeks nothing in exchange.

But for the Epicurean what is the actual context of such graceful engagement? He is not typically a family man, and there is no fragment in which Epicurus specifically speaks of giving to the poor. He did not make an ideal out of service to others. It seems to me that the central context for Epicurean generosity is in relations with friends. Here, we might consider how Seneca characterized friendship.

Seneca is criticizing the view that the purpose of having a friend is to have "someone to come and sit beside his bed when he is ill or come to his rescue when he is hard up or thrown into chains." Seneca instead maintains that the purpose is:

> On the contrary [that] he may have someone by whose sickbed he himself may sit or whom he may himself release when that person is held prisoner by hostile hands. . . . What is my object in making a friend? To have someone to be able to die for, someone I may follow into exile, someone whose life I may put myself up as security and pay the price as well. The thing you describe is not friendship but a business deal, looking to the likely consequences, with advantage as its goal.[153, 154]

Though Epicurus saw friendship as originating in self-interest, I believe he shared with Seneca this vision of friendship as a human relation in which the boundaries of interest between self and other are transcended. It was no accident that Epicurus found the secret of simple living within a community of friends, and it is instructive to understand just why this is so.

FRIENDSHIP AND GRACEFULNESS

It has long been known that a concern with how one will be seen by others is a central motive behind consumption. The language for talking about this differs, as do the specifics of the explanation. But, whether it is a matter of peer pressure, keeping up with the Joneses, or conspicuous consumption, avarice, envy, or coveting thy neighbor's ox, there has long been an awareness that both consumption and the pursuit of wealth are part of our relation with the Other.

We still struggle with these matters today, but it may be that Epicurus found the most effective response. Let me approach this indirectly, in a way that will explicate more fully the notion of gracefulness and its relationship to simple living.

In a passage in *The Wealth of Nations*, Adam Smith commented on the apparently universal link between the concern with self-as-seen-by-others and the specifics of our consumption patterns. Thus, Smith noted that, in the England of his day, a man needed to have a linen shirt to appear in public without shame, but this was not so in other societies—each having its own requirements. He noted that in England both men and women needed to be wearing shoes to avoid shame, in Scotland this applied only to men, and in the France of his day, both men and women could appear without shoes.

What varied between cultures were the norms with respect to wearing or not wearing clothing on our feet. But what was universal was the fact that in each culture there were norms with respect to what a respectable person should wear; and, further, that violation of these norms was experienced by the individual himself as revealing the inner self as lacking in value. This experience of the inner self as seen-to-be-without-value is the emotion we call "shame." It is the opposite of what the ancients referred to as "honor" and perhaps the more powerful motive.

One of the most fundamental and perplexing questions of human psychology is why we have this vulnerability to the viewpoint of the Other. The phenomenon is familiar. Our sense of well-being, our conception and opinion of ourselves, our sense of who we are, and our self-identity are fragile things dependent upon the views that others have of us. This is the umbilical point through which we are attached to our culture or subculture.

The great French philosopher Jean-Paul Sartre saw it as an inescapable feature of the human condition. For Sartre, a person is always in search of being, and is always coming up empty. This absence of being is itself the concomitant of being conscious and free beings. We can never have qualities the way things have them. Our identity is always slipping away from us. It is in flight from this void that we try to impose upon ourselves self-identities, and, in doing this, the perceptions of the other are central. Thus Sartre writes of our experience of being looked at by another:

Thus for me the Other is first the being for whom I am an object; that is, the being through whom I gain my objectness. If I am to be able to conceive of even one of my properties in the objective mode, then the Other is already given.[155]

Here Sartre is saying that it is only through the look of the Other that we can conceive of ourselves as having properties at all. He illustrates this dependence on being seen by others for our sense of who we are with respect to shame:

I have just made an awkward or vulgar gesture. This gesture clings to me; I neither judge it nor blame it. I simply live it. . . . But now suddenly I raise my head. Somebody was there and has seen me. Suddenly I realize the vulgarity of my gesture, and I am ashamed . . . the Other is the indispensable mediator between myself and me. I am ashamed of myself as I appear to the Other. . . . Nobody can be vulgar all alone![156]

What Sartre sees as an inherent part of the human condition, the ancient Stoic philosophers saw as human foolishness that the wise man would overcome. One of the keenest observers of these matters was the Stoic philosopher Epictetus. Of Epictetus, along with Epicurus (who was not a Stoic), Jefferson wrote that they "give laws for governing ourselves"[157] and this is exactly what Epictetus sought to do when it came to these matters of shame or honor. He wrote:

These reasons do not cohere: I am richer than you, therefore I am better than you; I am more eloquent than you, therefore I am better than you. On the contrary these rather cohere, I am richer than you, therefore my possessions are greater than yours: I am more eloquent than you, therefore my speech is superior to yours. But you are neither possessions nor speech. (XLIV)[158]

At issue here is our identity, and how having a clear vision of what is pertinent to our identity and what is not liberates us from a concern with externals. Here the specific advice concerns judgments of superiority such as "I am better than you"—but perhaps this is more powerful if framed in terms of avoiding judgments of inferiority, of not making a transition from "they have more than I do" to "they are better than I am."

Thus Stoicism supports the simple life by offering a challenge to conventional notions of social status based on income and wealth, and even those based on certain personal capacities. The Stoic does not allow such judgments to become internalized, but instead dismisses them as a form of ignorance. The intended effect is liberation from the dominant cultural emphasis on wealth and social standing.

Epictetus asks us to consider how foolish we are in our fears about what others think, and he seems to assume that when we see that we are foolish we will no longer be so:

> If any person was intending to put your body in the power of any man whom you fell in with on the way, you would be vexed: but that you put your understanding [probably better translated as identity or psychological well-being] in the power of any man whom you meet, so that if he should revile you, it is disturbed and troubled, are you not ashamed at this?(XXVIII)

If we start to see ourselves as important, as socially successful, or as a big fish in the pond, then we are setting ourselves up for a life of never-ending insecurity, and, ultimately, it is the effort to cope with that insecurity that drives us into the frenetic lives we lead.

The central arena that is transformed if we reorder our sense of identity is our relationship to the economic realm. What Epictetus has seen is that much of what we are doing in economic life is a process of identity construction and maintenance. If we get ourselves straightened out on that most basic psychological level, it transforms our relationship to the world of things.

To start on the road to psychological reconstruction requires that we are prepared to sacrifice for it, and that we are willing to be judged to be fools by others. Thus, he writes:

> If you intend to improve, throw away such thoughts as these: if I neglect my affairs, I shall not have the means of living. . . . For it is better to die of hunger and so be released from grief and fear than to live in abundance and perturbation. (XII)

And,

> If you would improve, submit to being considered without sense
> and foolish with respect to externals. (XIII)[159]

We must free ourselves from the judgments of others with respect to
externals—that is, with respect to the main objects of economic life: income,
wealth, fame, reputation, respect, and social status.

The claim is that to achieve tranquillity (a component of what I call
"gracefulness") requires that we march to a different drummer. You have to
live your life according to your own lights. If you cannot free yourself from
the internalization of the other's perception of you, then even if you do live
an externally simple life, it will not be one of inner tranquillity. Thus, you
must find a way to free yourself from what Sartre called "the gaze of the
Other." It remains an open question as to whether this is really possible.
Sartre thought it was not; the Stoics thought that it was—though they
admitted that few achieved such complete independence.

But to both Sartre and Epictetus we can contrast a beautiful and illuminating passage by the nineteenth-century American philosopher William
James, in an essay entitled "What Makes a Life Significant?":

> Every Jack sees in his own particular Jill charms and perfections to
> the enchantment of which we stolid on-lookers are stone-cold.
> And which has the superior view of the absolute truth, he or we?
> Which has the more vital insight into the nature of Jill's exis-
> tence, as a fact? Is he in excess, being in this matter a maniac? Or
> are we in defect, being victims of a pathological anaesthesia as
> regards Jill's magical importance?

And James answers:

> Surely the latter; surely to Jack are the profounder truths revealed;
> surely poor Jill's palpitating little life-throbs are among the won-
> ders of creation, are worthy of this sympathetic interest; and it is
> our shame that the rest of us cannot feel like Jack. For Jack real-
> ized Jill concretely, and we do not. He struggles toward a union
> with her inner life, divining her feelings, anticipating her desires,
> understanding her limits as manfully as he can, and yet inade-
> quately, too; for he is also afflicted with some blindness, even here.

> Whilst we, dead clods that we are, do not even seek after these
> things, but are contented that that portion of eternal fact named
> Jill should be for us as if it were not. Jill, who knows her inner life,
> knows that Jack's way of taking it—so importantly—is the true
> and serious way; and she responds to the truth in him by taking
> him truly and seriously, too.[160]

Here James has taken no position on whether our identity is inevitably
dependent upon the perspective of the other—rather he calls us, as the
Other, to take a certain generous stance toward each other. Rather than
thinking that we know who and what they are, he asks us to take the perspective, or at least honor the perspective, of Jill who sees in Jack something
remarkable and special.

James has put his finger on the most fundamental act of giving that we can
extend toward another—a generosity of perception in our apprehension of
the other. This generosity is not in the first instance about judgments: for
instance, whether to be critical. It is a more basic act of seeing the other as a
being of such importance that "its little life-throbs" are taken as "wonders of
creation."

There are two perspectives here: that of the one being perceived, and that
of the one doing the perceiving. For the one who is perceived to be the object
of a generous perception is to be affirmed, it is to be reinforced within one's
project of maintaining or attaining a positive self-identity. Whether this is a
project that constantly requires shoring up because it runs against an existen-
tial structure of being, as Sartre would have it, or whether it is valid and
enduring hardly matters. What matters is that in a world of generous perception, others are supported in the project of attaining self-worth, and,
being successful, they are relieved of further need to pursue success within
commonplace modes of acquisition of things and power.

From the point of view of the Other who does the perceiving, there is also,
perhaps, a gain in coming to find in the other person something of what Jill
saw in her Jack; something of wonder, interest, and value; and something
worthy of respect. Thus, there is a true graciousness, a recognition of the
other as a worthy end in himself, not in response to a Kantian imperative to
do so, but as the concomitant of an appreciation of that which is of value in
the other.

Thus gracefulness of being is inherently supportive of the simple life because generosity of spirit within the simple living community makes unnecessary the vast alternative project of attaining self-worth through consumption and social standing. This, I believe, is the key to the viability of Epicurus' Garden life. Essentially it was life within a community of friends who supported each other in their collective withdrawal from the dominant value system of their society and whose generous responsiveness to each other provided them with the ability to be different, as well as with the pleasures of their life together. When one has friends one has much of the wealth that the world can provide, and in forging these friendships one far more directly attains a sense of self-value, the search for which underlies much of our economic life. Thus, participation in a community of gracefulness, in the sense that includes this generosity of spirit, emerges not just as a particular kind of simple living, but as a central structure without which the project of the simple life is vastly more difficult.

It might also be maintained that this generosity of friendship, through which one experiences oneself as seen by the friend as a bit of "a wonder of creation," serves a psychological role similar to that of experiencing oneself as the central object of God's passionate concern. As noted above, this perspective is one that the Epicureans rejected.

One interesting paradox about Epicurus' Garden life should be noted. It may well be that the actual life that Epicurus lived was quite different from the life that he espoused and that presumably was attained by those in the Garden. Epicurus was the founder and director of a community. He was responsible for its financial viability. It was he who wrote fund-raising letters. It was he who must have supervised all facets of life within the Garden. Though he eschewed politics in the normal sense of the term, he was a social change activist. The creation of the Garden was not done merely for the well-being of a small set of inhabitants; it was intended as a form of education for the larger world as well. Thus, Epicurus wrote his 300 books and what must have been as many letters. These were all written by hand and intended to be circulated as part of a larger movement.

As anyone who has participated in such activities knows, life can get very complex and demanding. Perhaps Epicurus himself had achieved such inner tranquillity that he could gracefully carry demands that would frazzle the ordinary person. Or perhaps he made some trade-offs—sacrificing certain aspects of gracefulness (e.g., tranquillity) for a chance to give generously of himself to a larger project, thus giving his life a meaning that it might otherwise have lacked. If so, this is a useful reminder that as formal properties of life, gracefulness and simplicity still leave open the question of the substance of life.

THE GARDEN VS. THE SABBATH AS THE PATH TO GRACEFULNESS

With Epicurus' emphasis on pleasure, and his attack on otherworldliness, one might think that there could be little relationship between his vision of simple living and the Sabbath observance tradition put forward by the Israelites.

Yet these vast differences should not blind us to the common ground. How we see this depends, in part, on how we understand Sabbath observance. Even for the ancient Israelites this must have been a matter of contention; thus, the prophet Isaiah (Isaiah 58:13) instructs the people to "call it a delight"—a directive that would not have been necessary if everyone so understood the Sabbath. This understanding is carried forward within Judaism. Consider again the injunction: "Sanctify the Sabbath by choice meals, by beautiful garments; delight your soul with pleasure and I will regard you for this very pleasure."[161]

Here we are told that pleasure on the Sabbath is that which sanctifies it. We are instructed to "delight our soul with pleasure" and that we will be seen favorably in God's eyes for this very pleasure. This is a reconciliation of pleasure and religion that Epicurus never dreamed of. Here is a conception of God in which God is indeed deeply involved in the intimate specifics of how we live. This is a God who rewards and punishes. It is also a God who not only tells us that pleasure is allowed, but tells us that it is through pleasure that we give full religious significance to the Sabbath, and further suggests that as individuals or as a people we will be rewarded for this very pleasure taking!

Pleasure, of course, can mean many things. The pleasures of the Sabbath, like the pleasure of Epicurus' Garden, exclude the debauch of the Roman orgy. But at the same time, they are not restricted to the pleasures of the mind or spirit. We are told to sanctify through choice meals and by beautiful garments. Thus, the sensory delights to the palate, the eyes, and the nose are all filled with religious significance. We are again reminded of the God who created the beautiful, sensory world, separating the heavens from the earth and who looked back after each day's work and "saw that it was good."

Further, both the Sabbath meal and religious services on the Sabbath are done with others: with friends and relatives, with neighbors, and with congregants. Thus the pleasures of the Sabbath parallel those of Epicurus' Garden; they are taken together in a community of like-minded friends, neighbors, and loved ones.

If anything, the sensory element seems to have a stronger place in this Sabbath observance than it does in Epicurus' bread-and-water, vegetables-and-wine Garden life. As we saw earlier, Sabbath observance was not a form of simple living; it was rather a day of gracefulness, open to both the rich and the poor. As a one-day affair, rather than the six days of rest and one day of work that Thoreau proposed, it was not linked to the problem that both Epicurus and Thoreau were sensitive to: that high consumption entails long hours of beastly work.

For the Israelites the Sabbath was the one day off, the day of rest. For the Epicureans, the life in the Garden was life itself; there was no work outside it. It is not fully clear how the Epicurean communities supported themselves economically, but it seems they were dependent upon the larger society. They received contributions from wealthy members, but this was wealth amassed outside the Garden life. True, the limitation of desire that Epicurus recommends is the central tool for escaping from the curse of beastly labor, but even with the low levels of consumption within the Garden, it is not likely that they sustained themselves on the basis of their crops of home-grown vegetables.

The Israelites were not creating a garden within society; they were creating a way of life for the entire society. They, too, had their island of gracefulness. But theirs was not a physical garden within the larger city; it was an island in time that gave a rhythm and organization to the flow of time, and a weekly return to gracefulness that the entire society participated in.

Yet for the Israelites the garden theme was also prominent. It was in the Garden of Eden that mankind first experienced the simple life, and it was in virtue of disobedience that Adam was not only expelled from the Garden but placed under the curse of labor. Thus, God, in Genesis 3:17–19, speaks to Adam and says:

> "Cursed be the ground because of you;
> By toil shall you eat of it
> All the days of your life . . .

> By the sweat of your brow
> Shall you get bread to eat. . . ."

When the fourth commandment prescribes a day of rest, it is a partial reprieve from the curse of toil "all the days of your life." Thus, the Sabbath represents a partial overcoming of the consequences of the expulsion from the Garden. But only in some dimensions (e.g., not having to toil on that day) is the Sabbath a return to the Garden—for in the Garden there was an innocence of good and evil that was lost to the human condition.

But this loss is properly seen as a mixed blessing. When Eve sees the apple she sees it as "good to eat and as a source of wisdom." Thus it is the motivation toward wisdom, as much as any act of disobedience, that has taken us out of the Garden. There is nothing in the Jewish tradition that seeks to abandon that hard-won wisdom, or to retreat to an artificial world in which we disengage from mankind's struggle within a world of good and evil.

For Epicurus, the Garden life is achieved through recognizing that the gods do not intervene in our lives, that there is no afterlife, and that the wise man seeks pleasure in this life. For the Israelites there is also a separation from God, but it is this separation that leads us out of the Garden of simplicity. Yet God himself, at least once a week, bids his people back to gracefulness, not as simple creatures, but as a complex, developed civilization of the Book.

Epicurus' Garden was much like what a small subgroup might attempt today—to do for itself what might not be possible if everyone sought to do so. But could society as a whole be that Garden? What would happen if we all went into an Epicurean Garden? In ancient times such a society would have been overrun militarily by outside enemies as were the virtuous, simple-living bees in Mandeville's *The Fable of the Bees*. The fact that in the Greek world this would have meant enslavement of others illustrates how radically different are the small-group projects of Epicurus and the society-wide vision of the Israelites.[162]

One final point of comparison is worth noting. In the ancient world, slavery was the common practice and was generally the fate of defeated enemies. In the Israelite Sabbath the injunction to refrain from work applies to master, slave, and servant alike. The gracefulness of the Sabbath was not dependent upon having slaves and servants. Because it was within the one day of rest/six days of work pattern, it was part of the life of the rich and poor alike. However, in the Greek world the graceful life seems to have had a more intimate dependency on slavery, in particular upon slaves supplying domestic services. Thus, Aristotle had fourteen slaves, and in Epicurus' will he gives freedom to four slaves. We do not know if he had more than four, and some commentators believe that the slaves (who were domestic servants) participated in the life of the Garden—but it is unrealistic to believe that they did so on the same basis as others. Quite possibly, it is they who did the actual gardening, and they who undertook laborious tasks such as making simple fabrics out of raw wool.

We do not know enough about the role of Epicurus' slaves, nor about the actual finances and home economy of the Garden, to say that it was dependent upon slavery. Given that Epicurus was concerned for the continuity of the Garden and yet freed these four slaves at his death, perhaps it was not. Either way, it is important that we not idealize the Epicurean Garden, and that we remember that even there we find a complex relationship between power relations, desires, income, consumption, technology, work, domestic services, and graceful existence.

Chapter Eight

GRACEFUL OPULENCE VERSUS GRACEFUL SIMPLICITY

I have characterized gracefulness as a way of being, both in the world of things and in time. In doing so, I have called attention to its four interrelated facets: beauty, peacefulness, appreciativeness, and generosity of spirit. But why should gracefulness be presented as a form of simple living? Just as Sabbath observance is possible for the rich, so, too, it must be possible for the rich to live gracefully. Indeed, material abundance certainly seems the more natural ground for gracefulness. Why "graceful simplicity" rather than "graceful opulence"?

To explore this question an important distinction needs to be made between opulence and being rich. By a life of opulence I mean a life suffused with an abundance of goods and services. Opulence is not the same as being rich. Being rich is a relative matter, a matter of having significantly more than those around one. In this relative sense even in poor societies, and throughout human history, there have been those who have been rich. Since it is a relative notion, it is logically impossible that everyone would become rich—that everyone would have significantly more than most other people.

Of course, in its social aspects, the American Dream has frequently been characterized as one in which everyone gets rich. When America was envisioned with streets of gold, it was said that in America all would, or could, become rich. In relative terms this, of course, is impossible. In a land of opportunity perhaps anyone can become rich, but it is not possible for everyone to do that as each person's relative success implies someone else's relative failure.

Opulence on the other hand can be understood as an absolute notion, not in relation to what others have. Thus while we can't all be rich, we can all become opulent. The problem in defining opulence is to determine what counts as having a lot. Are we talking about living in the style that only the rich have today? Are we talking about living the way the rich lived 300 years ago? Mandeville, as we saw in his celebration of eighteenth-century England, maintained "the very Poor Liv'd better than the Rich before." Putting the poor aside, does the upper middle class today already live a life of opulence?

There is no nonarbitrary answer to this. Unlike "absolute poverty," which can be defined as a situation in which access to goods and services is so limited that life itself is in danger, "absolute abundance," or opulence, has no objective reference point. This arbitrariness is not necessarily problematic so long as we are aware of it. For present purposes let me simply stipulate a level of consumption such that consumption above that level is by definition opulent. Opulence then, by stipulation, is a sustained consumption level of the sort that is typical of those with an income of $200,000 a year (or more) for a family of four in 1998.

Why $200,000? There is no special reason for this particular number. It would have been equally possible to specify $500,000 or $1,000,000. I chose $200,000 because only a very small percentage of families, perhaps 1 or 2 percent, have incomes of this level. Thus, in these terms, America in 1998 is very far from being an opulent society. In 1998 the median family income for married couple families was roughly $50,000 (for single-parent families it is about half of that). But with steady growth of family income at, say, 2 percent per year (after adjusting for inflation), in seventy years median income for married couple families would rise to $200,000; half of these families would be opulent. Even if growth is very slow by American standards, say, only 1 percent a year, then in 140 years this level of general opulence would be reached. Were we to define opulence at the $400,000 level, then at 2 percent growth, it would take 105 years for half the population to become opulent.

Conventional thinking about what constitutes economic progress understands the difference between a successful economy and one that is floundering primarily in terms of its rate of passage toward opulence. Let us then assume many years of success culminating in such massive opulence. Would this "success" also represent a movement toward graceful existence?

If graceful existence means a life of beauty, peacefulness, appreciativeness, and generosity, then, of course, the answer is "not necessarily." All one has to do is to look at people who today have incomes of $200,000; having a high income does not guarantee that life will not be tawdry, hectic, anxiety ridden, avaricious, and self-absorbed. Gracefulness as an ideal of being is far too complex and too demanding to be brought about simply by income and consumption levels.

But this is not the interesting question. The interesting question is whether going from our present levels of $50,000 family incomes to opulent levels of $200,000 makes it substantially easier for people to live gracefully. Are we more likely to have a society with more graceful lives at opulent levels of consumption than at present levels?

This is not an easy question to answer, yet it is of tremendous importance. At present, our dominant approach to economic life sets this passage to opulence as the goal and gives great weight to how rapidly we move toward it. But if we would be no closer to a graceful form of life, then perhaps there is some other direction that we should be taking. Perhaps the central goals of economic policy rest on a misconception.

There is good reason to be skeptical about any claim that the passage to general opulence will bring us closer to graceful living. First, as some have discovered, having a household income of $200,000 has its demands, and we can almost hear the bickering as our opulent husband and wife try to sort out the tasks:

> Dear, the lawn has to be mowed,
> And the bushes screening us from the neighbors,
>
> Should really be thickened.
> Shouldn't we be refinancing the mortgage?
> Are you doing the taxes early this year?
>
> The paint on the ceiling in the living room is
> Flaking, and the drapes really should go;
> We need some wine!
> Are you making dinner? Or are we going out?
>
> The kids need new shoes.
> I'm taking Maddy to soccer.
> And Billy won't do his Suzuki violin practice unless
> Someone stands over him.

The kids need help with their homework,
And some prepping for that entrance exam.
To that school.
And remember,
You promised to drive them.

Oh, by the way, the BMW needs new tires,
A wash, and a vacuuming.
And the Volvo is on its last legs.
Ugh, shopping for a new one,
And selling the old,
And getting new plates.

The dishwasher needs to be repaired,
Will you call? And who will
Stay home for the repairman?

The plants need to be watered;
There is a loose brick on the patio,
And someone might trip,
And sue us.

Did you rake the leaves,
And clean the gutters?
And clear the garage?

I took the chairs to be reupholstered;
And made sure not to pay too much.

The recyling! I forgot.

And so on. The point is not that abundance is a curse, but that abundance
has its own demands that may indeed destroy the possibility of the life of
graceful ease to which one aspired in the first place.

One might say that the problem simply is that one is not rich enough.
When you are really rich then you can have all these things and have other
people do everything for you. Viewed from the point of view of any individual household this has an obvious appeal. One major part of the answer to

how to live gracefully with abundance is to have servants and service providers. Or more generally, to have not just an abundance of goods, but to consume as well an abundance of personal services sufficient to allow a life of ease.

If we let our imaginations roam and ask what kinds of personal services it would be most appealing to have, and we assume that we are talking now about an opulent two-career family with children, it certainly would be nice to have (a) a combination housekeeper and cook, someone who shops, cleans, and cooks, and (b) someone who watches after the children and perhaps does some educating as well, say a part-time governess/baby-sitter/grandmother/grandfather and (c) a combination chauffeur (for the children), dog walker, auto maintainer, house repairer, and groundskeeper, and perhaps (d) a person to hire and supervise the other three, while at the same time taking care of paying bills, opening junk mail, screening fund-raising calls, preparing taxes, maintaining record keeping for the household as a whole, looking after its financial options and investments, and dealing with the health insurance companies.

Suppose we had just two such persons at our disposal. With such assistance it should not be very hard to handle an abundance of possessions. But if anyone thinks this is more than we would need, they might consider that in the classic nuclear family of a few decades back, when the husband went off to work, the wife/mother was essentially in the role of the full-time provider of household services. Yet even for such middle-class families with far lower levels of consumption than what we are defining as opulent, it was clear that one full-time person providing services for the household was insufficient.

That classic household of the 1950s not only occasionally hired other people, it often worked women more than eight hours a day, five days a week. And it also pressed men with never-ending things to do. If we saddle that family with the additional service demands associated with, say, a tripling of real income, the idea that two full-time service providers are needed for graceful living is probably not too wide of the mark.

But if employing two full-time equivalents for personal services is part of what is needed for a household of graceful opulence, then clearly this is an impossible ideal for the society as a whole. There are several reasons why this is so.

If every household required two full-time providers of household services, this would mean that the entire adult population would be providers of household services. Essentially, we would be cooking, cleaning, driving, and baby-sitting for our neighbors while they were doing the same thing for us. Today only a small fraction of our labor force provides these household services for others. For the most part we provide them for ourselves. If the key to graceful living is to free ourselves from this burden of household service, it hardly represents a gain if we are free of it in our own home only to have to minister to the house next door.

This inherent limit to growth (no society can ever become so wealthy that everyone has servants to provide household service) may be obscured because, historically, in many societies the servant workers have been defined as outside the society. Either they were household slaves, or immigrant workers, or members of a social underclass that hardly counted. So long as this "external" labor pool provides the resources, in principle, all who are inside could potentially become rich enough to employ the required servants. But as soon as the pool "dries up," not necessarily because we do away with immigrant labor, but because our moral horizons widen so as to include all within our social ideals, it becomes clear that extensive provision of household services by others is an incoherent ideal.

The same phenomenon can be viewed in terms of income and wages. If everyone both hired a household servant and worked as a household servant, this would mean that everyone was paying all of their income (what they earned from their servant work) to the servant who worked for them. Servant classes can exist only when there is an enormous income differential between the wages for household service and the income of the employing population. For this reason, it is the middle class in very poor countries that today is more likely to have servants (and thus graceful opulence) than it is the middle class of the rich countries where, because of greater equality, the middle class can no longer afford servants.

One might have thought it would work out otherwise. Thus, with the vast historical reduction in the numbers of people engaged in agriculture, and with the sharp reduction in the percentage engaged in manufacturing, one might have predicted a flow of servant labor into the household. Yet this is exactly what did not happen.

One hundred years ago there were 1.5 million launderers, cooks, housekeepers, and other household workers. They constituted 5 percent of the workforce. Today there are about 800,000 household workers, constituting six-tenths of 1 percent of the workforce. In short, rather than expanding as a segment of the workforce, household workers have almost disappeared altogether.[163]

The central reason for this decline in household workers as a percentage of the workforce is that there was a shift in the pattern of income. When either the cost of servants rises, or the relative income of those at the top declines, people will simply be unable to pay the wages required in order to keep servants. If there is no change in income distribution, widespread growth of income will not result in a greater ability to hire servants.

In a few areas there has been a substantial increase in the extent to which people hire others to perform services for the household. These are services that are available outside the home. Thus, rather than having cooks and waiters live with us, they are set up outside the home, and we go to them. Thus consider the following[164]:

	1900	1996
Cooks (outside home)	117,000	2,061,000
Waiters and waitresses	107,000	1,375,000

Over the last hundred years, these two groups combined grew from seven-tenths of 1 percent of the workforce to close to 3 percent of the workforce. But this pattern applies only to selective areas. When one considers the multitude of tasks that fall on households, especially when they are opulent, it is clear that a general solution will not be found in hiring others to do it for us, whether we employ them inside the home or outside.

This is not to deny the obvious, that for any given individual household, a rise in *its* relative income makes things easier. A rise in relative income means that you are better able to hire others to do the work. This has always been the main way in which growth of an individual's income increases gracefulness, but it hardly serves as a general social goal. It offers little support to the idea that as a society we should try to go from $50,000 median family incomes to $200,000 family incomes.

This then is a critical problem: how to attain sufficient labor within the household so as to sustain graceful existence. If graceful opulence is the general objective, then other solutions need be sought.

THE PROBLEM OF HOUSEHOLD LABOR

In theory, many household tasks are things that can be part of a graceful existence. They are diverse in character. They allow for individual creativity. They can be done with complex skills. And they can result in households in which there is beauty in both the artifacts and practices of the household. Moreover, household activities often involve doing things with and for those we love.

A central factor that determines whether such tasks will be an inherent part of a graceful existence, or be radically antithetical to it, is the amount of available time. Gracefulness almost always requires that things be done slowly; it is incompatible with rush, with cutting corners, with time pressure, with expedience. Gracefulness pays its respect to things and persons by giving them the time that is their due.

One of the objectives of a politics of simplicity is to make it feasible for people to reduce their paid employment, thus providing themselves with greater time both for leisure activities and for household maintenance. There are large numbers of Americans who yearn to be able to do just that, often feeling that they can't.

As an alternative, Americans have looked to technological solutions. Outside the home, technology has vastly increased the productivity of labor. Can this not be done inside the home? Earlier, I discussed Aristotle's fantasy of machines that would act on their own. If there is an answer to the problem of achieving graceful opulence without slaves or servants, perhaps it lies just along the lines of Aristotle's fantasy, not with robots, perhaps, but with a steady increase in household productivity that allows a person to do in minutes what previously required hours.

In thinking about what machines can and cannot do in the provision of personal service tasks, distinguishing *service outputs* from the *service-time inputs* is important. This distinction may not be obvious since personal service jobs are often thought of as jobs that do not have any tangible output, as distinct from manufacturing jobs where there is some physical product produced. Nonetheless the distinction can be made. For instance, when someone cleans the kitchen, we can distinguish his performing the task of cleaning the kitchen from the outcome—the kitchen's having been cleaned. Often enough, it is the outcome that is important, not the provision of the labor input. The grass on the lawn has to be kept at a reasonable length.

Perhaps this means that someone has to mow the lawn; perhaps the lawn can be reseeded with a grass that will not grow more than three inches in length.

There are some services in which what is needed is not just the outcome, but the service itself. Thus, someone might say that they need a massage, meaning not merely that they need to have their muscles relaxed, but that they have a need for having some person actually massage them. This is an important point to which I will return, but for now let me put it aside and assume that much or most household service is really of the first sort, where the need is for the service result rather than for the labor service itself.

If there are truly sharp advances of this sort, then they might not only reduce the current need to devote inordinate time to household tasks, but further meet any expanded need for household service outputs that accompanies a general rise in opulence. Thus it is possible that, even with the growth of opulence, as a result of increased productivity in service delivery, so little will be needed by way of personal service time that more and more people can live gracefully.

In principle the continued expansion of such home technologies, coupled with a rise in income sufficient to purchase them, could render insignificant any increased demands for personal services associated with an increase in opulence.

But are there household technologies that can vastly reduce work time within the household? Can we reasonably expect that such technologies will emerge? What has our experience been?

One detailed study concluded that there was far less payoff from "time-saving" household technologies than might be imagined.[165] The explanation for this was that new technologies do not generally mean the simple substitution of one thing for another, but rather they change work processes in ways that can carry their own time demands. Thus, an automatic dishwasher may require scraping or rinsing dishes before putting them in, arranging the items properly in the machine, and then unloading the machine, plus any time associated with occasional breakdown and replacement. Further, with new technologies there has been a rise in the standards of decency. Thus, with vacuum cleaners more frequent vacuuming became the societal norm.

While this may have been the recent experience, there is no general rule that one can turn to. Without doubt certain changes in household technologies enormously reduce the amount of personal services that are required in the household. For instance, in some poor countries villagers have to walk a mile or more to a source of water. This might be a trip repeated several times a day. Having the water come directly into the house virtually eliminates this very significant time demand.

While we should not rule out the possibility of new technologies that seriously reduce labor time in the home, it is interesting to note that today there are no major time-saving technologies that rich people have, that middle-class people do not have. If technologies are to make any appreciable difference, they would have to be radically new technologies, and it is not obvious what they would be. Of course, the fact that our imaginations might not be adequate is insufficient reason to maintain that no solution along these lines is possible.

However, it should be remembered that our concern is with the possibility of graceful living. Not every technology that offers a way to reduce the time required for performing household activities contributes to gracefulness. For instance, it is quite true that if one is prepared to eat TV dinners that are cooked in the microwave, one can significantly reduce cooking time. Further, if one eats them in their disposable trays, and eats them with disposable plastic forks and knives, one can eliminate much of the cleanup time as well. But to eat in this way is not to take one's meals gracefully. The pace is wrong; the aesthetic is wrong; and the food is wrong.

Once graceful existence is seen as central to the good life, doing things more quickly loses its character as an unambiguous good. The perspective of gracefulness causes us to rethink the work/leisure distinction. Rather than eliminating work in favor of leisure, it is also possible to metamorphize work that is onerous into fulfilling human activity precisely by doing it more slowly. Not because time is an evil to be absorbed, but because doing things more slowly allows for a rehumanization of activity. Of course, time remains a limited resource, and there is no universal formula that can specify the appropriate pace for every activity. Thus, the time we give to things reflects our values. When everything is rushed, then everything has been devalued.

Consider the everyday preparation of a meal. From the perspective of efficiency and a busy agenda, the preparation of a meal is a pure means, or worse, an inherently onerous task. As such it is desirable to reduce the time involved to the barest minimum, and whenever possible, to get someone else to do it for you.

But from the perspective of graceful existence there is another possibility—that we live in ways such that there is sufficient time to turn the preparation of a meal into something quite different. When done together, in the right spirit, and with craft, the preparation of a meal (even a simple meal) can emerge as a social enterprise in which people come together in a joint productive and aesthetic endeavor that yields its delicious reward not just in the eating and savoring, but in the doing as well. Are monks who do a sand painting intending it to be destroyed when it is completed engaged in something inherently more poetic than making a salad?[166]

Thus, graceful existence puts certain constraints around the issue of time-reducing technologies. Essentially, it says that even if there were miraculous technologies that vastly reduced the amount of time needed for personal services, we would find that some of them destroy rather than enhance the possibility of gracefulness. At the same time, we should remain open to the possibility that some technological advances will make a difference. But such technologies do not presently exist, and it would indeed be foolhardy given the hectic world we presently live in, to have confidence in a technological fix.

SIMPLY LIVING AND SIMPLIFICATION

The discussion points in one direction: the widespread achievement of graceful living does require simplification. The demands of ordinary life are frequently overwhelming, and, all other things remaining equal, they are more likely to go up with a general rise in affluence than to go down.

Here, however, we come to an ambiguity in the concept of simple living. On the one hand simplicity is understood as the opposite of complexity and multiplicity. It means slowing down, focusing, prioritizing, and having fewer things cluttering one's mind and life. On the other hand, simple living has always meant a way of life that found the human good in something other than consumption. It advocates living on a modest income. It is about turning away from money and toward life's greater blessings. A politics of simplicity is about both of these things, and often in the literature on simple living they are amalgamated into one concept. These two elements need to be distinguished, however, and I will use the term "simplification" for the first (the less hectic, slower, focused life), and "simple living" for the life that has not merely undergone simplification, but in which consumption levels are quite modest.

At any income level it is always possible to undertake simplification. Thus, rather than multiplying the number of things one owns—adding more and more rooms to the house, filling the closets, adding a third car, a boat, and a vacation home—there is another way to use money.

If one is wealthy, one can have a very small stock of very beautiful things. One can opt for great quality over quantity. One can have one car, and it can almost always be a new car, without the headaches of older cars. One can have one house rather than two, but live in a place from which one is not motivated to escape. With enough money, one can live in a very expensive neighborhood, and find that life is in some ways simpler—for instance, the public schools are better. One's children might even walk to school. One might even send the kids out to play, without a fear in the world.

The great economic theorist Alfred Marshall made just this point—that additional money is better spent on quality than quantity, in particular, on aesthetic quality. He wrote:

> When the necessities of life are once provided, everyone should seek to increase the beauty of things in his possession rather than their number or their magnificence. And improvement in the artistic character of furniture and clothing trains the higher faculties of those who make them, and is a source of growing happiness to those who use them. But if instead of seeking for a higher standard of beauty, we spend our growing resources on increasing the complexity and intricacy of our domestic goods, we gain thereby no true benefit, no lasting happiness. The world would go much better if everyone would buy fewer and simpler things, and would take trouble in selecting them for their real beauty being careful of course to get good value in return for his outlay, but preferring to buy a few things made well by highly paid labour rather than many made badly by low paid labour.[167]

Here we have a case being made for "graceful simplification" rather than gracefulness as a form of simple (i.e., low-cost) living. From this perspective, much of the burden of opulence is self-induced by our failure to use our money for a few beautiful things. There is much truth in this. If opulence is used intelligently, to promote simplification and in the service of beauty, then opulence does not have to lead to expanded demands for personal services. Thus, it is not impossible to have a society in which everyone is both opulent and living gracefully.

Nonetheless, the general pursuit of opulence is antithetical to graceful existence for other reasons. The advantage of graceful simplicity over a simplified opulence has to do not with problems of being opulent, but with what it takes to *become* opulent. As Thoreau saw, because an opulent lifestyle requires significantly more income than does a simple life, it requires significantly more paid employment. Because graceful existence requires ample leisure, and because paid employment is so frequently antithetical to gracefulness, the demands of opulence interfere with the project of achieving gracefulness. Pursuing gracefulness through opulence commits one to its postponement, and possibly, as Aristotle and Thoreau warned, to self-destructive distortions as we dedicate our efforts to having more. This is foolishness if gracefulness can be achieved at far lower levels of income.

Take just the issue of postponement. Earlier I defined opulence as a consumption level of the sort found in families with an income of $200,000. As we saw, this represents a fourfold expansion of current levels of median family income, and would require perhaps seventy to one hundred years to attain depending on the growth rate. Moreover, even if it was attained, we would still face the problems we face now—insufficient time to make life graceful. If we are committed to opulent incomes, then we are committed to using whatever productivity increases occur in order to expand income, rather than to expand leisure. We condemn ourselves to more of what is most problematic with our current situation.

Just how thoroughly we do this is generally not seen because we tend to not think in terms of how long it takes for a society to increase its income. As individuals, if we hustle enough, we can generally move up. In ten years' time, a student might go from college to a $150,000 law practice. But this can't be replicated collectively. Over the course of the last century, the growth of per capita income in the United States has been 1.8 percent per year. Historically speaking, this is very rapid growth, unlike what has occurred throughout most of history. Yet it is quite different from what happens to an individual who is "moving up." For the most part, such "success" involves attaining a prized position in a game of musical chairs. If I have the seat, it means that you don't. When instead we look to broad-based economic growth, the time scale is very different. As a society, attaining general opulence takes a long, long time.

On the other hand, the simple living individualists, be they Thoreau or contemporary authors, maintain that, with the right attitudes and with wise personal choices, the good life—understood as a form of simple living—is presently within our grasp. I've been skeptical of the general applicability of this position. And in arguing for a politics of simplicity, I have maintained that although this is true in principle, it won't work for most people. The financial solutions are not as easy as advertised; the personal transformations and cultural shifts that are required ask more of people than they can (or will) provide; and some of these strategies involve us in far too much personal accountancy and far more concern with saving money, cutting corners, and worrying about budgets than seems compatible with gracefulness.

On the other hand, I agree with the individualists, that within a relatively short period of time, we can significantly change our way of life as a society. If we combine the personal with the political, we can make enormous progress. I've offered some examples—free college tuition, thirty-hour workweeks, simple living tax credits, neighborhood beautification and revitalization. With steps of this sort as the general background within which people pursue simple living, in only a few years we could find ourselves living quite differently.

Interestingly, if I were asked, "What is the primary obstacle that stands in the way of a politics dedicated not to expanded incomes but to expanding the opportunities for simple living?" I would answer that we, ourselves, are the problem. What stands in the way is how we see the world. For those who have advocated personal transformation, this has always been obvious, and they have always preached a new vision of self and life. But I would argue the very same obstacle of misguided vision stands in the way of a politics of simple living. What we need, whether we are talking about individual solutions or political approaches, is a coherent body of thought that allows us to see the world differently, be it a religion, a philosophy, or an ideology. We have to set our thinking about economic life within a larger vision of human life.

In the final two chapters I offer some ideas with respect to the fundamental questions that any such outlook must come to terms with: Are we simple creatures? What are our needs? What is real wealth? And how might we reasonably think about money?

Chapter Nine

ARE WE SIMPLE CREATURES?

It is widely accepted that everyone in America wants to get rich. This is not true, yet to suggest otherwise—that most people want something quite modest yet elusive, and that they are right in seeking something different from economic life—is always a bit suspect. To pose graceful simplicity as a general ideal has, to some ears, the trappings of "second best," of accepting limits, or of throwing in the towel on the American Dream.

In levering ourselves free of the dominant economic ideology we need to go back to basics, to the very concepts of income and wealth. Typically both income and wealth are measured in monetary terms, with wealth representing the stock of valuable things (assets) that a person owns at any given point in time. Income is a flow concept, the amount that is added (net or gross) to the individual's stock of valuable things during a given time period. Thus, one's wealth at a particular point in time (e.g., January 1, 1999) might be $500,000, and one's income during a particular time period (e.g., January 1, 1998–December 31, 1998) might have been $100,000. Income is either consumed, thus producing direct satisfactions, or it is saved, thus expanding the individual's wealth.

Before considering income and wealth for human beings, let us consider a simpler creature, the rabbit. What does a rabbit need for the good life? Perhaps only this:

Fresh water
Good grass

Nice weather
Other rabbits
Good health
Absence of predators

Once these needs are met, external conditions have contributed as much as they can contribute to the good life for a rabbit. Once these have been supplied, rabbit happiness can't be increased much further. Moreover, when this bounty is available to the rabbits, it is generally none of their doing. It is supplied by nature. Since there is little that rabbits can do to ensure these conditions, the rabbits do very little work, whether conditions are optimal or not. Like the Stoics at a banquet, they partake of the great dish as it is passed around, but (for the most part) if it has little on it, they accept that, too.

Suppose then a rabbit world in which these six desiderata are met. One day a rabbit toy is invented. One and all, the rabbits find it great fun. But to acquire it the rabbits must work to produce it. As a result they develop a production system and a system of markets, for labor, for extracting raw materials, and for selling the toys. In short, they develop an economy. And they measure the size of the economy in terms of how many of these rabbit toys (RTs) are produced. Suppose that these reach very substantial levels, and that these levels vary sharply as we go from rabbit community to rabbit community.

How are we to understand income, wealth, and well-being in the rabbit world? How are we to compare the well-being of the rabbits in one community with those in another, or to compare the time prior to the invention of RTs with the years afterward? The pleasure from the RTs is indeed real. If it were not, the rabbits would not work to attain them. Rabbit income could be measured in terms of the flow of RTs, and wealth in terms of the stock of RTs, or the capacity to produce RTs. Yet only the blind would imagine that rabbit well-being or rabbit standard of living is adequately captured by how many RTs the rabbits have. Even if each one of them represents some net advantage (the pleasure of having it minus the pains undergone in acquiring it), surely this would be only the thinnest icing on a very thick cake—a cake of fresh water, good grass, other rabbits, and good health. Of course the rabbits, taking the thick cake for granted, hardly notice it. Paying nothing for these critical factors, it slips from sight. They come to think that their well-being consists in how much icing they possess. But in this they are wrong.

Is it so radically different with people?

MONEY AND HUMAN NEEDS

Even in the world of RTs, rabbit well-being is largely a matter of health, good weather, grass, fresh water, other rabbits, and the absence of predators. Perhaps good health, good weather, basic food, fresh water, other people, the absence of predators, and a modicum of clothing also represent the bulk of what we humans need for our well-being. Might it not be that the income and wealth that the economy provides beyond that which addresses these fundamental needs constitutes only a thin icing of well-being? Might it not be that, like the rabbits, our true wealth consists of things other than what the economy can provide?

Yet, people are not rabbits. While the description of the constituents of rabbit well-being can serve as a rough description of the simple life as found in the Garden of Eden, we are not living in that Garden. And if we look more closely at the Garden of Eden story itself we see that perhaps even for Adam and Eve the Garden was not so perfect. Or at least not perfect for Eve.

What we remember most readily, of course, is that God tells Adam and Eve not to eat from the tree of knowledge of good and evil, but beguiled by the snake, first Eve and then Adam eat the forbidden fruit. So understood, they are seduced by the snake who is history's first huckster, its first adman suckering them into overconsumption. When they had limited desires, they were content. Then the snake intervened and flashed the shiny apple; he induced new desires, and with that they got into trouble.

But the story is really more interesting than that. If we read carefully we see that after the snake tells Eve that by eating the fruit "your eyes will be opened," and after he assures her that this is really a safe product to consume, Eve comes to her own conclusion: "When the woman saw that the tree was good for eating and a delight to the eyes, and that the tree was desirable as a source of wisdom, she took of its fruit and ate."

Why should Eve have been moved by the tree being a source of wisdom, and why should she have perceived it thus? The answer is clear. Even in the Garden of Eden, from the very first, as part of the inherent motivation of her humanity, Eve, if not Adam, was a seeker of wisdom. Here one may ask whether she had a *need* for wisdom; certainly she had no instrumental need for it—in the Garden, everything was taken care of. Eve's motivation toward wisdom must be seen as either a need (or a desire) for wisdom for its own sake. Thus, even in the Garden, in the original mankind of our central myth, we find human beings, or at least Eve, to be more interesting and complex than the truly simple creatures.

That Eve steals wisdom from God may be compared to the Greek myths in which Prometheus steals the secret of fire from the gods. Fire represents energy and technology. But how much more interesting is the Israelite myth in which Eve steals wisdom.

Actually, it is not even wisdom itself that Eve steals, but the categories that are central to the search for wisdom and for its attainment: good and evil. Thus, as an immediate result of eating of the fruit of the tree, neither Adam nor Eve shows any signs of having achieved great wisdom. The change they have undergone is evident only when God calls out to Adam, "Where are you?" and Adam answers, "I heard the sound of You in the garden, and I was afraid because I was naked, so I hid," and God, who is clever, but apparently not omniscient, responds, "Who told you that you were naked? Did you eat of the tree?" In the use of the word "naked" Adam reveals his internalization of moral concepts, and thus reveals that they had eaten the fruit.

Of course, eating of the tree could not produce wisdom, but merely the preconditions of wisdom, for the entire Torah (the first five books of the Bible) makes no sense if mankind is already possessed of wisdom, rather than capable of receiving it. And indeed, if in reading the Bible we drop our preconceptions of the nature of God (e.g., that merely in virtue of being God, God is all knowing, all powerful, all good) the storyline of the Bible makes clear that God, too, is in need of wisdom. He has much to learn about the human creatures He has created, and much to learn about how to educate them. For instance, in the story of Noah, after He reacts with rage and disappointment and wipes out almost all living things in response to human debauchery, He, for the first time, starts an effort at instruction, providing a few simple rules for life. In successive books the rules multiply vastly, and one might wonder if God still has not yet mastered the art of pedagogy. From a Christian perspective it might be maintained that it is only as expressed through Jesus that God achieves his fullness as a teacher. From an Islamic perspective one might say that this process reaches its fulfillment only in Mohammed. And from the perspective of Rabbinic Judaism one might say that it is the Torah itself and the institutions of communal inquiry that are the central elements in acquiring wisdom.

But, to return to the main point, human beings are not rabbits. Like Eve our needs are different. The key, however, is to understand the ways in which this is true and the ways in which it is not. Here we must distinguish material needs from higher-order needs. It is a fundamental mistake to think that human beings need only good food, clean water, good weather (or adequate shelter and clothing), and the absence of predators (human or otherwise). As we have seen, it may be very costly for us to even meet simple material needs (e.g., to live in a neighborhood free from predators); however our core economic needs are in themselves not so very different from those of the rabbit. The difference is that, like Eve, we have deeper needs that are unknown to the rabbits. But if this is so, then how do we manage to go so wrong, how do we manage to veer so far from this simple wisdom that has been articulated again and again within our traditions?

THE TRANSFORMATION OF NEED INTO DESIRE

One answer is that we have in addition to our material needs a set of fundamental psychological needs that, through various processes, come to be associated with the goods and services produced by the economy. There are numerous ways to conceptualize these ultimate psychological needs. We may speak of the need for positive self-identity, for self-respect, for being, for psychological security, for love, for self-worth, and so forth. For our purposes, the differences among these various conceptualizations are not essential.

Three factors are important. First, part of what it is to be a person is to be the object of one's own perception; people then develop a substantial stake in seeing themselves in particular ways. Second, how we see ourselves is to a considerable extent typically affected by how others see us. And third, to varying degrees, in human cultures, how people see others is partially determined by aspects of the person's economic involvement (e.g., how they consume, what they earn, what they do for a living).

Thus, from the point of view of the individual, the need to see oneself in a certain way is dependent upon how one is seen by others, and the factors that determine how others will see any given individual are to some extent cultural givens. If one internalizes these cultural norms, then even the actual perceptions of others may drop out of the equation, as one perceives oneself through the eyes of the culture or subculture.

We can, therefore, speak of a process of transmogrification through which an underlying need (e.g., a need for self-worth) is transformed into desires for specific marketplace commodities. The diagram that follows schematizes how, in a specific cultural context, a deep-seated need, such as the need for self-esteem, can be transformed into a desire for specific possessions (and thus for the income with which to acquire them).

Need	Psychological/Social Conditions
Level 1: Adam has an underlying need for self-esteem.	
	Context: Like most individuals, his self-esteem is highly dependent upon how he is seen by others.
Level 2: His underlying need for self-esteem thus emerges as a need to be seen by others as valuable.	
	Context: A specific group of people emerge for him as the reference group whose judgment really matters (e.g., parents, colleagues, peers).
Level 3: His underlying need for self-esteem now emerges as a need to be seen as valuable by this select group.	
	Context: The reference group has certain norms with respect to consumption patterns, such that the failure to meet these norms symbolizes failure, lack of decency, inadequacy.
Level 4: His need for self-esteem now emerges as a need to satisfy the consumption norms of the reference group.	
	Context: The reference group's definition of "decency" and "adequacy" mandates living in houses

Need	Psychological/Social Conditions
	with certain minimal conditions (e.g., a "good" neighborhood, at least two baths, bedrooms for each child, and a large kitchen).
Level 5: His need for self-esteem is now expressed as a desire for a specific kind of house and style of life.	
	Context: Market conditions price such houses at $200,000 or more. His ability to attain these financial resources is dependent upon his employment.
Level 6: His need for self-esteem is now expressed as a desire for employment that yields income sufficient to have a $200,000 house.	

The above diagram does not at first mention desires. The starting point was a need for self-esteem. The individual typically is not conscious of such a need, and its existence is not dependent upon his awareness of it. To say that he has a need for self-esteem is to say that, on a very basic level, something will go seriously wrong with him if he fails to develop self-esteem.

How this fundamental, and perhaps universal, need gets transformed into a specific desire for certain kinds of jobs, as well as a multiplicity of other desires, is a matter of social and economic context. As the underlying need becomes more concretely related to things that he can actually do to satisfy it (or that he believes will satisfy it), it moves more fully into a conscious desire. And this itself may be expressed in plans and intentions. For instance, in order to be able to have a particular kind of job he may seek to go to law school, and in order to get into law school he may seek to do well as an undergraduate. This desire, in turn, may proliferate into a thousand more concrete desires to do well on a test, to get to class on time, to get his assignments finished, and so forth. In the end, an enormously expansive orientation toward the day to day may emerge, all expressive of an underlying need for self-esteem.

The diagram, though simplifying processes that we don't fully understand, is useful in allowing us to distinguish among the levels at which different anticonsumerist orientations and philosophies propose interventions in order to block this process through which fundamental psychological needs give rise to the specific desires for money and commodities. Thus Stoicism, in its emphasis on individual self-sufficiency, might be understood as an effort to block the transformation of the general need for self-esteem into a need for the approval of others (level 2). Buddhism might be thought of as seeking change on an even more fundamental level, whereby the sense of self is so totally transformed that there is no longer a need for self-esteem (level 1). The formation of utopian communities might be thought of as the substitution of a different subculture as the group of relevant others (level 3). A broader social change movement, however, might take a different approach. Rather than trying to move the individual toward a different reference group, it might be trying to transform the norms of the entire society (also level 3). And finally, there are the more familiar, less ambitious social and economic policies that might simply seek to transform the market conditions. Thus, one might seek to make "decent" housing available at much lower income levels by controlling prices, subsidizing purchases, making low-interest loans available, and so forth. All of this so we might be more widely successful in attaining self-esteem (level 6).

There is nothing new in the existence of these processes whereby deep needs are transformed into desires for the goods and services that the economy can provide. We are talking about an ancient phenomenon that has existed and been noted among many cultures.

THE SNAKE IN THE GARDEN

What is new in our age is the existence of self-conscious efforts of other economic actors to enhance these linkages between deep psychological needs and desires for consumer goods.

One interesting example is *Why They Buy: American Consumers Inside and Out*, a book that was written explicitly for what the authors call "marketeers";

that is, people who specialize in getting consumers to want to buy specific products. What makes this book particularly interesting is its fine-grained approach to human needs. The authors identify some sixty specific psychological needs. These include the following:

    to be visible to others
    to accomplish difficult tasks
    to establish one's sexual identity
    to give care
    to engage in forceful (bodily) activity
    to exercise one's talents
    to be autonomous of others
    to be positively noticed by others
    to win over adversaries
    to be associated with others
    to win acceptance
    to see living things thrive
    to help others develop
    to protect one's charges from harm
    to be the recipient of nurturent efforts
    to receive and provide sexual satisfaction
    to maintain sexual alternatives without exercising them
    to avoid condemnation for sexual appetites
    to engage in the unusual
    to play
    to be amused
    to learn new skills
    to be amazed
    to teach
    to be free from threat of harm[168]

With respect to these needs, the authors identify the kinds of goods "that serve each kind of need." The author's advice is that if you want to succeed in marketing, it is essential to know your consumer, to understand what his needs are, and to know what needs your product serves. The marketeers are told that it is important for them to "instill purchase incentives in the minds of potential buyers" by "teaching consumers about what they will get."

Although one might want to challenge either the legitimacy or the very existence of some of these "needs," for the most part they do seem real, important, and valid. Moreover, even this enumeration, which is the most extensive I have ever seen, is clearly not exhaustive. For instance, the authors do not include a need to love and to be loved, or a need for insight into oneself, or a need for meaningful work, nor do they include a need for beauty or adventure, or a need for a comprehensive vision of life.

Considering a list of this sort, despite its source, is very useful. It helps dispel two notions to which critics of consumer culture (such as myself) are prone. The first misconception has already been mentioned, the mistaken belief that at bottom we are very simple creatures like the rabbits. The second is that our vast sense of what we need and our diverse set of desires emerge from our having been manipulated by these "marketeers." It is not that they would not like to manipulate us, and indeed, it is not that they do not often succeed, but rather that for all the billions spent on advertising, this is the smaller part of the story. The larger part is that we are creatures of considerable complexity, with highly developed and diverse needs. Like Eve with her need for wisdom, we are not the passive victims of the snake.

Moreover, I would go so far as to suggest that even the self-serving claims of marketeers that they are "educating" us about what will "serve" our needs, rather than manipulating us, have a significant element of truth to them. Thus, when the authors of *Why They Buy* go on to say that these needs can "be served" with distinct clothing, customized cars, and exotic foods and drinks, and with bizarre hairstyles and unusual jewelry, with "how to" books, with tools and with "do it yourself" manuals, and with plaques, and awards, and trophies, and school pins, and pet supplies, and garden products, and massages, and shoe shines, and sexy clothes, and perfumes, and films and videotapes, and exercise equipment, and bubble baths, and flavors, and toys and games, and recreational vehicles, and boats and sports equipment, and travel, and adult-education programs, and magazines, and soaps, and financial services, and alarms, and vitamins—when they say that all this "serves our needs"—they are largely correct. This enormous cornucopia of goods and services does serve our needs. And the alternative hypothesis, that our desire for all this is the creation of Madison Avenue or emerges from mere emulation of others, is distinctly implausible.

But in saying this, it should be recognized how little is conceded to the priests of consumption. Yes, we are complex creatures. And yes, of course, the vast array of goods and services in the marketplace is linked to our complex needs. But to say this is not to say that participation in this consumptionist form of life is the only way to meet human needs, or the best way.

The case for simple living does not require believing that we ourselves are simple creatures. Rather, it involves recognizing that the ways in which we are complex and subtle involve needs that the marketplace typically addresses inadequately or at extremely high personal and social costs.

Reviewing the entire diverse list of psychological needs itemized above, there is not one that cannot be satisfied by means other than the purchase of goods and services. The case for simple living is that there are better ways to satisfy our needs than through high levels of consumption. These other means are better in two ways. First, through them the need is more fully, deeply, and lastingly met. And second, it is met at lower cost—initially monetary cost—but this translates into time or life energy.[169]

If there are high-consumption and low-consumption forms of life that both address our diverse needs, even if they both address them adequately, the case for living simply is enormously compelling. Consumption requires income, and, for most of us, income requires labor, and labor is costly in two ways. First, for many people, beyond a certain level, it is distasteful, painful, unhealthy, or boring. Second, whether labor is pleasant, neutral, or distasteful, it takes time. It takes time to prepare for, time to get to, time to perform, time to return from, and time to recover from. Yet our time is relatively fixed. Time we devote to getting the means of consumption is time that is not available for other aspects of life.

Except when spending more time on the job is the most fulfilling use of one's time, to opt for a high-consumption rather than a low-consumption way of meeting the same need is to be wasting life. Put another way, we can say, "No we are not simple creatures like rabbits, and just because we are complex creatures with complex needs and capacities does not mean that we need to waste our time and energy in pursuit of material responses to the complexities, opportunities, and challenges of human life."

MONEY IS NOT THE ENEMY

How adequately do money and the things it can buy satisfy human needs? Consider in this regard a passage from an early manuscript of Karl Marx entitled *The Power of Money in Bourgeois Society*. Marx, following Aristotle, is explicating the distorting character of money. He tells us about a world where everything has its price:

> What I am and am capable of is by no means determined by my individuality. I am ugly, but I can buy for myself the most beautiful of women. Therefore I am not ugly, for the effect of ugliness—its deterrent power—is nullified by money. I, as an individual, am lame, but money furnishes me with twenty-four feet. Therefore I am not lame. I am bad, dishonest, unscrupulous, stupid; but money is honored, and hence its possessor. . . . Do not I, who thanks to money am capable of all that the human heart longs for, possess all human capacities? Does not my money, therefore, transform all my incapacities into their contrary?[170]

We should not accept this at face value. Actually, rather than the corrupting nature of money what we see here is the complexity of the role of money. The individual in Marx's passage suffers from a multiplicity of disabilities and characteristics. He is

+ ugly
+ lame
+ stupid
+ bad
+ dishonest
+ unscrupulous

How these characteristics play out in a monetarized world is determined in considerable part by whether the individual is rich or poor. In short, our interaction with the world is "mediated" by money (Marx's term), and, in particular, mediated by how much of it we have.

There are two queries that need to be distinguished: first, does having money really provide an alternative capability when natural capability is lacking, or does it represent only a capability to achieve a limited or perhaps false satisfaction of our needs; and second, is this a good thing or not?

There is no general answer to these questions. Having money may help us overcome being lame, but it never does so entirely. Yet, for what it does accomplish we should be thankful. Being lame does not make one less deserving of a good life. If money helps to overcome such obstacles, so much the better.

We might feel the same way about ugliness. One might be physically ugly through no fault of one's own, and while it seems "unnatural" that wealthy ugly people suffer the less for their looks than do those who are both ugly and poor, this is at least an understandable compensation for the rich. Here, too, we may wonder how adequately money actually does compensate for being ugly? Perhaps one can "buy" a beautiful consort, but this is not the same thing as being genuinely desired or genuinely loved. On the other hand, perhaps rich people who are not physically attractive get the benefit of a second look or a deeper look.

Marx may be largely right that social honor does go to the rich even if they are lacking in honorable character. This represents a different pattern from the above. Here, the social order is itself wrongfully distorted, yet the individual does, in fact, achieve through money that which he might never have achieved without it—social respect.

These varied roles and evaluations of the mediation of money should not be lumped together, for they show very different things. In some cases they are indictments of the social order; in other cases, they show the way in which a money culture can be more humane than a so-called "natural order." In some cases money leads to the genuine satisfaction of needs through alternative routes; in other cases it shows that money can only provide limited satisfaction; and, in still others, this is only an ersatz satisfaction.

When it comes to our most fundamental needs—for love, meaning, friendship, self-expression, understanding, esteem of others, and self-worth— money may, in the terms of the marketeers, be "of service," but it rarely provides the genuine article. Here we find that when money is central to the "servicing" of need, the result is either diversion or compensation from the fact that the need is not fulfilled, or a symbolic or false taste of the real thing.

But this is not to dismiss its importance. We make a very big mistake if we imagine that in walking away from a world of high consumption (or high relative economic standing) one is walking away from little. Finding genuine satisfaction for our deepest needs is not easy, and most people are at best only partially successful in this search. Even when we say that friendship can provide much of what we seek in life, this does not mean that it is easy. True friends are hard to find—or, to put it more constructively, building and sustaining true friendship is itself an art and a commitment. It, too, requires time and investment. And it is not so easy to succeed. Life can be filled with disappointment in others, and we may not come easily to the human capabilities that friendship requires. Indeed, it is far easier to be the love object of another than to be their friend. Any Jack may someday get lucky and find a Jill who falls in love with him—but if he depends on luck, or on looking cute, he may go forever without true friends.

What the marketplace often provides are second-best responses and comforts. In a world in which we may lack the human resources, or simply the good fortune, to attain the genuine article, second-best fulfillments, or even pleasant diversions, can be of substantial value. In that sense, to choose simple living is an act of courage. It is a decision to "go for it"—to not accept second best in life.

Chapter Ten

THE MONETARY ILLUSION

If money is not the enemy, if money sometimes helps us attain a safer second-best or third-best or fourth-best life, it must be acknowledged that money does contribute to our confusion. Part of the mystery of why we go so wrong in life lies in the "illusion of money," by which I mean the illusion that the price of things tells us much about their true value.

What is fascinating about money is that we all know that it does not offer a meaningful picture of genuine wealth. For instance, is it not indisputable that much of what is most important to us—our children, our reputation, the love of another—has no price. This is a commonplace, known to all at the first instant of reflection. Yet, the moment we get up from the easy chair, we seem to set aside our reflections. Or perhaps, even while sustaining them, we cannot break away from thinking about wealth in monetary terms. We use money to measure both the income and the wealth of individuals and society. We use monetary measures to consider how income and wealth are distributed, and we use it to make comparisons with respect to standards of living—between different individuals, or between countries, or between two points in time—whether in our own life, or that of society as a whole.

We suffer from at least two kinds of blindness. First, we tend to measure the value of things in terms of their price; and second, we tend not to see the value of things that have no price. Let us consider these in turn.

THE DIFFERENCE BETWEEN PRICE AND VALUE

Economists long ago pondered what initially seemed paradoxical, that some of the most valuable commodities, such as air and water, have little monetary value, while others, such as diamonds, are worth a great deal. In struggling with this anomaly, the distinction was made between exchange value and use value. *Exchange value* means the value that something has in virtue of its being exchangeable for some other item of value. We make these exchanges in the market, and in market economies we exchange labor and commodities for money, and money for commodities. Since money is the common element into which things are exchanged, exchange value can be measured by the amount of money that something exchanges for. The term we give to this is "price." When people inquire about the price of an item, they are asking, "How much money does one need to exchange in order to get it?" As economists came to greater clarity about these matters, explaining and predicting the prices of commodities emerged as a central task of economics.

Use value, on the other hand, was seen to mean the actual contribution to human welfare that the commodity makes. Everyone realized that when diamonds are compared to water, water is low in exchange value and high in use value, whereas diamonds were relatively low in use value but high in exchange value.

For a time, it was a challenge to economic theory to explain how this could be the case. Ultimately, the explanation was found in understanding that the price a commodity exchanges for is determined not by the importance of the commodity as a whole (e.g., water) but by its importance on the margin (e.g., one more gallon of water). Further, what was important on the margin was the cost of supplying one more unit, as well as the value to the purchaser of having one more unit.

Thus (assume that water is the only liquid), while one might exchange most of one's possessions for a gallon of water if none were available at all, one would give very little for an additional gallon if one already had plenty. Similarly, since an additional gallon can be brought to the market at very little cost, one need pay only a small price to induce the sale of an extra gallon. Whereas, if we reached a point at which bringing the extra gallon to market was very expensive (although water as a whole may remain inexpensive to provide), unless the price of water was at that high price, the last gallon would not be brought to market, and the same for the next to last and so forth. So, in order for any quantity of water to come to the market, its price must rise to the cost of supplying the last gallon. Thus, despite its almost infinite use value, water exchanges for little because it is abundant (we have limited desire for more) and because more can be obtained rather inexpensively.

What is sketched above is the solution that economists in the nineteenth century—the so-called marginalists, such as Alfred Marshall—found to the seeming paradox that things of great value (in use) could have little value (in exchange). But what is most interesting here is this: first, both before and after the paradox was explained, no one was in doubt as to the phenomenon—that there is no fixed correspondence between the market price and use value. And, second, *explaining the paradox made no difference.* We still continued to view the prices of things as adequate measures of their value, even though we knew they were not. Such is the hypnotic quality of money.

Suppose then that there are two people, and that they are in possession of exactly the same items, except that the second person has two of every item, whereas the first has only one. Thus, the second person has two houses, two cars, two blue coats, two refrigerators full of food, and so forth. The first person has only one house, one car, one blue coat, and one full refrigerator.

Insofar as we are measuring the extent of a person's assets by summing up the prices paid for the various items (or the price he could get if he sold them), the second person has twice the wealth of the first person. Having no doubt as to the difference between use value and exchange value, we know that this is nonsense. Moreover, if rather than two houses the person had a house twice as big, and rather than two cars, a car twice as long, it should be apparent to us that he still doesn't have twice the wealth of the first person. We know it is nonsense to believe that he does, yet we do so nonetheless.

The extent to which we suffer from such illusions is remarkable. It reflects something very deep about our culture, about how thoroughly our vision of things has been molded by markets and the exchanges that occur within them, and about how much of our life activity is organized around bringing things to market and bringing things back from market—most centrally, bringing ourselves (our labor, our skills) to market and bringing back home, in exchange, money or commodities.

Permanently dispelling the idea that the price you pay for something reflects its value is almost impossible. Nonetheless, it may help to reflect on the following:

- While the price of the physical necessities is often low and in some cases zero, their value is almost infinite. If they were in short supply, a billionaire would pay almost all he had for the food and water that you consume. Yet with these items of near infinite worth, having more than is necessary, or having fancy versions, is worth little more than having that which meets our needs.

- With respect to many of the commodities that we have, they would in fact be fantastically valuable (in monetary terms), if it weren't the case that they can be produced cheaply. Thus, consider your old car. Perhaps it is worth $2,000—but if, in fact, cars could not be made cheaply, or not made at all, your old car would be worth tens of thousands. If it were the only car, it would be worth millions. The same for your camera or your mirror or a pair of scissors, or a pencil or a piece of paper. Under some circumstances, these could be the most sought after, most amazing, most valuable (in monetary terms) items in the world.

- Whenever we buy something, we are doing so because we have judged that the thing is worth more to us than the price that is asked for it. That's the whole point of exchanging the money for the item. Sometimes this gap is enormous, and not merely with respect to necessities. Consider that it may only cost you $50 to buy a dog that you would not sell for thousands. What was the value of the $1 of painkiller that relieved the worst headache you ever had? How much was the best novel you ever read worth? The bicycle you had for ten years as a child—how did its value compare to the $50 paid for it?

THE VALUE OF THINGS THAT TYPICALLY HAVE NO PRICE

In the 1960s and 1970s the women's movement called attention to a certain blindness with respect to the value of women's labor in the home. The basic problem was that neither the existence of women's labor nor its contribution was recognized, neither within the family nor within the larger society. In response an effort was made to "price out" women's labor at home, to point out what it would cost to hire someone to perform all these tasks. To move in this direction, to focus on monetary equivalents in order to make us appreciative of value, is both wrongheaded and quite understandable. It is wrongheaded because the price we might have to pay for the labor is not a good measure of its value; and it is understandable because being blind to all else but monetary terms, what other language can we understand?

Unfortunately, neither pointing out the monetary illusions we suffer from, nor placing monetary values on that which is not monetized, seems to make a great deal of difference. We are so thoroughly embedded in our ways of seeing that probably nothing short of being reborn in a totally different culture would really free us from the hold that money exercises upon our minds.

Still, we must try.

Consider a familiar item without a price, the human body. What is it worth? Well, if we are talking about a dead body, then perhaps very little. Medical schools, as a rule, don't have to pay for the cadavers they teach from; they are donated free of charge.

But this is not our question. Our question is not about the value of an extra body, but rather about the value of one's own body. We are not really concerned with market prices, since those reflect only the supply and demand of that which is actually brought to market. What we really are interested in is the value of one's own body to the person himself.

Were it possible, what would someone pay to retain one's body, or perhaps to replace it? That, of course, depends on its condition and the condition of the replacement. Would an eighty-five-year-old billionaire with a life expectancy of five years pay a billion dollars to exchange bodies with someone who had fifty years to live as opposed to five? How many twenty-five-year-olds with healthy bodies would rather have a billion dollars plus an eighty-five-year-old body? No doubt some, but not most people. I'd expect most people would not, for virtually any amount, exchange their bodies for significantly older, significantly less healthy bodies. I would imagine that most eighty-five-year-old billionaires would give virtually all that they own to be able to trade for a young, healthy body. Our body—our thinking, feeling, living body—is our natural wealth. It is our great property. It is from this property that our flow of experience emerges. It is this that enables us to enjoy all we enjoy, to feel all we feel. It is this that enables us to do and to be.

In this wealth, with the exception of people with illnesses, we all start out relatively equal. Each of us is given a gift that is worth billions. However, we are cursed at the same time; it is a worth that starts to dissipate the moment it arrives. It flows away from us at a steady rate, like a hole in the bank account—365 days are lost every year. There are some things we can do to make it last a bit longer, but one way or another, we end our lives completely broke.

One of the reasons that very few people see things this way is the simple fact that there is no technology for exchanging bodies. Medical science can, however, replace body parts, even vital ones, but not entire bodies. Even with respect to vital body parts, markets are largely undeveloped or underground—one cannot go out and buy a young heart.

But we are likely not far from technologies that will allow us to exchange full bodies. Let us say that we can do this, retaining perhaps enough of the brain so as to ensure continuity of memory and identity. Suppose then that body swaps between consenting adults become a real possibility. Under those conditions I expect that we would all be greatly more aware of the fundamental equality of our present situation, as well as, ironically, of the fundamental inequality; some will be buyers of sound bodies, and others will be sellers. Of course having (or occupying) a living body is not all much of a muchness—its value can vary widely. Certainly a person facing only prolonged captivity and torture might value his living body less highly than otherwise. There are always deeply troubled, saddened, and lonely persons for whom being alive has lost all value.

Like all wealth, the wealth we have in our living body represents only the *capability* of what is good in itself. Merely being alive is never sufficient for valued living. This wealth in our body is however necessary for any valued human functioning and experience. It is this dependence of all good experiences upon having a living body that imparts tremendous derivative value on whatever is itself necessary to sustain the life and health of that body. Thus, as noted, food, and water, and air, taken in the first increments without which life is not possible, are of extraordinary value to the individual, however little they may cost.

One implication, however, of recognizing the tremendous value of small amounts of life-sustaining necessities, and of the great wealth that we all have in our bodies, is that it seems to call into question the extent of the relative differences in income and wealth of the rich and the poor. If the marginal value of money declines rather rapidly, then the actual value of the goods possessed by the poor is substantially closer to that of those possessed by the rich than a comparison of market costs would indicate. (The use value of a liter of tap water that costs less than a penny may not be so vastly different than that of a liter of fine wine that cost 20,000 times as much; and that of a $50 bicycle may not be vastly different from that of a $30,000 car.) While this conclusion initially may be disconcerting, it takes on a different aspect when we realize that the transition we seek is not from poverty to wealth, but from poverty to simple living.

WHEN DOES MONEY REALLY MATTER?

One clear circumstance where the income of the poor and the income of the rich differ enormously in value is when their income differences translate into differences in years of life. Clearly this is true in very poor countries where the life expectancy at birth of the rich and the poor is enormously different. The poor may be exposed to infant mortality rates of 1 in 5 while the rich might face rates of 1 in 100. In terms of life experience, that means that if you are poor, there is a good chance that one of your babies will die, while this is a rare tragedy if you are rich.

Consider the following table, which shows the relationship between per capita income and life expectancy for various countries in the world.

COUNTRY	1994 PER CAPITA GDP (PPP $)	LIFE EXPECTANCY AT BIRTH
Luxembourg	34,155	75.9
United States	26,397	76.2
Japan	21,581	79.8
Canada	21,459	79.0
Denmark	21,341	75.2
France	20,510	78.7
Australia	19,285	78.1
Finland	17,417	76.3
Ireland	16,061	76.3
Israel	16,023	77.5
Spain	14,324	77.6
Mauritius	13,172	70.7
Portugal	12,326	74.6
Korea S.	10,656	71.5
Chile	9,129	75.1

COUNTRY	1994 PER CAPITA GDP (PPP $)	LIFE EXPECTANCY AT BIRTH
Mexico	7,384	72.0
Costa Rica	5,919	76.6
Brazil	5,362	66.4
Turkey	5,193	68.2
Poland	5,002	71.2
Jordan	4,187	68.5
Egypt	3,846	64.3
Morocco	3,681	65.3
Peru	3,645	67.4
Congo	2,410	51.3
Senegal	1,596	49.9
Kenya	1,404	53.6
India	1,348	61.3
Nepal	1,137	55.3
Haiti	896	54.4
Niger	787	47.1
Chad	700	47.0
Sierra Leone	643	33.6
Ethiopia	427	48.2

Source: Human Development Report, 1997, United Nations Development Program.[171]

The table suggests a few generalizations:

- Income matters. People in countries with higher average incomes tend to live longer.
- Income isn't all that matters. There are some countries with modest income levels, such as Costa Rica, in which people live as long as in the United States, although incomes are less than one-quarter of our level.
- Income level seems to matter less and less as income rises. Thus, comparing countries with less than $1,000 per capita income with those at about $5,000, there is a life expectancy gap of at least fifteen years. But between countries at the $5,000 level (excluding Costa Rica) and those at the $10,000 level, the gap is around nine

years, and comparing those at the $10,000 with those at the $15,000 level, the gap is only around four years. Between those at the $15,000 level and those at $20,000, it is approximately two years. Above the $20,000 level there seems hardly any relationship at all between average income and life expectancy.

These, of course, are numbers for countries as a whole. They do not say anything about the differences within the country. Thus, we must not assume that for individuals within a country, higher income translates into longer life up to the $20,000 per year level, but no further. Unfortunately, data on the relationship between income and life expectancy are not abundant. One study that was done for Canada compared the life expectancy at birth of those in the top one-fifth of the income spectrum with those in the bottom one-fifth. It found that in 1986 the life expectancy difference was 5.6 years for men and 1.8 years for women.[172] Income inequality in Canada is less than in the United States, and access to health care is greater. Thus, one would expect to see a somewhat bigger gap for the United States. One study of mortality in the United States for the period 1979–1985 concluded that, between the highest and lowest income groups, there was a difference for white men of about 10 years and for white women of 4.3 years.[173] For all the races together, these differences would be greater. This general picture is supported by a recent study that compares life expectancy of Americans, depending on what county they live in within the United States. It found a gap of about fifteen years, ranging from a low of about sixty-five years to a high of about eighty years.[174] This gap can at least be partially explained by differences in income, whether understood in its bearing on the quality of medical care available to low-income people or on the levels of homicide in the neighborhoods low-income people can afford.

On the other hand, one should not jump to the conclusion that the only reason for the gap is that the things money can buy result in higher life expectancy. Part of the explanation for the gap may lie in lifestyle choices, such as smoking, which is more prevalent at lower income levels. In part people with certain problems (e.g., self-hatred) may be both destroying their health and destroying their careers. Sometimes the link between income and health emerges not because money can sustain health, but because people who have health problems (for whatever reason) can't earn much money, sometimes being unable to work at all. Thus, in assessing the contribution that having a higher income contributes to life expectancy, these differences in life expectancy should be viewed as somewhat overstated upper limits to the importance of income. The actual significance of higher income is no doubt less, though still quite real.

In relating household income to life expectancy within countries, we can expect to find a structure similar to that found between countries: income matters, income is not all that matters, and there is a declining marginal benefit in life expectancy associated with each increment of income.

While we do not have precise figures, we can develop an informed picture of what the relationship looks like for the United States, again remembering that not all of the correlation is due to the effect that higher income has on health.

**Estimate of How Money Matters
in the United States in 1999**

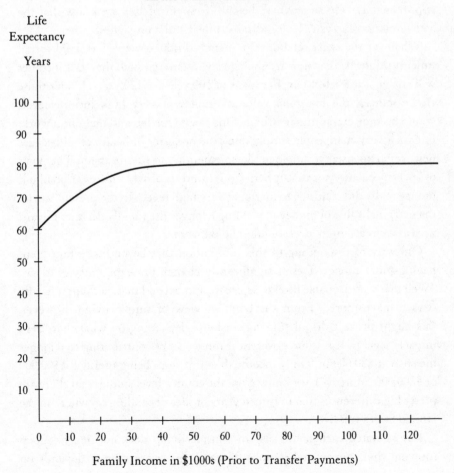

Family Income in $1000s (Prior to Transfer Payments)

There is a clear advantage to being born into a higher-income family. Measured in terms of life expectancy, this value is of diminishing significance as income levels rise. I would conjecture that it reaches zero somewhere around family incomes of $100,000, but is quite small well before that. This, of course, is a guestimate, but it seems plausible to me.

That there is a declining marginal effect of income on life expectancy must be true. Thus, assume that at levels of family income of $10,000, each increment of $1,000 resulted in a gain in life expectancy of 1 year, and that at the $10,000 level life expectancy at birth was 65 years. If the incremental value did not decline, then at the $60,000 level of annual income life expectancy would be 50 years greater or 115 years long, and someone with $1,010,000 in annual family income would be living until they were 1,065 years old. Because we know that the effect of income on life span has reached approximately zero somewhere below life spans of 100, we know that the actual relationship can't look radically different than my guestimate.

Whatever the exact relationship, it should not be viewed as fixed for all time. It might be that new technologies will emerge such that vast incomes will enable, for a select few, life spans of 100 years or 120 years. Under those circumstances, the marginal value of money at very high income levels would become extraordinarily high. One can go further and imagine a world in which very rich people simply don't die or suffer ill health at all because new, very expensive technologies keep emerging to sustain them. The point of such speculations is that it helps to remind us of what it *would* be like if money really did continue to matter at very high levels. In the present world, the marginal value of money in yielding a longer life rapidly declines toward zero as we reach high levels of household income.

One way of responding to this recognition that beyond a certain point having more money doesn't significantly change life expectancy is to say, "Well that's a reasonable level to aspire to, and beyond that, perhaps it hardly pays to have more." From the point of view of simple living, however, this might prove a disquieting conclusion—depending on what that "zero impact" level is. It is quite different if money stops contributing to a longer life span at $20,000 in family income than if it stops being useful at $100,000 or $200,000. Moreover, we know from the county-level studies that there are pretty big differences (ten to fifteen years of life) depending on where in the United States you live.

But as stated earlier, the case for simple living does not depend upon showing that money makes no difference, any more than it depends on showing that consumption makes no difference in responding to complex human needs. Rather, the case for simple living is that high income is not necessary, either to live well or to live long. Thus, from the point of view of simple living, the conclusion is twofold: first, beyond a certain level (whatever that is), having more money yields little benefit; and second, if one lives properly, one can attain those benefits at much lower levels of income.

Here, what is important is the existence of the examples of countries like Costa Rica where, with an annual average income of about $5,000, people live as long as in the United States. As was noted above, in Canada, money seems to matter less when it comes to its contribution to life expectancy. We can have a society in which money stops making a contribution to longer life spans at very low levels of income. Such a society facilitates simple living, and is one of the objectives of a politics of simplicity.

THE VALUE OF UNPRICED PERSONAL SERVICES

Beyond having a healthy body and a long life expectancy, in what else does human wealth reside? As we have seen, the Greek philosopher Epicurus identified friendship as that which was most important to human happiness. In this he was right. Clearly it is our relationships with other people that truly matter; having a loved and loving life partner, having good friends, having loved and loving children and relatives. We do not use the word "property" in these cases, nor do we speak of ownership. Yet we do sometimes speak of our friends and loved ones as our true wealth, or more commonly as our treasures or treasured ones.

When we own something, we have certain specific property rights with respect to it: a right to use it as we please; a right to exchange it for something else; a right to sell it; a right to whatever of value emerges from it; a right to restrict the access of others to it; a right to give it away; a right to destroy it. These property rights are what constitute economic ownership.

When it comes to other people, we have no such rights. Yet even with respect to physical property, such rights themselves confer little of economic value unless they can in fact be exercised. Where there is no expectation that such rights can be exercised, ownership is empty and, in market terms, will yield nothing. It is like being told that you own a million shares of stock in a gold mine, but no one will ever be allowed to mine the gold. The shares are worthless. Ultimately, what gives economic value to the things we own is the belief or expectation that such ownership can be transferred into a flow of things of value: in the first instance into a flow of income (through sale, rent, investment), and then, secondarily, into a flow of valued goods and services through the expenditure of that income. If not the second assumption, then the flow of monetary income is itself without economic value. Thus, it is the potential for transformation into a flow of valued goods and services that gives economic value to what we own.

How then are our human treasures, our very most valued relationships, related to goods and services? To goods, hardly at all. But what we get from each other when we have the *right* others is a unique flow of services. Consider just three of the many things that the other, beloved and true, might provide:

+ partner: someone with whom you can act in concert, not just doing things together but having a joint project
+ companion: someone with whom one can share the events of the day, someone who listens, who responds, who understands, who helps you see things more clearly and more fully
+ affection: someone who has genuine concern, someone who thinks of you, who does things that make you feel valued, who helps you see your own worth.

The illusion of money is such that we self-blind ourselves toward these unpriced personal services, just as we do with unpaid household labor. How are we to move out of our restricted way of seeing economic life? How can we find human touchstones for thinking about political economy? How can we relate these "services" that friends and loved ones provide to the questions of wealth and income? A starting point is to rethink the notion of personal services and home production.

PERSONAL SERVICES AND HOME PRODUCTION

It has long been recognized that in nonmarket economies much of what is produced is never brought to market, but is intended for home consumption and thus falls outside normal income accounting. Thus, in some Third World countries one might find, as was once the case in the United States, that 70 percent or 80 percent of the population lives on small land holdings, and that most of what they produce is used by the family itself. Thus, a very substantial portion of their income comes not in a monetized form, but rather in the goods and services directly produced.

In order to develop a more adequate picture of consumption and income and either to allow comparisons with more marketized economies or to make historical comparisons where the degree of marketization has changed, economists have sought ways of placing appropriate monetarized value (i.e., exchange value, price) on these outputs of home production. When the item in question is a good that is itself subject to market transactions (e.g., a kilo of rice, a bushel of wheat), or when it is a clear substitute for a market good, then it is easy enough to simply adjust the income and consumption figures for home production/consumption by using these market prices.

When no market price exists, an effort sometimes is made to attempt an estimate of what such items might bring if brought to market, or alternatively to estimate what price the family might have to be offered so that they would place the item in question on the market.

This all makes good sense. For most purposes our interest in income or consumption is about something more basic than the amount of money earned or spent by the household, and we can more adequately evaluate the household situation by making these adjustments for nonmarketed goods and services.

What has not been generally recognized, however, is just how wide such a principle of admission truly is. For instance, if we have agreed, as I think makes sense, that the unpaid household labor and services of women (whether as Third World farmers or in rich country homes) are both part of the income of the household and part of what it consumes, then what basis is there for not similarly treating the very same services when members of the household provide them for themselves? Thus, if it is part of the household income when the homemaker cleans five rooms, it is similarly part of household income if her husband cleans his own room, or cooks a meal for himself. In short the entire array of household tasks that encompass housework, no matter who does them, are part of the home production of the unit, and part of what must enter into a full notion of economic well-being.

But this only scratches the surface. When we think of housework we think of those activities that are somewhat arduous and often unpleasant. But this is not a defining characterization of work or of income-producing activities. Some people love their jobs; productive activity can be activity that would be done in the absence of external reward. Moreover, in wealthy economies much of our consumption expenditures are for leisure time activities. In one society a person goes out to work, earns some money, and then provides to the family a TV for their evening entertainment, indirectly paying others for a multitude of entertainment services; in another society an elder mesmerizes the children with ancient tales told around a campfire. This, too, is a contribution to family income. Once we accept the idea that goods and services produced or performed at home which substitute for market goods and services are part of family income and consumption, the range of activities that can be so viewed is wide indeed.

Often when economists attempt to adjust income numbers for home production they limit themselves to those goods and services that have a clear market substitute. But this is a matter of convenience, not because having a market substitute is a necessary condition for having economic value. Often, the absence of a clear marketplace substitute for home activities, rather than impugning the value of the home activity, is an indication of the inability of the market to actually generate a viable substitute. The most graphic examples of this occur in the area of human relationships (e.g., spending time with friends). When the market tries to provide substitutes (e.g., escort services, prostitution), they are poor imitations of the real thing, yet their prices are often very high. The high prices paid reflect the high value placed by consumers on the real thing. And of those things for which it is near impossible for the market to provide a substitute (e.g., things that have value only when provided free of monetary motivation), one is dealing with things of the greatest value.

Thus, the idea that a marketplace substitute is necessary to show that a nonmarketplace activity is of value has things backward. The economic history is typically that marketplace items take on their value by being substitutes (generally imperfect) for what is produced or done for self or others outside the market. Most of what is truly valuable are personal services, things that people do for each other or for themselves. We are drawn into market economies because of their vastly greater efficiency, even when it means that the services and, to some extent, the goods are less meaningful. Those areas that are of greatest value, or where the personal service relationships are unique, are typically areas in which market provision is so inadequate that it is not undertaken at all.

Consider then the differences between these two lists of personal services.

In the first what most people seek (and need) is the engagement of a particular person who is of importance to us:

+ intimate conversation
+ sex
+ dinner with the family
+ sitting on your father's knee
+ hearing what happened with your daughter at school today
+ having a holiday dinner
+ watching TV together
+ holding hands
+ having a game of catch with your son
+ playing chess with an old friend

Most of what the very wealthy hire household workers to do does not fall into these categories. Rather, it is typically the case that others are hired when the personal service has some *clear output* that is the actual objective of importance, not the doing itself by a particular person. Though people differ, rich people hire others to do things such as these:

+ cleaning the house
+ painting the house
+ mowing the lawn
+ fixing the roof
+ paying the bills
+ cooking dinner
+ shopping for food
+ taking the car in for repair
+ driving the kids to soccer practice

With respect to those person-centered services (the first list) in which the value of the activity resides in the fact that it was done by or with a particular other person (a friend, a parent, a loved one), the rich are no better positioned than the poor. Neither can hire someone else to do it for them. Yet it is these person-centered services, which markets cannot provide, that are of the greatest value.

Moreover, the household is not the only nonmarket source of personal services; friends and other nonhousehold relations also help meet our personal service needs. Thus, the market can be thought of as servicing a residue of needs that remains when we subtract those needs that are met by all non-market providers, be it oneself, others within the household, friends, and neighbors.

With respect to simple living, the core wisdom is that the provision of person-centered services can under certain circumstances be, not a demand on a person's time, which subtracts from their ability to live well, but rather an opportunity for them to have a meaningful existence. It is to be able to do this that we need time.

One of our deepest personal needs is the need to provide significant personal services to others. Having the psychological capacities to do that and having the social opportunities to use those capacities are among our greatest forms of wealth. Here we might remember Seneca's point that we want a friend because we need someone to sustain when he is in need. This is a major part of the contribution to our wealth that having children contributes—it gives us an opportunity to develop into our higher selves and to express those selves by giving to others.

At bottom a successful form of economic life is one that figures out how to organize society so that we are each performing and receiving such services from each other. The existence of social roles that allow this to occur is a form of national treasure; these roles are the value infrastructure that make it possible for what is truly valuable in human life to emerge. Without knowing what we do, we often sweep away such forms of human interaction in the name of a false efficiency.

This may become more obvious when we remember that fewer and fewer workers are actually engaged in the production of commodities; most are providing services, and increasingly these are personal services. For the most part economic life is merely the exchange of services, whether within the marketized segment of life or outside.[175]

Understanding the value of nonmarket services casts the familiar distinctions we make between opulence and simple living in a different light. It appears a distinction that functions only on the more superficial level of goods and marketable services. Once we reach down toward what is most valuable, the chance to give and the opportunity to receive those forms of personal services that are themselves nonmarketable, we find that the simple life can be inherently opulent if it is a life in which human bounty is constantly increased through giving to one another.

SIMPLE LIVING: WEALTH AND POVERTY

When in the first chapter I discussed the difference between simple living and poverty, I suggested that the most useful way to make the distinction is to ask, "What is it for a life itself to be impoverished?" From that perspective we were able to distinguish the following:

+ material and physical impoverishment
+ intellectual impoverishment
+ spiritual impoverishment
+ aesthetic impoverishment
+ social impoverishment

When a form of simple living is advocated, it is generally because it is believed that, by living simply on the material level, one can live best in one or another of the nonmaterial dimensions.

The concept of wealth can be captured within this same framework. Being wealthy means having the diverse "assets" that allow us to live a life that partakes of diverse forms of richness: material, intellectual, spiritual, aesthetic, and social.

Once approached from this angle it becomes clear that genuine wealth resides in an extraordinarily broad range of "assets":

+ in our social relationships, our friendships, loves, and families
+ in our psychological capabilities, our abilities to build relationships, our ability to find meaning, to take aesthetic pleasure
+ in our cognitive capabilities, our ability to read, to understand, to learn, to reason
+ in our creative capacities, our ability to make something beautiful, to contribute something different
+ in our political rights, our ability to be a citizen of one country rather than another, our ability to build our own life, according to our own lights
+ in our historical and cultural legacy, in the riches of insight and experience that have been preserved from previous human lives and that are embodied in the great elements of human culture, be they forms of life and traditions, or great literature

✦ in our natural and man-made physical environment, the beauty of Florence, or the view from the back porch

Material wealth is not irrelevant, but its role is largely instrumental, largely in terms of how it facilitates our ability to access other forms of wealth. With clarity about genuine wealth, we may recognize how wealthy we really are (or in some cases, how poor) and, as a result, be better able to choose time rather than money, or make better use of both time and money.

The life of graceful simplicity is not a life that one can live merely by deciding to do so. To live well is an art, and to live gracefully in time is to be particularly accomplished in that art. It involves drawing on our internal capacities for creativity, appreciation, and generosity; it involves having attained some substantial level of inner peace, of security of identity and freedom from anxiety. And it involves having the good fortune of an external environment in which there is good grass and clean water and an absence of predators, but most essentially having a space that is abundant in beauty and friendship.

ECONOMIC LIFE FOR THE TWENTY-FIRST CENTURY

Even for those of us who are successful, there is something wrong with the way we live our lives. Yet it is not easy to say exactly what the problem is. In trying to gain perspective, this study has taken a wide sweep, an approach perhaps not inappropriate as we begin both a new century and a new millennium.

There is an ancient dichotomy that appears in the earliest reflections on human affairs. It is well captured in Aristotle's discussion of the two ways of thinking about money and in radically different responses to economic growth and technical change. While Thucydides was a progressivist who embraced social and material transformation, Seneca thoroughly rejected the fruits of technological advance. And in a similar spirit Epicurus created a self-help community that retreated from the worlds of politics, economics, and religion to seek the good life in friendship and intellectual community.

Although the issue was not always framed in terms of simple living, from the very point at which Western civilization became conscious of technological progress, there have been fundamentally different perspectives on the relationship of material accumulation to the good life. The term "progress" is inherently value loaded. But what specifically are those values? This has been in dispute for more than two thousand years. What is at stake is the larger story of human history. Depending on how one defines progress, the story comes out quite differently. In this recurring debate, the issues of moral virtue, beauty, and creative power were once central to the definition. But in the end, they were sequestered into a corner of human experience as preferential weight was given to scientific advance, technological achieve-ment, and economic growth. Thinking of the economic realm in this way, as of value independent of its meaning for a larger conception of human life, is what defines the modern world. When first articulated by Mandeville it was shocking, but today we take it for granted.

We need to recover and fuse the insights of Aristotle and Condorcet: Aristotle's conception of self-actualization in meaningful activity that is largely independent from economic necessity and Condorcet's vision of his-tory as the story of ordinary people. For Aristotle graceful living was indeed possible, but it was built upon the enforced servitude of women, slaves, and ordinary workers.

The real progress of humankind lies in overcoming such servitude and injustice. The real meaning of technological change and economic growth is that it has opened the possibility of graceful existence for the entire society. Ironically, however, as we continue to undergo the multiple liberations from inequality based on race, gender, and economic class, contemporary life has taken on particularly hard edges. We find it in the overburdened two-career family; we find it in the increasingly egalitarian scramble for the better places in our socioeconomic order; we find it in the continued tense relations between races. Sadly, at a point at which it should be possible to have a soci-ety that is both egalitarian and graceful, we not only fail to take advantage of our collective potential, we have lost much of the ability to articulate any ideal other than having more.

Aristotle was right about money: while it is a necessary means to the good, it is of rapidly diminishing value. Our central wealth lies not in our financial assets but in our selves, our character, our bodies, our mental and physical health, and in our relationships with others, our friendships, our loves, our social roles.

There is no single version of the good life. It can be found with family and friends, in meaningful work, in service to others, in pursuit of knowledge, in creative endeavor, in religious pursuit, or more likely, in the achievement of a harmony among such realms.

Yet these diverse forms have certain points in common. None of them is strongly dependent upon high levels of consumption. Each of them requires genuine commitment to something beyond oneself. Each of them re-quires ample time to do things at a serious pace, typically slowly and with care. This slower, simpler life is modest in its material dimensions precisely so that it may be unusually rich in other respects.

Looking at middle-class life in America, one finds strikingly few people who are actually living the good life. Instead we live at a frantic pace. We live lives filled with anxiety, filled with hassles and headaches and hard edges. What is most absent from our lives is gracefulness. This I have understood in terms of beauty, an aesthetic of time, inner peacefulness, appreciativeness, and generosity of spirit.

No government and no set of social policies can deliver gracefulness into people's lives. To live gracefully is to have mastered an art of living—and as with most art, true mastery requires inner development. Yet while achieving gracefulness is accomplished one life at a time, no social environment is neutral with respect to gracefulness. The social and economic world we inhabit either facilitates graceful living or frustrates it. Thus, there is no such thing as a separate realm of economic life, and because this is so, economic policies and social institutions can be made subject to a broader criterion: are they making it easier to live lives of graceful simplicity? This is the perspective of a new politics.

There have always been philosophies and religious outlooks that have explained how the individual, independent of the social and economic environment, can achieve simple living in one or another of its higher forms. And it is often maintained that in "Affluent America" this is most certainly the case. Here, it is said, we suffer from a disease of overconsumption. We are the victims of Madison Avenue and an inflation in our sense of necessity.

I have challenged this story, not because it is completely false, but because it misses the big picture for people of average means. The society we live in is one in which it is very expensive to meet core economic needs. While it is indeed unfortunate that as a society we abandoned the project of reducing the workweek and expanding leisure time, we did not do so because we were hooked on artificial desires. Unfortunately, we live within a strikingly inefficient social world, one in which great sums of money are required to meet ordinary needs, such as getting to work and living in a safe neighborhood with good public schools.

In response I have proposed a politics of simplicity—an approach to social and economic policy that would offer a new paradigm of the purpose of an economy. Rather than seeing the goal as higher and higher levels of income, it would assess economic and social performance in terms of expanded leisure time and an increased ability to meet core needs at modest levels of income.

The central task of this new politics is to bring people to ask different questions and to seek different objectives from our collective life. A specific

agenda and specific policies come later and should be subject to healthy dispute. I, for one, favor expanding the number of three-day weekends and
eliminating tuition at all public colleges and universities. And I would place
the reclamation of urban environments at the center of any effort to make it
easier for people to live well with modest incomes. Further, I would stress
the creation of beauty and the release of creativity in all our social programs.

But these are specifics and, at this point, not the most important matter.
What is important is to turn the healthy individualistic impulse of the simple
living movement toward a wider perspective, one that retains the insight
that finding the good life is an essentially personal endeavor, but that also
recognizes the need to join with others in creating a world in which it is
possible.

THE TWENTY-FIRST CENTURY

Graceful simplicity offers a new vision as we begin the new century, a vision
in which the central social objective is to make simple living feasible for all.
But "Why in America?" Of all the countries in the world, one might think,
the United States is the one place where this does not make sense, the one
place on the planet that is least likely to shift to a different paradigm. So
why here?

First, as we have seen, simple living has always been part of the American
consciousness. There have always been two American Dreams, one a dream
of riches, the other of simple living. What has changed is the content given to
simple living. For the Puritans it was not what it was for those like Samuel
Adams, who feared that self-absorption was incompatible with democratic
government. And Ben Franklin's focus on frugality, saving, and financial
independence was quite different from the Quaker theorist John Woolman,
who saw the pursuit of high levels of consumption as the underlying force
that gives rise to oppression and injustice. Different still was Thoreau, with
his concern for self-discovery and his understanding of how expansive consumption commits us to the self-enslavement of labor, and his advocacy
of a reversed Sabbath pattern—six days of leisure and one of work. Today
we need a framework that can foster and accommodate these multiple
American traditions.

Second, simple living resonates with American egalitarianism. In a society
that affirms the principle of equal dignity, there is no place for the sharp class

distinctions implicit in the notion of great and complex estates. Of course, there has always been an enormous gap between American ideals of equality and the American reality; yet at the same time in America today there is little acceptance of subservience. But without subservience, the old forms of gracefulness are, thankfully, no longer possible. We need a simple living society.

The widespread pursuit of simple living can occur in the United States because this is a country that has enormous potential for change. Our own insularity, in its way, reflects a strength, a self-confidence. We are a nation that rarely looks outside itself in deciding how to be, and thus is freer than most to march to a different drummer. In part this has been grounded in an economic self-sufficiency. And while it is true that in recent decades the United States has become vastly more integrated with the rest of the world economically, its very affluence gives it wider options than other countries may possess.

Having achieved substantial material abundance, many Americans are intimately aware of its limitations. America as an affluent society is in search of a new organizing conception, both in understanding itself and in presenting itself to the world. On an individual level, this same affluence has already given rise to a greater interest in simple living. Were we to begin to conceptualize the purpose of economic life in different terms, we would discover that the changes in social and economic policies needed to facilitate simple living are well within our grasp, if we are bold enough to make the transformation.

NOTES

1. Aristotle, *Politics,* trans. Ernest Barker (New York: Oxford University Press, 1961), p. 26.
2. Ibid., p. 280.
3. Ibid., p. 280.
4. Ibid., p. 280.
5. Ibid., p. 281.
6. Ibid., p. 26.
7. Ibid., p. 27.
8. Contemporary economic thought, taken in formal terms, can accommodate almost anything. Thus, the distortion of personality can be viewed as "an externality" generated by market transactions, adding to the costs of every market interaction. But virtually no economists have expanded the idea of externalities to include distortions of personality. It remains a formal possibility, but consideration of such impacts, central to earlier eras, is largely outside of the way we think of the economic realm.
9. Aristotle, *Politics,* p. 37.
10. Ibid., p. 10.
11. This is wonderfully explicated in David Shi's study *The Simple Life: Plain Thinking and High Living in American Culture* (Oxford: Oxford University Press, 1985), and I have drawn heavily upon Shi's account for this summary.
12. John Woolman, "A Word of Remembrance and Caution to the Rich" in *Words That Made American History*, ed. Richard N. Current and John A. Garroty (Boston: Little, Brown and Co., 1965).
13. "The Way to Wealth" in *Benjamin Franklin, Autobiography and Other Writings* (Cambridge, Mass.: The Riverside Press, 1958).
14. Yaacov Oved, *Two Hundred Years of American Communes* (New Brunswick: Transaction Books, 1988), pp. xiii–xiv.

15. Henry David Thoreau, *Walden* (Princeton: Princeton University Press, 1973), p. 9.
16. Ibid., p. 4.
17. Ibid., p. 6.
18. Ibid., p. 11.
19. Ibid., p. 14.
20. Ibid., p. 14.
21. Ibid., p. 8.
22. Jimmy Carter, "Energy Problems: The Erosion of Confidence," *Vital Speeches* XLV (15 August 1979): 642, 643 as excerpted in David E. Shi, *In Search of the Simple Life* (Salt Lake City: Gibbs M. Smith, 1986).
23. Joe Dominguez and Vicki Robin, *Your Money or Your Life: Transforming Your Relationship with Money and Achieving Financial Independence* (New York: Penguin Books, 1993), p. 269.
24. As it turns out, this 5 percent real rate of return is perhaps similar to what one would expect if one accepted the advice and outlook of the authors. At present Treasury bonds are paying 6 percent interest. The authors tend to dismiss the significance of inflation, arguing that the danger of inflation in the items that one relies on in a simple life is vastly overstated. In Chapter 3, I offer a very different way of viewing the problem of the rising cost of necessities.
25. See Arlie Hochschild, *The Time Bind* (New York: Henry Holt, 1997).
26. Epictetus, *The Manual*, XVII, in *Discourses of Epictetus*, trans. George Long (New York: A. L. Burt, 1930).
27. Julie V. Iovine, "Padding the Empty Nest," *New York Times,* 4 September 1997, p. C. 1.
28. The India figure is the purchasing power equivalent; using the more conventional exchange rate method, per capita GNP is $450. These are 1999 figures, taken from the 2000/2001 *World Development Report,* United Nations Development Program.
29. In 2000 the figures were as follows:

Housing	32.4%
Transportation	19.5%
Food	13.6%
Personal insurance/pensions (includes Social Security)	8.8%
Health care	5.4%
Clothing	4.9%
Entertainment	4.9%
Other	10.5%

30. Bureau of Labor Statistics, *Consumer Expenditure Survey for 2000.*
31. Calculated from Bureau of Labor Statistics, *Consumer Expenditure Survey 2000* (Washington: U.S. Department of Labor, 2001).
32. Ibid.

33. Author's calculations based on Bureau of the Census, *Money Income in the United States, 2000* (Washington, 2001), table H. Social Security taxes are not treated as expenditures.

34. Single-parent families have significantly lower income levels, many at or below poverty level. The median income for female-headed households with no husband and with children is considerably lower: $24,693 in 2000 (Ibid.)

35. U.S. Department of Commerce, *National Income and Product Accounts Tables.*

36. Bureau of the Census, *Money Income in the United States, 2000* (Washington, 2001), table F-7.

37. In *The Overworked American* (New York: Basic Books, 1991), Juliet Schor suggests that if we had taken all the productivity gains since the 1950s in the form of more leisure time rather than higher income, we could have reduced the workweek to half its present level.

38. The historical picture has not been one of steady growth, however. For instance, median family income in 1996 ($42,300) is little changed from that of 1979 ($41,530 in 1996 dollars, *Economic Report of the President,* February 1998, table B-33). It is important to bear this sharp break in trend in mind. The thirty years following the end of World War II showed largely uninterrupted growth of income and consumption. In the last twenty or so years, this has not been the case. Per capita consumption figures still show some growth, while median family income figures hardly do. This difference is attributable to several factors, including an increase in income inequality as well as a reduction in family size. Nonetheless, the big picture for the last half century is one of dramatic steady growth in consumption for three-plus decades following World War II, and relatively little for most people in the subsequent decade and a half.

39. The statistics often appear to show conflicting pictures of more recent years. For instance, hourly compensation in the nonfarm business sector went up by 80 percent between 1959 and 2000 (*Economic Report of the President,* February 2001, table B-49). But there is a very important difference between the compensation levels just cited and actual earnings. Compensation includes employee benefits paid as well as Social Security taxes. Between 1959 and 2000 hourly earnings went up by a modest 22 percent and actually fell by 4.8 percent between 1978 and 2000 (*Economic Report of the President,* February 2000, table B-47). While this explains some of the differences between competing images of American affluence, it doesn't alter the basic fact of increased consumption over the long historical view. For example, between 1950 and 1970 per capita consumption expenditures rose by 53 percent, while distribution of income was relatively constant. We do consume at much higher levels than previous generations, yet we do not feel much room for significant cutbacks.

40. We can compare societies in terms of "the social efficiency of money," meaning the extent to which money is converted into need satisfaction. Societies differ markedly in this respect. A general formula can be derived as follows:

$$(1) \text{ needs satisfaction} = \text{needs satisfaction}$$

Then, multiplying the right-hand side by one (per capita income/per capita income), we have:

(2) needs satisfaction = needs satisfaction × (per capita income/per capita income)

Then, rearranging the terms of the right-hand side of the equation:

(3) needs satisfaction = (per capita income) × (needs satisfaction/per capita income)

This is a tautology, but one that is interesting to ponder. The last equation tells us that the extent to which a society has satisfied core needs depends on two factors, the level of income per capital, and (needs satisfaction/per capita income).

The first part of the result, that the degree of need satisfaction depends on the level of income, is, of course, no surprise. It fits perfectly with our intuition that, all other things being equal, the needs of the rich are more adequately satisfied than the needs of the poor, and that the poorer you are, the more likely it is that your basic economic needs are unsatisfied.

What is interesting, however, is that the last equation says that the there are two factors involved. The first is income, but the second is the ratio of needs satisfaction to income level. This last term (needs satisfaction/per capita income) is a measure of efficiency, though not the kind typically investigated by economists. We can term it "the social efficiency of money."

41. How long a commute is reasonable? Well, thirty minutes each way is five hours a week, or 250 hours for a fifty-week year. That is more than six weeks of forty hours each.

42. *Statistical Abstract, 1999,* table 1205.

43. Bureau of the Census, *Historical Income Tables,* table F-11.

44. Bureau of the Census, *Historical Income Tables*, table F-11.

45. For black males in the District of Columbia, the 1990 life expectancy was 57.9 years. See "Death Knocks Sooner for D.C.'s Black Men," *Washington Post,* 4 December 1997, p. 1.

46. See Eva Sharp and Stephanie Shipp, "A History of U.S. Consumer Expenditure Survey: 1935–36 to 1988–89," *Journal of Economic and Social Measurement* 19 (1993): 59–96.

47. Author's calculations from data in *Economic Report of the President* (January 1993), tables B-5 and B-111.

48. Calculated from Bureau of Labor Statistics, *Consumer Expenditure Survey for 1991* (December 1992), table 5.

49. Amount is in 1991 dollars. *Money Income,* table B-11.

50. Eva Jacobs and Stephanie Shipp, "How Family Spending Has Changed in the U.S.," *Monthly Labor Review* (March 1990), table 2.

51. Author's calculations based on *Consumer Expenditure Survey,* 2000, National Income data.

52. Author's calculations based on *Statistical Abstract, 1997,* table 157, and SAUS, 1995, table 156.

53. Historical levels taken from Jacobs and Shipp, "How Family Spending Has Changed in the U.S.," table 1.
54. The point may well be made that prior to their entry into the labor force, women had critical unmet needs, or that over time new needs emerged. My point is more limited; it is simply that whatever the reasons for women's entry into the labor force, this brought with it higher NRI with respect to the long-standing need that employed parents have for child care that allows them to be away from home.
55. *Statistical Abstract, 1997,* table 248.
56. *Statistical Abstract, 1997,* table 631.
57. *Statistical Abstract, 1997,* table 632.
58. *Statistical Abstract, 1992,* table 600, and *Statistical Abstract, 1995,* table 615.
59. *Money Income, 1997,* table F-13.
60. *Statistical Abstract, 1997,* table 730.
61. Author's calculations based on *Statistical Abstract, 1992,* table 269, and *Statistical Abstract, 2000,* table 311.
62. See Eric Wee, "Students Go the Extracurricular Mile for Admission to Elite Colleges," *Washington Post,* 8 May 1996, p. 1.
63. Calculated from Bureau of Labor Statistics, *Consumer Expenditure Survey for 1994.*
64. *Statistical Abstract, 1997,* table 730.
65. Reported in Richard Morin and Megan Rosenfeld, "With More Equity More Sweat," *Washington Post,* 22 March 1998.
66. Herbert Spencer, *Essays: Moral, Political and Aesthetic* (New York: D. Appleton and Co., 1878), p. 313.
67. As quoted in Shi, *The Simple Life,* p. 183.
68. "The Hardship of Accounting," in *Robert Frost, Poetry and Prose,* ed. Edward Connery Lathem and Lawrence Thompson (New York: Henry Holt, 1972), p. 125.
69. Aristotle, *Politics,* 1323a 14–17. See also Martha Nussbaum, "The Good as Discipline, the Good as Freedom"; David Crocker, "Consumption, Well-Being and Capability"; and Jerome Segal, "Living at a High Economic Standard: A Functionings Analysis," all in *Ethics of Consumption,* ed. David Crocker and Toby Linden (Lanham, Md.: Rowman and Littlefield, 1997).
70. This should not be taken as self-evident. There are those who maintain that society is hopelessly divided about how people should live, and thus that it is best merely to provide a system that is neutral to different versions of the good life, and just gives people an opportunity to live the lives they desire. The problem here, however, is that no system "merely provides opportunities"—every real-world system makes some ways of living more difficult and other ways less difficult to achieve. While it is not desirable to compel people to live one way rather than another, we do have to decide which forms of life to make accessible.
71. See Benjamin Hunnicutt, *Work Without End* (Philadelphia: Temple University Press, 1988).
72. Data is from the U.S. National Center for Education Statistics. The cost would actually be less, as the $22 billion includes tuition paid through Pell grants. Further, the cost would be less if the proposal were restricted to undergraduate

education; the $22 billion figure covers all tuition payments paid to public institutions of higher education.

73. Frithjof Bergmann of the University of Michigan has given new currency to thi. term, as part of his notion of "new work."

74. The distinction between machines and tools is pursued in my book *Agency a Alienation: A Theory of Human Presence* (Lanham, Md.: Rowman and Littlefie 1991).

75. R. H. Tawney, *Religion and the Rise of Capitalism* (Harmondsworth, UK: Pelican Books, 1938), p. 126.

76. I have specified this as an ideal, and have added the proviso "with more efficient use of money for need satisfaction" because with the present way in which needs are satisfied in the United States, it would require a very substantial family income to satisfy needs. If, for instance, it required $50,000 a year, then on two twenty-five-hour jobs, this would require a wage level of $20/hour. Both politically and economically this is virtually impossible as a minimum wage.

77. *The Instruction of Duauf,* quoted in Arnold Toynbee, *A Study of History,* Volume IV (Oxford: Oxford University Press, 1951), p. 419.

78. Homer, *The Iliad,* trans. Robert Fitzgerald (Garden City, N.Y.: Anchor Press, 1974), p. 150.

79. Ibid., p. 154.

80. Ibid., p. 526.

81. Ibid., p. 526.

82. Kitto, *The Greeks* (Baltimore: Penguin Books, 1951), p. 44.

83. Ludwig Edelstein, *The Idea of Progress in Classical Antiquity* (Baltimore: Johns Hopkins Press, 1967), p. 35.

84. Simone Weil, "The Iliad: Poem of Might" in *Simone Weil Reader,* ed. George A. Panichos (New York: David McKay Company, 1977), p. 183.

85. Frederick Teggart, "The Idea of Progress: An Historical Analysis" in *The Idea of Progress,* ed. Frederick Teggart (Berkeley: University of California Press, 1949).

86. Nisbet also rejects the idea that the "rediscovery" of the classical world occurred in the Renaissance; but what is important here is that that was the Renaissance perception.

87. Thucydides, *History of the Peloponnesian War,* trans. Rex Warner (New York: Penguin Books, 1980), pp. 34–42. I was made aware of the significance of Thucydides for a history of the idea of progress by reading Robert Nisbet, *History of the Idea of Progress* (New York: Basic Books, 1980).

88. As quoted in J. B. Bury, *The Idea of Progress* (New York: Dover Publications, 1960), pp. 13–14. I draw heavily on Bury's account.

89. As quoted in Nisbet, *History of the Idea of Progress,* p. 46.

90. Seneca, *Epistulae Morales,* in Teggart, *The Idea of Progress,* pp. 95–96.

91. Ibid., p. 98.

92. An earlier consideration of the relative merits of the ancients and moderns can be found in Jean Bodin's *Method of Understanding History*, which was published in 1566. Bodin cites various modern discoveries unknown to the ancients. See Nisbet, *History of the Idea of Progress,* p. 122.

93. In the seventeenth century Turgot and Adam Smith stand out among those who

argued that nothing was more detrimental to economic growth than the deliberate efforts of the state to manipulate the economy.

94. Bury, *The Idea of Progress,* p. 87.
95. Jonathan Swift, *The Battle of the Books* in *A Tale of a Tub* . . . (Oxford: Clarendon Press, 1958), p. 246.
96. Ibid., p. 258.
97. Bernard Mandeville, *The Fable of the Bees*, ed. F. B. Kaye (Oxford: Oxford University Press, 1966), p. 17.
98. Ibid., p. 24.
99. Ibid., p. 25.
100. Ibid., p. 26.
101. Ibid., p. 34.
102. Ibid., p. 35.
103. Ibid., p. 148.
104. Ibid., p. 169.
105. See Amartya Sen's essay in *Ethics of Consumption*, ed. David Crocker and Toby Linden (Lanham, Md.: Rowman and Littlefield, 1997).
106. Mandeville, *Fable of Bees,* p. 169.
107. Ibid., p. 170.
108. Ibid., p. 171.
109. Ibid., p. 171.
110. Ibid., p. 248.
111. Bernard Mandeville, "An Essay on Charity and Charity-Schools" in *Fable of Bees*, p. 311.
112. Ibid., pp. 314–17.
113. Nicolas Condorcet, *Sketch for a Historical Picture of the History of the Progress of the Human Mind* (New York: The Noonday Press, 1955), p. 4.
114. Ibid., p. 102.
115. Here, as elsewhere, he seems to be anticipating Marx. Would it be too much to say that Hegel found Condorcet standing on his feet, and stood him on his head, only to have Marx set him upright again?
116. Condorcet, *Sketch,* pp. 170–72.
117. Note that in this passage Condorcet speaks of societies at different "stages of their political existence"; in this general statement of the doctrine of the indefinite perfectibility of mankind, he spoke of "the different stages of their development." Because of the centrality of enlightenment and because for Condorcet the issue of enlightenment is inextricably a political issue, he can be said to have a conception of development as political development.
118. Condorcet, *Sketch,* p. 189.
119. Ibid., p. 187.
120. Ibid., p. 181.
121. Ibid., p. 199.
122. Abraham Joshua Heschel, *The Sabbath* (New York: Farrar, Straus and Giroux, 1951), p. 10.
123. Ibid., p. 13.
124. Ibid., p. 14.

125. Ibid., p. 18.
126. Deuteronomy rabba 3,1; quoted by Heschel in *The Sabbath*, p. 19.
127. Heschel, *The Sabbath,* p. 23.
128. Ibid., p. 28.
129. As quoted in Shi, *The Simple Life,* p. 143.
130. Heschel, *The Sabbath,* pp. 30–31.
131. Ibid., p. 29.
132. One does not have to choose between these strategies in the abstract. One or another may be suited for any given person at any given time; and, of course, it is possible, as most people do, to try to strike a middle course—though it may be argued that this brings only the worst of both worlds.
133. Shi, *The Simple Life,* p. 143.
134. Lucretius, *On the Nature of Things,* Book V, in *The Stoic and Epicurean Philosophers,* ed. William Oates (New York: Modern Library, 1940).
135. From Jefferson's letter of October 23, 1819, to William Short, *The Life and Selected Writings of Thomas Jefferson,* ed. Adrienne Koch and William Peden (New York: Random House, 1944), p. 693. I owe this reference to William Hilber, *Happiness Through Tranquillity* (Lanham, Md.: University Press of America, 1984), p. 83. This letter made me think perhaps I was not so idiosyncratic in selecting specific thinkers from the past—Jefferson herein indicates his esteem for four of them: Epicurus, Epictetus, Seneca, and Condorcet.
136. *The Stoic and Epicurean Philosophers,* Vatican Collection XXV, p. 41.
137. See H. D. Kitto, *The Greeks* (Baltimore, Md.: Penguin Books, 1966), p. 127.
138. *The Stoic and Epicurean Philosophers,* Vatican Collection LVIII, p. 43.
139. Ibid., LXXXI, p. 44.
140. Ibid., XLIV, p. 42.
141. Ibid., XVIII, p. 40.
142. Ibid., *Principal Doctrines* VIII, p. 35.
143. Ibid., Vatican Collection LI, p. 42.
144. Ibid., *Principal Doctrines* XXI.
145. Ibid., *Letters to Unknown Recipients,* p. 41.
146. As quoted in Shi, *The Simple Life,* p. 134.
147. *The Stoic and Epicurean Philosophers,* p. 46.
148. Ibid., p. 50.
149. Ibid., Vatican Collection XXXIII, p. 41.
150. Ibid., Vatican Collection LII, p. 43.
151. Ibid., *Principal Doctrines* XXVII, p. 37.
152. Ibid., Vatican Collection XLIV, p. 42.
153. Seneca, *Letters from a Stoic,* ed. Robin Campbell (Middlesex: Penguin Books, 1969), p. 49.
154. Ironically, in this passage, Seneca was criticizing a view of friendship that he ascribed to Epicurus. In this I believe he was in error. Epicurus said, "All friendship is desirable in itself, though it starts from the need of help" (*The Stoic and Epicurean Philosophers,* p. 63). And in his *Life of Epicurus,* Diogenes Laertius attributes to Epicurus the view that the wise man "on occasion will even die for a friend" (Ibid., p. 43).

155. Jean-Paul Sartre, *Being and Nothingness* (New York: Philosophical Library, 1956), p. 270.

156. Ibid., pp. 221–22.

157. *The Life and Selected Writings of Thomas Jefferson,* pp. 693–94.

158. The quotations in the section on Stoicism are from Epictetus, *The Manual.*

159. Ibid.

160. William James, "On What Makes a Life Significant" in *Talks to Teachers* (New York: Norton and Co., 1958), p. 171.

161. Deuteronomy rabba 3,1; as quoted by Heschel, *The Sabbath,* p. 19.

162. Whether or not the Israelites were allowed to fight in self-defense on the Sabbath was at one point a contentious issue. Under the leadership of the Maccabees, this interpretation of Sabbath restrictions was overcome.

163. Bureau of the Census, *Historical Statistics of the United States* (Washington, 1975, Series D). For recent years, see *Statistical Abstracts of the United States.*

164. Ibid.

165. Ruth Schwartz Cowan, "More Work for Mother—The Ironies of Household Technology from the Open Hearth to the Microwave" (New York: Basic Books, 1983).

166. Here we see the limitations of some recent inquiries into the purely quantitative issues of work—are people working more or less—this does not tell us enough if the inherent qualities of the work are what determines whether more is a positive or a negative thing. It is not as if there awaits for us some special nirvana in so-called leisure time activities—what we seek and need most of all are life's central activities, done right.

167. Alfred Marshall, *The Principles of Economics,* 8th ed. (London: MacMillan, 1936), p. 137.

168. Robert B. Settle and Pamela L. Alreck, *Why They Buy: American Consumers Inside and Out* (New York: John Wiley and Sons, 1989), pp. 24–27.

169. The term "life-energy," as the cost of consumption, is introduced by Vicki Robbins and Joe Dominguez in *Your Money or Your Life.* Thoreau had a similar concept.

170. Karl Marx, *The Economic and Philosophic Manuscripts of 1844,* ed. Dirk J. Struik (New York: International Publishers, 1964), p. 167.

171. The income figures are provided in terms of "purchasing parity," which seeks to compare income levels in different countries based on what one can buy with them rather than through reliance on international currency exchange rates.

172. R. Wilkins, O. Adams, and A. Branker, "Changes in Mortality by Income in Urban Canada from 1971 to 1986," *Health Reports* 1(2) (1989): 137–74.

173. E. Rogot, P. D. Sorlie, and N. J. Johnson, "Life Expectancy by Employment Status, Income and Education in the National Longitudinal Mortality Study," *Public Health Reports* 107(4) (Jul-Aug 1992): 457–61.

174. David Brown and Avram Goldstein, "Death Knocks Sooner for D.C.'s Black Men," *Washington Post,* 4 December 1997, p. 4.

175. We are actually well beyond the point in which most people are engaged in providing services rather than growing or manufacturing things. In 2001, the number of people employed in various occupations was as follows:

Total employed civilians	135,073
Managers	20,338
Professionals	21,556
Technicians	4,497
Sales	16,044
Administrative support	18,503
Household and protective	3,193
Other service (food, health, cleaning, hair)	15,166
Transporters	5,638
Precision production, craft, and repair	14,833
Machine operators, fabricators, laborers	17,698
Farming, forestry, and fishing	3,245
Handlers, helpers, and laborers	5,326

It is only in the last four categories that we have people involved in making, growing, and building things. There were 41,102 (41 million) people with occupations of this sort in 2001, constituting 30.4 percent of those employed.

When viewed by industry, independent of exactly what the people themselves might be doing, we get a similar picture.

	1979	1992	2005 (pro)
total	101,363	121,093	147,484
Nonfarm wage and salary	86,491	107,888	132,960
goods prod excl agr	26,461	23,142	23,717
mining	958	631	562
construction	4,463	4,471	5,632
manufacturing	21,040	18,040	17,523
service producing	63,030	84,746	109,243
transport, comm, util	5,136	5,709	6,497
wholesale trade	5,221	6,045	7,191
retail trade	14,972	19,346	23,777
finance, insur, real est	4,975	6,571	7,969
services	16,779	28,422	41,788
business services			
health services			
educational			
legal			
amusement			
auto repair			
government	15,947	18,653	22,021
Agriculture	3,398	3,295	3,325
Private households	1,264	1,116	802
Nonag self-emply/unpaid fam	7,210	8,794	10,397

SAUS, 1995, table 654, Employment by selected industry with projections

As a percentage of the total, those employed within agriculture or goods-producing industries is projected to fall to 18 percent within a few years (from 26 percent in 1992). As recently as 1979, those in agriculture or goods-producing industries was 29 percent of the workforce. This is a totally different world than that of, say, 1920, when those in agriculture or goods-producing industries comprised 62 percent of the workforce, or 1850 when it accounted for 81 percent of the workforce (*Historical Statistics of the United States* Series D. 152–166 Industrial Distribution of Gainful Workers. 1820–1940).